BESTSELLING
BOOK SERIES

Human Resources Kit For Dummies, 2nd Ed

D0472461

Key Federal Laws

ADEA (Age Discrimination in Employment Act – 1967)

What the law does: Prohibits discrimination against employees 40 or older based on age. Although this law originally covered employees until age 65, it was amended to age 70, and then an age limit was completely removed. Also see OWBPA later in this list.

Who the law applies to: All private sector employers with 20 or more employees who work 20 or more weeks per year. Also covers labor unions (25 or more members), employment agencies, and state and local governments.

AC-21 (American Competitiveness in the 21st Century Act – 2000)

What the law does: Raises limits on number of temporary visas issued for highly skilled labor. Includes increased training and educational opportunities for American citizens.

Who the law applies to: Any company.

ADA (Americans with Disabilities Act – 1990)

What the law does: Prohibits employers from discriminating against individuals with disabilities. Requires employers to provide "reasonable accommodation," including modification of existing facilities, equipment, and work schedules so long as they do not impose "undue hardship" on business operations.

Who the law applies to: All private employers with 15 or more employees.

COBRA (Consolidated Omnibus Budget Reconciliation Act – 1986)

What the law does: Provides certain former employees, retirees, spouses, former spouses, and children the right to temporary continuation of health coverage at group rates.

Who the law applies to: Companies with 20 or more employees. (Some states also have their own version of COBRA, such as California's CAL-COBRA.)

Equal Pay Act (1963)

What the law does: Prohibits any discrepancies in pay between men and women and who are assigned to do the same job.

Who the law applies to: Private employers or labor organizations who have two or more employees, and who are engaged in the production of goods for interstate commerce.

FLSA (Fair Labor Standards Act – 1938)

What the law does: Establishes the minimum wage, requires overtime pay for certain employees, restricts the employment of children, and requires certain recordkeeping.

Who the law applies to: Most companies, with a few exceptions in certain retail and agricultural industries.

FMLA (Family and Medical Leave Act – 1993)

What the law does: Grants qualified employees a total of 12 work weeks of unpaid leave during a 12-month period for health-related reasons, including childbirth, family illness, or personal health reasons that preclude handling the job's duties. In most cases, employee is guaranteed return to work in the same or comparable position. Company must communicate terms and provisions of this act to employees.

Who the law applies to: Private employers with 50 or more employees within a 75-mile radius.

HIPAA (Health Insurance Portability and Accountability Act – 1996)

What the law does: Establishes guidelines for protecting private personal information. Covered entities such as an employer's health plan, healthcare providers, and healthcare clearinghouses must protect identifiable health information. Individuals have control over how their information may be used.

Who the law applies to: All employers.

(continued)

Human Resources Kit
For Dummies, 2nd Edition

(continued)

IRCA (Immigrant Reform and Control Act 1986, 1990, 1996)

What the law does: Bans employers from hiring illegal aliens — and establishes penalties for such behavior. Employer is responsible for determining legality of employee's status.

Who the law applies to: All employers.

OWBPA (Older Workers Benefit Protection Act – 1990)

What the law does: Amended version of 1967 Age Discrimination in Employment Act, prohibiting discrimination against workers age 40 or older. One provision gives employees a time frame (at least 21 days) to consider a company's offer that includes a promise not to sue the company for age discrimination. It also gives employees seven days to change their minds.

Who the law applies to: All private sector employers with 20 or more employees.

Patriot Act (2001)

What the law does: Enhances federal government's ability to conduct investigative and surveillance activities. Implication for employers: Need to implement new procedures to maintain employee privacy rights while also allowing release of information requested by the government.

Who the law applies to: All employers.

SOA (Sarbanes-Oxley Act – 2002)

What the law does: Creates stronger forms of fiscal accountability, including enhanced financial disclosure, increased corporate responsibility, and commitment to ethical behavior. Strongly recommends establishment of a company code of conduct/behavior.

Who the law applies to: Publicly held companies and private firms considering conducting an initial public offering (IPO) of their stock.

Title VII of the Civil Rights Act (1964)

What the law does: Prohibits practices that discriminate against people on the basis or race, sex, color, religion or national origin.

Who the law applies to: Private employers with 15 or more employees, as well as virtually all government institutions, employment agencies, and labor unions.

WARN (Worker Adjustment and Retraining Notification Act – 1988)

What the law does: Offers protection to workers, families, and communities, requiring employers to provide notice 60 days in advance of mass layoffs or plant closings.

Who the law applies to: Generally covers companies with 100 or more employees.

Five HR-Savvy Web Sites

American Society for Training & Development (ASTD) www.astd.org Good information on training programs — from in-person to online — for all employee levels.

Bureau of Labor Statistics (BLS) www.bla.gov Superb resource for studying trends in economics, demographics, employment, and more.

Occupational Safety & Health Administration (OSHA) www.osha.gov Extensive information on laws, safety, and other critical matters.

Society for Human Resource Management (SHRM) www.shrm.org Comprehensive HR center, including papers, studies, articles, updates, and discussions.

WorldatWork www.worldatwork.org Offers a variety of valuable HR materials. Exceptionally informative in matters related to payroll and benefits.

For Dummies: Bestselling Book Series for Beginners

Human Resources Kit

FOR

DUMMIES®

2ND EDITION

by Max Messmer

Wiley Publishing, Inc.

Human Resources Kit For Dummies,® 2nd Edition

Published by
Wiley Publishing, Inc.
111 River St.
Hoboken, NJ 07030-5774
www.wiley.com

For general information on our other products and services, please contact our Customer Care Department within the U.S. at 800-762-2974, outside the U.S. at 317-572-3993, or fax 317-572-4002.

For technical support, please visit www.wiley.com/techsupport.

Wiley also publishes its books in a variety of electronic formats. Some content that appears in print may not be available in electronic books.

Library of Congress Control Number: 2006934827

ISBN-13: 978-0-470-04930-3

ISBN-10: 0-470-04930-8

Manufactured in the United States of America

10 9 8 7 6 5 4 3 2 1

2O/RU/RR/QW/IN

WILEY

About the Author

As chairman and CEO of Robert Half International Inc., the world's largest specialized staffing firm, Harold M. "Max" Messmer Jr. is one of the foremost experts on human resources and employment issues. His entire business is built on the premise that the success of any company is based on the extent to which attracting and keeping outstanding talent is a top priority.

Messmer has written several critically acclaimed books, including *Staffing Europe* (Acropolis Books Ltd.) and *50 Ways to Get Hired* (William Morrow and Co.), as well as *The Fast Forward MBA in Hiring, Job Hunting For Dummies, Managing Your Career For Dummies,* and *Motivating Employees For Dummies* (Wiley Publishing, Inc.). Messmer's expertise has been featured in major business publications such as *Fortune, Forbes,* and *The Wall Street Journal.* He also has written countless articles and columns on job seeking, employment, and management topics.

In 2006, Messmer was named one of America's top CEOs by *Institutional Investor* magazine. He also was named 2003 CEO of the Year by Morningstar, an independent research firm. Messmer is a member of the board of directors of Health Care Property Investors, Inc., and previously served on the boards of Airborne Freight Corp., First Interstate Bancorp, NationsBank, Pacific Enterprises, and Southern California Gas Co., among others. During the Reagan administration, he served on the President's Advisory Committee on Trade Negotiations.

Messmer was valedictorian of his graduating class at Loyola University and graduated cum laude from the New York University School of Law. In 2000, he received the Alumni Achievement Award from NYU's Law Alumni Association. Messmer's community involvement includes service on the board of governors of the San Francisco Symphony and the UCSF Medical Center Executive Council, as well as the board of overseers of the Hoover Institution at Stanford University.

Robert Half International (NYSE: RHI) is a member of Standard & Poor's widely tracked S&P 500 index. The company has repeatedly been listed on the Forbes Platinum 400 list of the best big companies in America, ranking as one of the top U.S. business services firms for investor returns and growth. RHI also has consistently appeared on *Fortune* magazine's list of "America's Most Admired Companies."

Founded in 1948, RHI is a recognized leader in professional consulting and staffing services and is the parent company of Protiviti, a leading independent internal-audit and risk consulting firm. The company's specialized staffing divisions include Accountemps, Robert Half Finance & Accounting, and Robert Half Management Resources, for temporary, full-time, and project professionals, respectively, in the fields of accounting and finance; OfficeTeam, for highly skilled temporary administrative support personnel; Robert Half Technology, for information technology professionals; Robert Half Legal, for legal personnel; and The Creative Group, for advertising, marketing, and web-design professionals. The company serves its clients and candidates through more than 400 staffing and consulting services locations worldwide.

For expert advice on the legal issues currently impacting HR, *Human Resources Kit For Dummies,* 2nd Edition incorporates the sage counsel of O'Melveny & Myers LLP, one of the world's largest and most preeminent law firms and a leading specialist in labor and employment law. The Los Angeles–based firm was founded in 1885 and today has offices throughout the United States and abroad. O'Melveny & Myers's capabilities span virtually every area of legal practice: Antitrust/Competition; Appellate; Class Actions, Mass Torts & Aggregated Litigation; Corporate; Corporate Finance; Electronic Discovery; Entertainment & Media; Global Enforcement & Criminal Defense; Health Care & Life Sciences; Insurance; Intellectual Property & Technology; Labor & Employment; Mergers & Acquisitions; Private Equity; Project Development & Real Estate; Restructuring; Securities Enforcement & Regulatory Counseling; Securities Litigation; Strategic Counseling; Tax; and Trial & Litigation. Of particular value were the contributions of one of the firm's senior partners, Scott Dunham, a top employment law expert.

Dedication

To my wife, Marcia, and my sons, Michael and Matthew, who are my daily reminders that people are the most important source of inspiration — in life and in work.

Author's Acknowledgments

In preparing this second edition of *Human Resources Kit For Dummies,* I relied on the advice and assistance of a number of talented individuals whose contributions made this book possible. I want to thank Allen Scott, Joel Drucker, and Robert McCauley for their research and recommendations on the fast-changing world of human resources management. I also want to acknowledge the valuable insight of Reesa McCoy Staten, Vice President of Corporate Communications at Robert Half International Inc., and thank the many other professionals at Robert Half International who provided their expertise, including Linda Blandford-Beringsmith, Amanda Beck, Frank Lyons, Lynne Smith, Marilyn Sohmer, and Mark Wagoner. I would also be remiss if I did not acknowledge those individuals who made the first edition of *Human Resources Kit For Dummies* possible, most notably Barry Tarshis and Lynn Taylor. In addition, I'm indebted to Stacy Kennedy, Acquisitions Editor, at John Wiley & Sons, Inc., who saw the need to provide new insight on this important subject, and to the editors and reviewers whose efforts carried this second edition through to completion: Kelly Ewing and Debbie Casados.

My sincere thanks also go to the highly respected law firm of O'Melveny & Myers, whose collaboration was essential to the whole project. As legal issues continue to shape key HR practices, I believe our readers will benefit greatly from the insights provided by Scott Dunham, one of the firm's senior partners and a leading employment law expert.

A final acknowledgment goes to the founder of our company, the late Robert Half, who was a close friend. Bob established a corporate motto years ago — "Ethics First"— two words that continue to be the indispensable cornerstone of any successful business.

Publisher's Acknowledgments

We're proud of this book; please send us your comments through our Dummies online registration form located at www.dummies.com/register.

Some of the people who helped bring this book to market include the following:

Acquisitions, Editorial, and Media Development

Project Editor: Kelly Ewing
(Previous Edition: Tim Gallan)

Acquisitions Editor: Stacy Kennedy

Copy Editor: Kelly Ewing *(Previous Edition: William A. Barton)*

General Reviewer: Debbie Casados

Media Development Specialist: Kate Jenkins

Media Project Supervisor: Laura Moss

Editorial Manager: Michelle Hacker

Editorial Supervisor: Carmen Krikorian

Editorial Assistant: Erin Calligan

Cartoons: Rich Tennant (www.the5thwave.com)

Composition Services

Project Coordinator: Ryan Steffen

Layout and Graphics: Carl Byers, Lavonne Cook, Denny Hager, Barry Offringa, Lynsey Osborn

Anniversary Logo Design: Richard Pacifico

Proofreaders: John Greenough, Jessica Kramer, Susan Moritz, Ethel M. Winslow

Indexer: Techbooks

Publishing and Editorial for Consumer Dummies

Diane Graves Steele, Vice President and Publisher, Consumer Dummies

Joyce Pepple, Acquisitions Director, Consumer Dummies

Kristin A. Cocks, Product Development Director, Consumer Dummies

Michael Spring, Vice President and Publisher, Travel

Kelly Regan, Editorial Director, Travel

Publishing for Technology Dummies

Andy Cummings, Vice President and Publisher, Dummies Technology/General User

Composition Services

Gerry Fahey, Vice President of Production Services

Debbie Stailey, Director of Composition Services

Contents at a Glance

Table of Contents

Introduction

....

A company's ability to grow and stay on top of customer demand has always depended heavily on the quality of its people. Today, this relationship is even more relevant. In bottom-line terms, employees represent the intellectual capital that can make or break a firm's efforts to remain competitive. Businesses are now, more than ever, recognizing that a highly skilled and motivated workforce is pivotal to success.

But finding and keeping top talent can be a challenging task. In any job market, competition exists for the most desirable candidates, and, once hired, they are only a headhunter's phone call away from leaving you. Recruiting and managing a first-rate staff hasn't gotten any easier, either. As business has become more complex, so has the human resources function, now encompassing everything from assessing staffing needs more strategically to launching effective training initiatives, interpreting federal and state codes, and implementing policies and benefits that safeguard workers while protecting company interests. And the stakes are high. The legal and economic consequences of a major HR misstep can be enormous.

Managers and business owners with teams that consistently delight customers and make money for the firm aren't hard to spot. They are the ones who thoroughly understand the company's most important needs, know how to attract the best people and are intent on improving their work environment so their employees feel free to draw on all of their competencies. In short, they're very good at managing human resources.

For many, human resources management is an intimidating prospect, especially for executives and business owners at fast-growth companies who find their HR responsibilities are suddenly far more complex. Today's businesses — especially small and midsize ones — need a practical yet comprehensive resource with information, insights, and tools to help align their companies' HR practices and policies with their overall business objectives. That's why I decided to write *Human Resources Kit For Dummies.*

Some companies are lucky enough to have their own HR professional or even an entire HR department. Most of these HR specialists have developed their skills through years of education and on-the-job experience. In writing this book, my aim is not to pretend that I can magically turn you into a seasoned HR professional by the time you're finished reading this book. I *do* believe, though, that I can give you a fair representation of the issues HR people deal with, how the best of them approach these challenges, and enough background to help you better handle the HR function for your organization — both today and as you continue to grow.

About This Book

As you can see from the table of contents, human resources is a very broad and varied discipline, and one book can't possibly tell you everything you need to know about this continually evolving subject area. So don't worry. I don't overwhelm you with information. On the contrary, everything you read in this book and every tool available on the CD-ROM directly relates to the operational issues most companies deal with daily.

What can you expect to gain from this book? For starters, you'll be better able to

- ✔ Evaluate your company's current HR policies and practices to prepare for the business challenges of the next decade.

- ✔ Understand the HR-related issues (changing demographics, for example) that will impact the workplace of the future — and make the necessary long-term plans for success.

- ✔ Develop and implement a human resources program that responds to the needs and resources of your firm.

- ✔ Interpret the key regulatory issues that affect every business owner and manager and thus be in a better position to guard against costly legal disputes.

- ✔ Develop a strategic staffing mindset, ensuring that hiring practices and decisions are linked to long-term and short-term business objectives.

- ✔ Examine what today's most successful and progressive companies are doing with respect to such basic HR areas as recruiting, benefits, training, performance management, and staff retention.

- ✔ Gain insight into practices (flextime and telecommuting, for example) that have become basic components of today's "employee-friendly" workplace, determine which ones are right for your company, and administer them successfully and cost effectively.

Regardless of your role, this book provides general guidelines on how to set up and implement successful HR practices, as well as actual tools — forms, templates, Web site links, and so on — that you can put to immediate and productive use. *Human Resources Kit For Dummies,* in other words, is not simply a book to read; it's a book to use.

Conventions Used in This Book

If yours is a business that currently has a small number of employees, you may be handling all company and staff HR needs yourself. In other words, you serve as hiring manager, trainer, mentor, performance evaluator, and motivator for every individual your company employs. In this case, the suggested guidelines in this book apply to processes you will not only establish but also *implement.*

On the other hand, if your company has many employees — or grows to have many employees — you won't be able to handle all these functions on your own. In this case, all the advice in this book still applies to you, but for certain functions, as I discuss throughout the chapters, you'll serve as *counselor* to group, departmental, or "line" managers as to how to manage and bring out the best in the employees who report directly to them.

Foolish Assumptions

In writing *Human Resources Kit For Dummies,* I had to make certain assumptions about you — the reader. Because I'm not sure of exactly what your background and needs are, I've written the book with two broad audiences in mind:

- ✔ Business owners who find that their growing companies are demanding a greater portion of their time and attention in managing one or more of the most common HR functions, such as hiring, benefits administration, performance evaluation, training, and regulatory issues.

- ✔ Individuals in small to midsize companies who have only a limited knowledge of HR functions but whose management has asked them to take on some or all of these roles. While seasoned HR professionals may find much of the information a handy reference, my primary audience is people who are new to the field or are eager to discover new HR practices to gain competitive advantages for their companies.

I focus quite a bit on the operational, functional components of the practice of HR. But this is not my only purpose. First and foremost, I want to address you as a businessperson — someone who, after reading the book, is knowledgeable not only about the nuts and bolts of HR but also knows how to approach the function with the goal of becoming a strategic player in helping to run your company.

As you progress in your role, you may find another of my books, *Motivating Employees For Dummies,* helpful.

How This Book Is Organized

Human Resources Kit For Dummies consists of 22 chapters and a CD-ROM with forms, templates, and other tools that correspond to the topics in particular chapters. For the most part, each chapter deals with a single aspect of the HR function as it relates to today's workplace, and each chapter contains not just information but also concrete advice on how to put this information to practical use.

Part I: Building the Framework

In this part, I give you with an overview of key issues impacting human resources administration. I also alert you to the legal minefields in today's increasingly regulated environment and highlight relevant legislation to help you understand how these issues affect your company.

Part II: The Right People in the Right Places

This part deals exclusively with the staffing process. Successful staffing in today's workplace is a multistage process, with each phase linked to the others.

Part III: Retention: Critical in Any Business Environment

This part covers policies that can enhance — or impede — your ability to retain valued staff once you've attracted them to your organization. I cover issues such as wages, benefits, training, and company culture. I also focus on one of the most important trends in staffing today: the growth of the contingent workforce. You find out about the changes that have vastly increased the number of temporary and project workers today and discover how to successfully capitalize on this expanding pool of talent in your business.

Part IV: Keeping Things Together: Monitoring Ongoing Performance

In this part, you discover ways to maximize the employee performance appraisal process, as well as inspire extraordinary performance in employees. You also get a crash course on what to do when things go awry.

Part V: The Part of Tens

The final chapters of the book provide you with useful supplementary information, including a summary of laws affecting HR, the keys to HR success in the future, Web sites to access, and steps to take to increase your effectiveness as an HR specialist.

Appendix

One last thing: I also include an About the CD appendix that covers — you guessed it — how to use the CD included with this book.

The CD-ROM

From job application forms and sample employee policies to performance appraisals and benefit plan worksheets, you get everything you need to implement a state-of-the-art HR operation.

Icons Used in This Book

When I want you to pay close attention to a specific piece of information, I place little pictures, called icons, next to the text in the margin. Here's what the icons mean:

This icon flags what I consider to be good and practical advice.

I flag important conceptual information using this icon.

This icon indicates that if you don't heed what I'm telling you, you may get into legal trouble.

Whenever I mention a document that you can reference on the CD-ROM, I use this icon.

Part I
Building the Framework

In this part . . .

1 provide an overview of what HR is all about. Chapter 1
deals with some key, overarching concepts, such as the
transformation of the HR function, factors changing the
face of today's workplace, and a look at the HR software
tools available to help you carry out your responsibilities.
Chapter 2 discusses the many HR-related regulations, programs, and legal issues, such as nondiscrimination and
equal-opportunity laws, with which you must help your
company comply.

Chapter 1

The Big Picture

*M*ost people in business agree that being sensitive to — and doing your best to meet — the "people needs" of your employees is in your best interest as an employer. But a good deal of debate has always existed over just how much responsibility a company needs to assume — and how much time (and money) a company must devote to the needs and priorities of employees as opposed to the needs and priorities of its business operations and customers.

That's where *you* come in.

As a human resources manager (or as a business owner or senior executive responsible for the HR function), your job is to focus on the practices and policies that directly affect the welfare and morale of your company's most important asset — its employees. It's up to you to help your firm strike the optimal balance between the strategic needs of your business and the basic people needs of your workforce. The way your business manages your employee base can make all the difference in your ability to differentiate yourself from the competition.

Striking this balance has never been easy. But most people in business would agree that not only is the task harder to achieve today than in the past, but it's also more important as well. In short, human resources has become a business unto itself. And the principal asset of this particular business is people.

Scoping Out the HR Role

Human resources management is the phrase that nearly everyone uses to describe a set of functions that once fell under the category of "personnel administration" or "personnel management." Regardless of the name, you can sum up this particular aspect of business as the decisions, activities, and processes that must meet the basic needs and support the work performance of employees.

The most common areas that fall under HR management include the following:

✔ **Staffing:** Strategically determining, recruiting, and hiring the human resources you need for your business.

✔ **Basic workplace policies:** Orienting your staff on policies and procedures, such as schedules, safety, security, and so on.

✔ **Compensation and benefits:** Establishing effective — and attractive — wages and perks.

✔ **Retention:** Continually assessing the quality of your workplace and HR policies to ensure people want to stay with your company.

✔ **Training and developing employees:** Ensuring that your staff grows in knowledge and experience to help your company expand and continue to meet the changing needs of customers.

✔ **Regulatory issues:** Complying with the ever-increasing number of federal, state, and local regulations.

Human resources management is all about people: finding and recruiting them; hiring them; training and developing them; paying them; retaining them; creating an environment that's safe, healthy, and productive for them; communicating with them; and doing whatever is reasonably possible to find that delicate balance between what best serves the basic needs of employees and what best serves the market-driven needs of the company.

Throughout this book, I cover the organizational aspects of human resources management. However, I must stress that no cookie-cutter formulas for effective HR management are available. Every company — regardless of size, location, or purpose — must deal with human resources issues in a way that's best suited to its needs and situation.

If you run a small business, for example, you probably function as your own HR manager — that is, you personally oversee and conduct all the classic human resources functions of your company: You recruit and hire. You set up the compensation and benefits package. You write the paychecks and keep the appropriate records.

The chances are good, too, that you're the person responsible for training and developing the people you hire. And although you may not need to publish a company newsletter to keep the people who work for you informed about what's going on in the company, you probably make a point to keep them in the loop.

Bigger companies face the same basic challenges and carry out the same general activities. The only difference is that larger companies employ individual specialists — or sometimes entire departments — to handle these same functions.

True, after they reach a certain size, most companies feel virtually obligated to create a human resources department — even if it consists of only one person. Because of the increasing complexity of HR issues today, larger companies have boosted the size of their departments and typically employ specialists in areas such as benefits administration or 401(k) retirement plans. But smaller firms that don't have the resources for such specialization must ensure that the people who handle their HR functions are solid *generalists* — that is, they possess skills in several areas of HR rather than in one particular specialty. If your business is on the smaller side and you want to meet the needs of your employees today, you'll need to know a lot about a lot of things— and the more you know, the better.

The human resources function in general has undergone enormous changes in the past 20 years. Some companies still take a highly structured, largely centralized approach to human resources management. The majority of companies today, however, take a far more decentralized approach, with HR practitioners and line managers working cooperatively to set basic policies and carry out programs.

The following sections offer a brief summary of key themes, trends, and issues that are currently affecting the human resources function the most and that are likely to continue influencing the field in the near future.

Strategist versus administrator

The key theme of this book is the increasing recognition in corporate America that the most important asset a company has is not its products, factories, or systems, but its people. Companies no longer take the "human" side of business for granted. And that's why the human resources function itself has begun to assume so much more importance.

For several decades now, people responsible for the human resources function have ceased to be viewed merely as "personnel administrators" or strictly "support." The shift in terms from "personnel" to "human resources" reflects this thinking. But today's HR professionals are assuming an increasingly broad role in their companies, becoming strategic advisors to the senior management team. Top company managers now look to HR for help in formulating long-term staffing strategies, as well as introducing and following through on practices that help ensure that employees get the support and training they need to meet the increasing demands of their jobs. In short, senior management is looking to HR for insights on how to tap into the potential of every individual within the organization.

This expectation creates many new opportunities for you. One key skill you need to develop is the ability to think strategically. No doubt you've heard the term strategic thinkers. But what does it really mean?

Certainly, strategic thinkers spend plenty of time setting objectives and getting work done, but they also do much more. At heart, strategic business thinkers try to look ahead, attempting to anticipate which issues and information will be most relevant. They don't look at their work merely as a series of tasks or simply react to events; they also examine trends, issues, opportunities, and long-term needs — and shape what they discover into policies and recommendations. To borrow from the restaurant industry, strategic thinkers do more than cook; they help shape the menu.

How does the concept of strategic thinkers apply to the HR world? In effect, strategic HR professionals act as consultants to the rest of the business. They help set a path — that is, a vision of how to ensure HR effectively delivers on its mission. It's not easy to deliberate when you're in a hurry to move forward, but they know it's wise to look before they leap, and this philosophy helps them offer valued counsel. Before merely saying "yes" to a proposed direction, they carefully examine and explain the long-term cost-benefit ratio. They expand the range of people they talk and listen to, drawing insights not just from departmental colleagues but from finance, marketing, legal counsel, manufacturing, sales, and other areas who can help them better understand what makes their company tick. And they do so with people at all levels, ranging from experienced senior managers to entry-level employees.

Taking this approach is not easy. Still, you've got a great opportunity — the chance to be regarded not just as an HR person, but as a vital source of counsel and a central part of your firm's management team. Even taking just 15 minutes a day of solitary "think time" and research time can make a big difference in effectively shaping your work.

Adapting to the changing workplace

Most everyone is aware that companies today are smaller, leaner, and not as hierarchically structured as they were 20 years ago. But the most significant change in the organizational makeup of most companies has less to do with the infrastructure and more to do with the fundamental *nature* of jobs — and the working arrangements of the people who hold those jobs.

What's happening, in short, is that you can no longer think of today's workplace as the specific building or piece of real estate where employees perform their jobs. Today is the age of the telecommuter and the virtual office. Thanks to wireless connections, the Internet, video conferencing, mobile phones, and other technology tools, many businesses can run efficiently even though the key players never meet face-to-face more than once or twice a month. Eighty-seven percent of executives surveyed in a 2005 OfficeTeam study said that they believe telecommuting will increase in the next 10 to 15 years. According to a special report by *The Futurist,* by 2015, more than 100 million people will be telecommuters. But telecommuting is only one aspect of this new workplace.

Today is also the age of flexibility, with many companies providing some or all of their employees with an opportunity to modify the normal nine-to-five schedule in ways that suit their particular family situations or lifestyles. Work hours vary greatly, as does the philosophical approach people take to their work. No longer does an employee simply walk away from the office and stop thinking about his job. The OfficeTeam study revealed, for example, that 86 percent of executives believe workers in the future will be more connected to the office while on vacation. And only 9 percent think employees will be working fewer hours in the future.

Perhaps most important is the rise of the *contingent employee:* The man or woman who, instead of having one full-time job with a single employer, may work part-time or on a contract or project basis for a variety of companies in a given year.

The percentage of professionals in today's workplace who are working on a temporary or project basis is rising rapidly — and for a variety of reasons. The ability to call on contingent workers on an as-needed basis enables many companies to avoid the disruptive cycle of hiring and layoffs. Companies can hire and develop a core team of full-time employees and then, as additional needs arise, bring in supplemental people on a temporary basis.

Then, too, more and more professionals these days voluntarily choose to make their "full-time" job a series of temporary assignments. They like the flexibility, variety, and learning opportunities this option affords them.

To take full advantage of contingent employees, you need a strategy in place to help ensure that these workers bring the necessary skills to the table and are smoothly integrated into the existing work environment. For a detailed discussion of contingent workers, see Chapter 13.

Easing the work/life conflict

Is your company employee-friendly? It had better be if you want to attract and keep top performers in today's job market. Being *employee-friendly* means that your scheduling and general operating policies take into reasonable account the personal needs of employees — in particular, their desire to balance job responsibilities with family responsibilities. Most survey data today indicates that being able to maintain more control over schedules has become a priority for most workers, parents especially. And it has become increasingly apparent throughout the past decade or so that family-oriented policies do more than simply enhance a company's recruiting initiatives. They also produce a number of bottom-line benefits, such as reduced absenteeism, fewer disability claims, and fewer workplace accidents. Chief among the practices and policies that are typically found in companies actively pursuing work/family initiatives are flexible scheduling, telecommuting arrangements, employee assistance programs (EAPs), and benefits programs that enable employees to select the benefits (child care support, for example) relevant to their needs (see Chapters 11 and 12).

Avoiding the baby boom bust

Probably no generation has more greatly influenced the history of American business than the baby boomers, the 76 million men and women born between 1946 and 1964. Increasing numbers of them are nearing retirement age, creating a potential drain of knowledge within your corporation and the need to ensure proper training for the next generation of leaders. A great many of these boomers occupy the *sandwich generation,* meaning that their financial, emotional, and mental resources are spread thin as they attempt to simultaneously care for their children and parents. And others who've been focused on their careers for many years are beginning to ponder different directions. All these factors have profound implications for the kind of HR programs you build — from management skills training to flexible work arrangements to broader, strategic initiatives that help shape your firm's overall culture.

Workforce diversity: Making it work

The baby boomer's influence is just one element of the changing demographics of the workforce, a key issue affecting the work of HR professionals today. As nearly everyone knows, the American workplace is a far cry from what it looked like 50 years ago, when more than half the American workforce consisted of white males who were the sole breadwinners in the household. Consider just this fact alone: The Bureau of Labor Statistics predicts that by 2008, women and minorities will make up 70 percent of all new entrants to the workforce.

In addition, trends such as delayed retirement, second careers, and increased longevity mean that the age spread of workers is greater today than ever before. These professionals range from the *Silent Generation* — comprised of people born before World War II — and baby boomers to *Gen-Xers* (born between 1965 and 1980) and now *Generation Y* (sometimes called Millennials or Netsters), whose members were born in the early 1980s.

Diversity means a wider range of people are bringing a greater variety of approaches to work, ideas, and lifestyle issues to the workplace. If, as they say, variety is the spice of life, then the workplace is getting more vibrant by the minute. Your HR policies must address these differences in order to attract, retain, and maximize the contributions of all members of the changing workforce.

One example is how diversity is changing the way human resources professionals are structuring and administering their benefits packages. A "one-size-fits-all" benefits plan doesn't exist. The trend today is toward cafeteria-style offerings, which give employees the opportunity to choose among a variety of benefits that best match their particular life and workstyle arrangements.

By mid-2005, working mothers accounted for almost one-fifth of all employed individuals, and nearly three-fourths of employed mothers were usually working full time — a statistic that helps explain why child-care assistance is now a highly requested benefit. And because people are living longer today, an increasing number of employees are taking on the responsibility of caring for their aging parents or other relatives — a trend that's introduced a new term to the employee benefits vocabulary: *eldercare*.

In addition, the intergenerational workforce requires a new way of thinking about staff management. Each generation has unique priorities, perspectives, skill sets, and work styles. Each tends to respond to different motivations, seeks different types of support from managers, and reacts in different ways to company programs and policies.

The challenge to companies in general is not simply to adapt to diversity but to capitalize on it and embrace the ways it can enhance creativity and productivity. Many companies today are discovering that when you're competing in the global marketplace, with customers from all over the world, workforce diversity — especially at the managerial level — can be a significant competitive advantage. (See Chapter 3 for more on building diverse teams.)

Rising healthcare costs

The proper management of employee healthcare costs is an increasingly challenging business issue. According to a recent benefits study conducted by Hay Group, company medical costs rose ten percent in 2005, marking the sixth year of double-digit rate increases. This increase is significantly higher than the rate of inflation. The *average* contribution for family coverage in 2005 was $2,600. For a number of reasons — from aging employees to administrative issues within healthcare providers to the cost of procedures and prescription drugs — prices will likely continue to rise, significantly impacting your firm's payroll and bottom line.

But healthcare isn't merely a line item to be managed. The overall health and well-being of *everyone* in your company is arguably the HR department's most important responsibility. As you work with benefits experts, insurance advisors, legal counsel, and others to create viable healthcare programs, a number of issues must be addressed. They relate not only to how your healthcare plans are set up financially, but also to the factors within your firm's culture that promote — or don't promote — a healthy workforce. In large part, addressing healthcare from this big picture vantage point is central to the notion of the HR professional as a strategist. I give a detailed look at the nuances of healthcare in Chapter 11.

Keeping pace with technology

As it has in many fields, technology has been a revolutionary development for people in HR management. E-mail has replaced the cork bulletin board as the primary communication between management and employees — and gone on to serve far more functions. Computers have streamlined the administrative aspects of every HR function. And, of course, the Internet, company intranets and other online resources now play a significant role in employee training.

But you still face a challenging side to this otherwise rosy picture. As I explain later in this chapter in "Staying Ahead of the Curve with HR Software," the software that enables companies to process large amounts of information is complex (and often expensive). Furthermore, it has introduced training and security issues that HR professionals didn't need to concern themselves with in the days of the typewriter.

Then, too, as work processes have become more technically sophisticated, the need for skilled employees is intensifying. *Knowledge workers* is a term used to describe employees who possess the skills and knowledge needed to perform the jobs and functions most affected by technological advances, tasks that in turn require significant levels of education. These positions include analysts, database administrators, programmers, systems analysts, technical writers, academic professionals, librarians, researchers, lawyers, and teachers, as well as scientists and students of all kinds. According to the U.S. Bureau of Labor Statistics' 2006–2007 Occupational Handbook projections, more than 75 percent of the 25 fastest-growing occupations require a college degree. Companies are looking more and more to their HR departments to simultaneously enhance the skills of existing employees and identify job candidates who possess the necessary level of expertise.

Rules and regulations: Ethics first

In the 21st century, a workplace that's free of hazards, sexual harassment, and discrimination is no longer considered a "benefit." It's something that employees have every right to expect. In recent years, federal, state, and local government agencies are using their powers of enforcement to ensure that workers are protected.

If you don't already have an HR background, one of your biggest challenges is to familiarize yourself with the many government-mandated regulations and programs with which your company must comply. At first glance, the task is staggering. More than 35,000 programs exist, which in many cases are subsets of laws. Don't worry; you don't need to know the details of every one of them. But you do need to pay attention to the areas in your company that are covered by these regulations, as well as the laws you must keep track of in order to stay in compliance.

Government-mandated regulations touch almost every aspect of the human resource function, including safety and health, equal-employment opportunity, sexual harassment policies, pension reform, and environmental issues. Among recent legislation, the Sarbanes-Oxley Act of 2002 has had a widespread effect on workplace cultures. The primary objective of the act was to create stronger forms of financial accountability and internal controls in organizations. But the overall spirit of Sarbanes-Oxley is one of ethics and responsibility. To that end, it mandates that every publicly traded company create and articulate a strong code of conduct. Many private companies, attuned as well to the spirit of the legislation, are voluntarily complying with some of the regulations, including placing a stronger emphasis on the ethical behavior of their employees. No single department is better equipped than HR to deliver on this vision through company-wide communications, training programs and careful, ongoing monitoring efforts.

I can't stress enough the importance of ethics to an organization. We live in a dynamic business world that presents a great many challenges and opportunities. With all this flux and potential for reward, it's tempting for even an entire corporation merely to pay lip service to integrity. In the HR role for your company, you have the chance to be front and center in creating a corporate culture of accountability and personal integrity with a strong spirit of ethical behavior at its heart. Helping your organization understand the importance of putting ethics first is a way in which you can begin to make HR more than a function as you take on the role of strategic counselor.

Making HR a Strategic Partner

Nearly everything in the chapters that lie ahead focuses on specific aspects of the human resources function and what you need to do to manage these aspects effectively. The following list offers some general guidelines on how to be more successful overall in your HR efforts:

✔ **Become business savvy.** Make it your personal goal to find out everything you possibly can about your company's business, particularly in terms of revenues and profits. Keep in mind that the more broad-minded you can be in how you approach everything you do in your job, the more credibility you will have as a strategic business professional — and the easier it will be to get senior managers and line managers to endorse the development initiatives you recommend.

✔ **Don't ignore the basics.** Regardless of how committed you are to bringing new ideas to the organization you work for, don't overlook the traditional needs (such as policies regarding benefits, computers and the Internet, dress code, and privacy) that are all but universal among employees. At the very least, make sure that every employee in the company is familiar with your company's basic practices. If there's an employee manual, make sure that it's up to date. If the company doesn't have an employee manual, make it a priority to create one.

✔ **Make quality hiring a priority.** Make a personal commitment — and try to secure a similar commitment from other managers in every department — that your company will devote the time and energy needed to ensure that each new employee you recruit and hire is the right person for that particular job.

✔ **Keep your ear to the ground.** One of the most valuable contributions you can make to the senior managers of your company is to keep them apprised of all workplace issues and concerns that may affect your company's ability to meet the needs of customers. Taking on this role doesn't mean that you're constantly looking over the shoulders of the line managers in your company. It does mean, however, that you always have your hand on the staffing pulse of your company. You're aware, for example, when morale is starting to slip, or when the workload is starting to burn out people. You smell the smoke before a big fire occurs.

✔ **Stay current.** Make it your business to be aware of new developments in human resources administration, including technological advances and key trends in pay practices and benefits programs. When you come across new and promising ideas, make sure that you let senior management know. Be particularly diligent about keeping pace with what is going on in the legal and regulatory side of HR, making sure that you're aware of any laws or regulatory changes that apply to your company.

Staying Ahead with HR Software

Computer software has been very good to HR professionals over the last few decades. Many labor-intensive functions — time reporting, payroll calculation, tax computation, and tax reporting — are now processed quite rapidly.

The scope, flexibility, and versatility of HR-related software — formally known as Human Resource Information Systems (HRIS) — continues to accelerate at a dizzying pace. The new generation of training and development software, for example, not only tracks such aspects of training as scheduling, enrollments, vendor data, and costs, but it also integrates that data with information relating to career development and assessment.

To be sure, nobody who remembers the way it used to be in the typical human resources department is brooding over the fact that so many of the purely administrative tasks of HR management are now automated. There's no question, either, that the evolution of HRIS has not only enhanced the efficiency of HR operations in general, but it has also enabled HR departments to lower their administrative costs and make better and more timely use of data in strategic planning.

Unfortunately, however, an inherent challenge exists in this otherwise upbeat picture. The problem is that, with so many products and applications evolving at such a rapid pace (the number of HR-related software products on the market, according to WorldatWork, now exceeds 3,000 and shows no signs of ebbing), it has become increasingly difficult for HR professionals to make basic buying decisions. This challenge is no small matter. Depending on the size of your company, the level of customization you require, and the number of functions you're interested in automating or integrating, the cost can run anywhere from just under $500 to more than $1 million. And that sum doesn't include what you may have to spend on additional computer hardware, the time it takes your employees to learn the new system, or the potential operational problems during the transition period.

In other words, the challenge you face when you're in the market for an HR software application is not simply a matter of deciding which product has the niftiest features or which vendor is the most supportive. It's much more a matter of figuring out an overall strategy to ensure that the transition from the old way to the new way goes as smoothly as possible.

It's a given that all software decisions should be driven by the strategic and operational needs of the business — as opposed to the capabilities of the software. This axiom takes on special significance when you're considering buying software that will combine and integrate functions that currently operate as separate tasks. Regardless of how elegantly the software is designed, how easy it is to use, and how fast it runs, the system must ultimately produce a business payoff — whether it's through increased productivity, cost savings, quicker response time, or improved employee morale.

This advice may seem obvious, but it's worth mentioning nonetheless. You may get so swept up in the remarkable capabilities of today's HRIS products that you lose sight of what the technology is meant to do: help your company operate more efficiently and profitably. So before you move ahead on any software initiative, be prepared to go through a rigorous and disciplined needs assessment, followed by a cost/benefit analysis. In other words, rather than think about this purchase as an administrative matter of implementation, step back and assess it strategically. A new HR application may not represent the only means of achieving a given business objective. You may be able to achieve the same result more cost-effectively through some other means, such as outsourcing or using contingent workers. The key point: Don't jump the gun on any major software decision. Think it through.

Ask the following key questions when you're going through this process:

- ✔ What business benefits does your company stand to gain once the software is in place?
- ✔ How much is the software going to cost?
- ✔ How long will it take before the investment is recouped?
- ✔ What can you expect in terms of downtime or reduced productivity while employees are learning the new system?
- ✔ Is the new system compatible with the company's existing hardware and software, or will it need a complete upgrade?

Become an educated buyer

You don't need to be a computer programmer to make intelligent HRIS buying decisions. But if your company is seriously exploring a major software purchase, you should have at least a general idea of what various products are meant to do and what features distinguish one system and one vendor from another.

The Internet offers a wealth of information on technology products. Two useful Web sites to explore are the Society for Human Resource Management (www.shrm.org) and hrVillage (www.hrVillage.com). Each of these sites contains useful information about HRIS, including data from vendors and tutorial advice on how to best implement HRIS. Also included may be *white papers,* which, in the business world, are reports on major issues affecting a particular industry that companies produce to educate customers or other stakeholders.

No secret formulas ensure that your HRIS buying decisions will give you the results you seek. But the following suggestions stack the odds in your favor.

- ✔ **Instead of taking on sole responsibility for making the final decision (or assigning it to your information technology department), put together a cross-functional team** — a half-dozen or so employees who represent different constituencies in the company (IT staff, department managers, end users, and so on) and who have the time and the desire to take part in the process. This type of group can be more helpful in investigating and reviewing issues of compatibility and implementation more than researching vendors.

- ✔ **Find out everything you can about vendors you're thinking of using:** how long they've been in business, how established they are (you don't want to buy an HRIS product from a company that may not be around in six months), how committed they are to research and development, and how diligent they are when it comes to support.

- ✔ **Insist that any vendor who wants your business demonstrate how the software you're considering performs those specific functions that you believe are most important to your business.** The vendor should be able to demonstrate through case studies or pilot programs that their solution addresses your specific business needs.

- ✔ **Ask specific questions about how the product was developed.** Find out, in particular, whether the development team included people who were familiar with those business functions that are your chief priority.

- ✔ **If the IT investment is significant, get the names and telephone numbers of at least five current users of any product you're considering to get a real-world perspective.** When you talk to those users, ask for additional names that weren't given to you by the vendor.

- ✔ **Include as part of your overall strategy some mechanism that gets users excited about the system you're considering implementing.** Identify early on those people who may be resistant. Start training before the system is implemented.

HR software: A features checklist

When (and if) the time comes to compare two or more integrated software products on a feature-by-feature basis, you should focus on two considerations: the specific feature being compared and how important that feature is to your needs. The following list provides a general idea of features that normally differentiate one product from another. It's up to you to determine how important each feature is to your business.

✔ Response time (How long does it take users to access information, especially during peak periods?)

✔ Scope of search capabilities

✔ Report and audit capabilities

✔ Internet and intranet compatibility

✔ Scanning and OCR capabilities

✔ Security and self-service capabilities (Can employees update it without compromising security?)

✔ Flexibility (Can it run in a variety of environments — local area network and stand-alone?)

✔ Ease of use

You can find a lot of information about HR software through directories, Web sites, and publications:

✔ **Advanced Personnel Systems (www.hrcensus.com):** An online directory of vendor-provided information specializing in providing objective information on most types of HR systems, this Web site typically monitors 2,500 products from 1,500 vendors.

✔ **The International Association for Human Resource Information Management (IHRIM) e-Journal (www.ihrim.org/resources):** Published six times a year and available in a PDF format, this publication includes reviews of timely articles and books aimed at senior executives in HR and IT. Though primarily aimed at extremely large organizations ($1 billion or more in annual revenues), smaller companies can often apply many useful principles by studying the approaches taken by larger companies.

✔ **Society for Human Resource Management (www.shrm.org), WorldatWork (worldatwork.org) and hrVillage (hrVillage.com):** These three Web sites contain a lot of useful information, such as case studies, tutorials, white papers and information on vendors.

✔ **Workforce Online (www.workforceonline.com):** Although much of the HRIS information on this Web site is vendor-provided, it is comprehensive and organized attractively into categories that list database compatibility, current clients, and price range. Each listing includes a link to the vendor's Web site.

Chapter 2

Law and Order: Navigating the Legal Minefield of Hiring and Managing

*T*he legal aspects of HR are complicated, and, yes, they can be more than a bit daunting — especially when you first encounter them. Laws affect virtually everything you do in the field of HR: hiring, determining compensation, choosing how to evaluate employee performance — and many more tasks. All these activities carry significant legal implications. Failing to fully understand the law can prove costly.

You're not alone if you find this topic intimidating. However, with ample preparation (and frequent contact with legal counsel when it's called for), you should do just fine.

In this chapter as well as in other parts of the book, I cite what I believe to be the most up-to-date and legally sound information available, largely based on the advice and recommendations of the prestigious law firm O'Melveny & Myers LLP. Together, we share with you our knowledge of the most successful policies. But, just like heart surgery, the practice of law is not something you should do yourself. Consult an attorney. The information contained in this chapter gives you an overview, but it is no substitute for the specific and tailored advice of your own legal counsel.

Legal Matters: The Big Picture

The legal issues covered in this chapter require careful deliberation for the following reasons:

- **Daily changes:** I'm not kidding. Every day, new statutes are passed by federal and state governments, new regulations are adopted by federal and state agencies, new ordinances are adopted by local governments, and courts are ruling on existing statutes, regulations, and ordinances. The discussions in this book help make you aware of these topics, but you still need to have your own lawyer review all of your forms and procedures.

- **Vague definition:** It would be nice if all laws were as clear as the posted speed limit. If the sign says the speed limit is 65, you're safe if you're driving 64 and know you can get a ticket if you're driving 66. Most employment laws aren't so clear. For example, many laws specifically require you to do what is "reasonable." What is reasonable in a specific situation? The law doesn't tell you. Just because you think you're acting reasonably doesn't mean that the courts, the administrative agencies, or your employees will agree. If a dispute arises between you and one of your employees over whether you have acted reasonably, don't expect it to be resolved quickly by some easy-to-reach arbiter. You may instead face a long and expensive process of finding out whether your actions were reasonable. And if the court or agency eventually decides that you didn't act reasonably, you can be liable for large sums of money.

- **Inconsistency:** If only one government were involved and all the laws involving HR practices were adopted at the same time, you might have an easier time. But laws and regulations are adopted by the federal government, states, counties, cities, air quality districts, water districts, and so on, and they don't consult with one another. Often, the law of one entity contradicts the law of another. In addition, each law is adopted at a different time, and efforts aren't always made to be consistent. In fact, new laws often conflict with old laws without repealing them.

My advice to you is simple: Don't be your own lawyer. Most laws are defined, refined, and clarified by agency regulations and court rulings that cover areas that the average person wouldn't anticipate. For example, if a law applies only to businesses with 25 or more employees, does it apply to your business? That depends on how the law defines "employee." Do part-time employees count? Do temporary or supplemental employees count? Do independent contractors count? What if you never had more than 23 people at a time, but, because of turnover, 40 different people worked for you at various times during the last year? Each law answers this question differently, and the answer may change often.

It sounds scary, but keep in mind that lots of companies are surviving and thriving in this environment. You can, too, if you just use a little common sense. This chapter gives you that common-sense guidance. However, this information is no substitute for legal advice. Get a lawyer and talk to that lawyer often.

Keeping the Peace

The extent to which you need to concern yourself with labor relations in your company, both formally and informally, depends mainly on two things: the number of people in your company and whether the company is unionized.

If your company is unionized, chances are that you may spend a considerable amount of your time negotiating and administering labor agreements. What's more, you're likely to be the person that union representatives approach whenever they have grievances.

If you're in a non-union company, you can't take anything for granted. People are people, and this being the case, thinking that the absence of a union is going to guarantee that occasional disputes won't pop up between employees and their managers and among employees is naïve. You may have never thought of yourself as a peacemaker. Get used to the idea.

Discrimination

Many federal, state, and local laws make it illegal to discriminate on the basis of a number of factors, including, but not limited to, race, religion, sex, age, disability, veteran status, pregnancy, and marital status. Some states, counties, and cities prohibit discrimination on the basis of sexual preference. But the laws don't stop there.

Take employee appearance, for example. Section 12947.5 of the California Government Code makes it unlawful for an employer to prohibit women from wearing pants in the workplace. Hairstyles, tattoos, and body piercings have also been issues in lawsuits. Jonathan W. Yarbrough, managing member of the law firm Constangy, Brooks & Smith LLC, who led a session at the 2006 SHRM Annual Conference titled "What Do You Mean I Cannot Wear My Nose Ring at Work?", stresses that understanding applicable laws that influence an employer's decisions about employee appearance and conduct is the key to preventing these types of lawsuits.

Of course, discrimination laws cover many areas besides employee appearance. My point here is that, no matter how trivial an issue may seem to you, *all forms of discrimination are unacceptable,* and it's your responsibility to be familiar with federal, state, and local laws which address discrimination.

So how should you deal with these laws? The answer is simple: Make all your hiring, promotion, and other decisions solely on the basis of ability to perform the job, and you should generally be okay.

Disparate Impact

The laws against discrimination extend not only to intentional acts by you *(disparate treatment),* but may also cover actions that aren't intended to discriminate but have the effect of doing so, which is called *disparate impact.*

For example, assume that you own a trucking company. If you decide that you won't employ people of a certain race, sex, or religion, you're practicing disparate treatment, which is illegal from the standpoint of federal, state, and many local laws. Even the 2001 Patriot Act, which is primarily focused on matters of national security, takes this form of discrimination very seriously. It condemns discrimination against Arab and Muslim Americans and Americans from south Asia on the basis of religious, ethnic, or racial background.

On the other hand, suppose that you don't intentionally discriminate, but you require all your truck drivers to speak French. If it turns out that this requirement results in limited hiring of members of a certain race, sex, or religion because, for whatever reason, few members of that particular race, sex, or religion speak French, you may be guilty of disparate impact discrimination. You haven't intentionally adopted a policy against a group, but an apparently neutral policy impacts one group adversely.

What happens if you are challenged on this policy, and a disparate impact is shown? If you can then demonstrate that speaking French is a *bona fide occupational qualification* (BFOQ) for the job, then you will not be guilty of discrimination. For example, if your trucking company is based in Vermont and all your drivers, as part of their routes, have to drive across the border into Quebec (the part of Canada where French, and not English, is the official language and appears on all signs), you may be able to establish that the ability to speak French is a BFOQ. However, if your trucking company is located in Arizona, and the drivers drive only between Arizona and Mexico, speaking French will not be considered to be a BFOQ, and you will be guilty of disparate impact discrimination if the requirement results in too few members of one group being employed by you.

Your determination of what is a BFOQ will almost certainly be second-guessed. Your good faith belief isn't enough to guarantee that you'll win if challenged. And the court or administrative agency reviewing the situation doesn't have to agree with you. Therefore, you need legal advice when establishing any job requirements that you think may be open to question.

The Equal Employment Opportunity Commission (EEOC)

The *Equal Employment Opportunity Commission* (EEOC) is the federal agency responsible for enforcing federal antidiscrimination laws in employment.

Regardless of how disciplined you are in your company about following equal opportunity employment principles, you must meet these three key requirements:

✔ Post federal and state Equal Employment Opportunity notices.

For EEO posting requirements and a sample EEO posting, see the CD-ROM.

✔ Depending on the size of your company and the nature of its business, you may be required to file an annual form (known as the Employer Information Report, EEO-1) that communicates to the EEOC the demographics of your company's workforce broken out into specific job categories.

✔ Keep on file copies of all documents (job applications, payroll records, discharges, and so on) that may conceivably become relevant in the event your company is ever involved in a discrimination suit. The recommended minimum period for maintaining these records is three years. Keep on file records of hiring practices, identifying total hires within a particular job classification and the percentage of minority and female applicants hired.

Hopefully, it'll never happen (fingers crossed!), but in the unlikely event that an employee or group of employees decides to file an equal employment opportunity complaint against your company, you should at least have a basic idea of what to expect.

According to the EEOC, in 2005, employees filed more than 75,000 cases of discrimination. Though EEOC research indicates that nearly 80 percent of these cases result in no benefit to the individual filing the charge, you need to understand the steps involved in case you need to interact with the EEOC. What follows is a rough description of the sequence of events that typically takes place after a claim is registered with the EEOC.

1. **The EEOC receives the charges.**

   EEOC will, in nearly every case, accept a charge for filing. The EEOC doesn't investigate and evaluate a charge when it's clear, for example, that the EEOC simply doesn't have jurisdiction.

2. **The EEOC notifies you of the charges.**

   The EEOC promptly notifies you that a charge has been filed and provides a copy of the charge. The EEOC generally requests information about the allegations in the charge, including a statement of the company's position on the merits. The EEOC also invites you to participate in mediation/conciliation to try to settle the charge immediately.

   If you choose not to participate, skip to Step 4.

3. **The parties try to hash it out.**

   Someone from your company (probably you) talks with both the person who filed the charge and an EEOC staff member. The plaintiff gets a chance to tell his side of the story — that is, why the person feels that he is the victim of discrimination. Your company's representative then gets to give the company's side of the story — why, in your view, your company did not discriminate. The EEOC staff member tries her best to resolve the issue. (Note that the resolution may involve, for example, giving a dismissed employee another chance or additional severance pay.)

4. **The investigation begins.**

   If Step 3 is unsuccessful (or you choose not to participate), the EEOC requests that you provide the information and the position statement requested in Step 2. The EEOC may follow up this step with requests for more information, which can include interviews of witnesses and a review of documents at your facility.

5. **The EEOC makes a determination.**

   If, on the basis of the investigation, the EEOC finds "reasonable cause" that your company discriminated against the individual, the EEOC notifies you and, once again, solicits you to participate in a conciliation process (as in Steps 2 and 3). If the conciliation process fails (or you choose not to participate), the EEOC then decides whether to take you to court itself or to issue the individual a *right-to-sue notice* so that he can sue you. (Note that if the EEOC finds no reasonable cause, it will so advise you and the individual but still issue a right-to-sue notice to the individual.)

In the event that the complaint leads to EEOC action, you'll quickly find yourself with a difficult choice: You have to either go along with EEOC proposals or gird yourself for a legal fight that may take years and cost your company millions in court costs, damages, and negative publicity. Even if the EEOC doesn't take the case, the individual claimant can proceed on his own, and you may find yourself in the same predicament.

The individual can — and often does, when already represented by an attorney — short-circuit the administrative process by requesting and generally receiving an immediate right-to-sue notice.

The EEO Family: A Closer Look

More than a dozen pieces of major, HR-related federal legislation have passed since 1963, all relating in some way to equal opportunity. In addition, the local, state, and county levels have passed hundreds of statutes, and guidelines as well.

The focus of this legislation and the type of business covered by each piece of legislation vary, and a good deal of overlap occurs. The following sections offer a quick glimpse of the key federal actions over the past several years.

ADEA: The Age Discrimination in Employment Act (1967)

What the legislation does: Prohibits discrimination against employees who are age 40 or older. This law originally covered employees until age 65, was amended to age 70, and then had the age was completely removed. Also see the upcoming section on the Older Workers Benefit Protection Act.

Who the legislation applies to: All private sector employers with 20 or more people who work 20 or more weeks per year. Also covers labor unions (25 or more members), employment agencies, and state and local governments.

For a summary of the Age Discrimination in Employment Act and other discrimination guidelines from the EEOC, see the CD-ROM.

AC-21: American Competitiveness in the 21st Century Act (2000)

What the legislation does: Seeks to help the American economy in both the short and long run by a combination of temporary visa increases issued for highly skilled labor as well as training and education initiatives.

The act benefits both job seekers and employers. It allows individuals whose employers are trying to get them an extension on their visas to stay in the United States until a decision is made on their cases rather than forcing these persons to leave the country. The act also includes training and educational opportunities for American citizens. In addition, it exempts from the cap visas obtained by universities, research facilities, and graduate degree recipients to help keep top graduates and educators in the country.

Who the legislation applies to: Any company.

ADA: Americans with Disabilities Act (1990)

What the legislation does: Gives people with physical or mental disabilities greatly increased access to public services and requires employers to provide reasonable accommodation for applicants and employees with disabilities.

Who the legislation applies to: All private-sector employers with 15 or more employees.

Additional details: Employers in recent years have taken major steps to accommodate otherwise qualified disabled employees by outfitting the workplace with certain features (such as wheelchair ramps, for example) specially designed for disabled people or modifying schedules or training programs with an eye toward the special needs of disabled persons.

For a copy of the Americans with Disabilities Act, see the CD-ROM. The text of this act also can be found on the ADA Web site (www.ada.gov).

COBRA: Consolidated Omnibus Budget Reconciliation Act (1985)

What the legislation does: Provides certain former employees, retirees, spouses, former spouses, and children the right to temporary continuation of health coverage at group rates.

Who the legislation applies to: Companies with 20 or more employees.

Unquestionably, healthcare is an extremely important part of the world of human resources. I cover the topic more extensively in Chapter 11.

Equal Pay Act (1963)

What the legislation does: Prohibits any discrepancies in pay between men and women who are assigned to or perform the same job.

Who the legislation applies to: Private employers or labor organizations who have two or more employees, and who are engaged in interstate commerce or in the production of goods for interstate commerce.

FMLA: Family and Medical Leave Act (1993)

What the legislation does: Grants to qualified employees the right to unpaid leave for specified family or health-related reasons without the fear of losing their jobs. Employees who are seriously ill or who have seriously ill immediate family members are eligible for up to a total of 12 work weeks of unpaid leave during any 12-month period. This act also applies to the birth and care of a newborn child of the employee and the placement with the employee of a son or daughter for adoption or foster care.

Who the legislation applies to: Private employers with 15 or more employees.

Keep in mind: FMLA makes the company responsible for communicating the provisions of this act to employees.

For a list of these requirements, see the Key Provisions of the Family and Medical Leave Act on the CD-ROM.

FLSA: Fair Labor Standards Act (1938)

What the legislation does: Establishes the minimum wage, requires overtime for certain employees, provides restrictions on the employment of children, and requires certain forms of record-keeping.

Who the legislation applies to: Most companies.

FUTA: Federal Unemployment Tax Act (1939)

What the legislation does: Stipulates that employers must contribute to a government tax program that offers temporary benefits to employees who have lost their jobs. In most cases, includes both a federal and state tax.

Who the legislation applies to: Generally, companies that paid wages of $1,500 or more in any calendar quarter.

Tax rate: The current maximum tax imposed is at a rate of 6.2 percent on the first $7,000 paid annually by employers to each employee.

HIPAA: Health Insurance Portability and Accountability Act (1996)

What the legislation does: Establishes guidelines for protecting private, personal information. Covered entities, such as an employer's health plan, healthcare providers, and healthcare clearinghouses, must protect identifiable health information. Individuals have control over how their information may be used.

Who the legislation applies to: All employers.

Again, more information on healthcare is provided in Chapter 11.

IRCA: Immigration Reform and Control Act (1986, 1990, and 1996)

What the legislation does: Bans employers from hiring illegal aliens — and establishes penalties for such behavior.

Who the legislation applies to: Any individual or company, regardless of size or industry.

Determining the legality of the employee's status is the employer's responsibility. Matters related to immigration and security are even more important since 2001, when the Department of Homeland Security was established and the Patriot Act (see the section later in this chapter) was passed.

OWBA: Older Workers Benefit Protection Act (1990)

What the legislation does: Prohibits age-based discrimination in early retirement and other benefit plans of employees who are age 40 or older.

Who the legislation applies to: All private-sector employers with 20 or more people who work 20 or more weeks per year.

Additional details: One provision of this law gives employees a time frame (at least 21 days) to consider a company's offer that includes a promise not to sue the company for age discrimination. It also gives employees seven days to change their minds.

Patriot Act (2001)

What the legislation does: Expands the federal government's ability to conduct investigative and surveillance activities.

Who the legislation applies to: All employers.

Key implication: Complying with the Patriot Act requires vigilance in two areas. On the one hand, you need to maintain your employees' privacy rights. But you also must comply as requested by the government. Meeting these two demands requires thoughtful discussions with attorneys who can help you clarify and articulate the Patriot Act's legal implications for your employees. You should also work with computer, telecommunications, and security experts who can assist with everything from ensuring a safe internal communications environment to creating proper, secure, means for employees to enter and exit your offices.

Pregnancy Discrimination Act (1978)

What the legislation does: Requires employers to regard pregnancy as a "medical condition" and not to exclude pregnant employees from same benefits and medical leave policies.

Who the legislation applies to: Employers with 15 or more employees who work 20 or more weeks a year.

And remember: The act covers both married and unmarried women. Also, both female employees and pregnant spouses of male employees can receive pregnancy benefits. (The spouse receives benefits if she is covered by the husband's health plan, but the employer isn't required to pay for a spouse's leave of absence, which is the duty of the spouse's employer if she is working.)

For a comprehensive summary of this act, see the Discrimination Guidelines on the CD-ROM.

Rehabilitation Act (1973 and 1998)

What the legislation does: Protects disabled persons from discrimination. (A *disabled person* is defined as any person who has a physical or mental impairment which substantially limits one or more major life activities.) In 1998, Congress amended the Rehabilitation Act to require federal agencies to make their electronic and information technology accessible to people with disabilities.

Who the legislation applies to: Employers with federal contracts and sub-contracts worth more than $2,500.

Special requirements: Requires written affirmative action programs from employers of 50 or more people and with federal contracts worth more than $50,000.

Sarbanes-Oxley Act (2002)

What the legislation does: Requires publicly held companies to be more straightforward in reporting their financial results and how they were calculated. Also requires more stringent company controls to ensure the ethical behavior of all employees.

Who the legislation applies to: Publicly held companies and private firms that are considering becoming public companies through an initial public offering (IPO) of their stock.

Strong recommendation: Sarbanes-Oxley requires the establishment of a company code of ethics for its senior financial officers. By extension, many companies seek to uphold the spirit of the law by requesting that their HR teams update and communicate the firm's code of conduct for all employees.

Title VII of the Civil Rights Act (1964)

What the legislation does: Prohibits any employment and other practices that discriminate against people on the basis of race, sex, color, religion, or national origin.

Who the legislation applies to: Almost all government institutions, employment agencies, labor unions, and private employers with 15 or more employees who work 20 or more weeks per year.

Notable amendment: The Civil Rights Act of 1991 gives employees who believe they've been intentionally victimized by discrimination the right to seek compensation and damages before a jury.

For a copy of Title VII in full, see the CD-ROM. The text of this act also can be found on the EEOC Web site (www.eeoc.gov).

WARN: Worker Adjustment and Retraining Notification Act (1988)

What the legislation does: Offers protection to workers, families, and communities, requiring employers to provide 60 days' notice of mass layoffs or plant closings.

Who the legislation applies to: Companies with 100 or more employees.

Sexual Harassment: Keep Your Workplace Free of It

Sexual harassment became a major HR topic in the late 1990s, triggered by several landmark lawsuits that resulted in significant settlements. The settlement in one case exceeded $100 million.

The definition of *sexual harassment,* on the surface, seems fairly straightforward. It's any form of harassment that has sexual overtones. Then again, maybe not. According to language originally set forth in 1980 by the EEOC in guidelines under Title VII of the Civil Rights Act of 1964 (for more information on Title VII, see "The EEO family: a closer look," earlier in this chapter), not only is the sexual behavior at issue in identifying what constitutes sexual harassment, but also the *intent* behind the behavior. Also at issue is the connection between the behavior and the working circumstances and conditions of the person who is being harassed. Sexual harassment is really about power — abuse of power — in the workplace.

In its definition of sexual harassment, the EEOC labels the behavior as follows: "Unwelcome sexual advances, requests for sexual favors, and other verbal or physical conduct of a sexual nature." But the law adds some fine print that muddies the waters. It lists three situations in which these unwelcome advances rise to the legal definition of sexual harassment:

- ✔ Submission to such conduct is made either explicitly or implicitly a term or condition of an individual's employment.
- ✔ Submission to or rejection of such conduct by an individual is used as the basis for employment decisions affecting such individuals.
- ✔ Such conduct has the purpose or effect of unreasonably interfering with an individual's work performance or creating an intimidating, hostile, or offensive working environment.

You don't have to be a linguistic scholar to figure out that these guidelines are loaded with terms that are highly dependent on perceptions and interpretations. And that's one of the chief problems that arise when harassment complaints are filed. People (courts included) have varying ideas of what is implicit and different perceptions about what factors make a workplace intimidating or hostile.

I can make one statement with certainty: No company today can afford to ignore this issue, and no one with HR responsibility can afford to forget that what one person may view as a harmless joke may well be perceived by another as an aggressive and unwelcome sexual advance. Sexual harassment is one area of HR management in which you can never be too careful. To point you in the right direction, the following section offer guidelines that may help you develop a proactive — and effective — sexual harassment policy in your own company.

For a sample policy on Harassment, including sexual harassment, see the CD-ROM.

Spread the word

It's no longer enough to simply declare in writing your company's commitment to prevent sexual harassment. You need a written policy that spells it out clearly, and you need to state, in no uncertain terms, the penalties for flouting the policy — innocently or otherwise.

Your company is responsible for making sure that everyone in the organization — supervisors, managers, and employees — recognizes that sexual harassment is wrong and will not be tolerated in the workplace. How you communicate and educate people about this policy (by using classes, educational videos, literature, and so on) is up to you. Just do it.

A Supreme Court case involving the city of Boca Raton, Florida, proved the importance of aggressively communicating a company's sexual harassment policies. The Court held that the City of Boca Raton, Florida, was liable for the actions of two male lifeguard supervisors who were alleged to have created a sexually hostile environment for female lifeguards by making offensive and lewd remarks. While the Court conceded that Boca Raton did indeed have a formal antiharassment policy, it concluded that Boca Raton city officials hadn't gone far enough to communicate the policy to employees and didn't inform employees that they had a right to bypass their harassing supervisors in order to file the complaint.

What the Court was saying, in other words, is that it's not enough to simply adopt and publish a sexual harassment policy. It's also the company's responsibility to communicate the philosophy and procedures associated with it to everyone in the company.

Publicizing your policy on sexual harassment can be accomplished yearly. Set a date during the same month each year and send copies of your policies to every employee. You may also consider developing an online sexual harassment policy manual and training course that you can deliver to every employee annually.

In certain states, further sexual harassment awareness training is required by law. For example, in California and Connecticut, all companies with 50 or more employees must provide all supervisors and managers with at least two hours of sexual harassment awareness training. This example shows how state law can affect mandatory training requirements.

Create a reporting process

Employees are not required by law to report sexual harassment to their employer before going to the EEOC or to court. You should, however, encourage employees to report internally so that the company can take care of any problems without "help" from the government. Identify several different sources for employees to use to report harassment, such as their supervisor, an HR representative, or an anonymous, toll-free phone line.

Treat all complaints about sexual harassment seriously

Regardless of how frivolous you may consider a sexual harassment complaint, you must take it seriously and, at the very least, look into the charge. If an incident ultimately spirals into a court case, and the fact comes out in testimony that management was aware of the complaint but didn't act on it, you may, as a result, have to pay more in damages.

Take decisive action

After you've established that sexual harassment is taking place, your company must investigate and take any reasonable action that will end it and prevent it from happening again. The value of the employee's work doesn't matter. Doing nothing or being too lenient can put your firm at great risk and, at the very least, create the impression that you're condoning the behavior. This impression won't do much to help your company recruit or retain good employees and will expose the company to increased monetary damages.

Document every complaint

Every sexual harassment complaint, no matter how trivial it may seem and how quickly or easily it is resolved, should be documented. Don't view paperwork as a burden. It can be your company's best defense. Documentation of discipline demonstrates that your company is serious about the problem and the solution. Getting detailed statements from the person making the harassment charges, as well as from the accused, is paramount.

International Expansion: Stranger in a Strange Land

Legal issues become increasingly complicated when your company expands. Many laws, regulations, and tax codes differ in various municipalities and states throughout the United States. But the matter of compliance grows by leaps and bounds when you add offices and employees in other countries.

Proper legal and financial counsel is mandatory for understanding the accounting and taxation policies and procedures of another nation. But as I explain throughout this chapter, laws are often subject to a wide variety of interpretations.

In large part, laws are an extension of culture — a nation's values, priorities, and history. The United States, for example, has always placed a strong emphasis on equal opportunity. This commitment to equal chances for all is one reason many of the laws that matter most for HR professionals in the United States ban discrimination, helping in some ways to flatten hierarchical distinctions and creating a business culture that's more informal than those of some other nations. In a nation like Japan, for example, while avoiding discrimination is important, laws and practices reflect the role that hierarchy and formality play in business. Whereas it's not uncommon in the United States for an initial meeting to be scheduled via telephone, in Japan it's expected that executives will arrange their initial business meetings in writing, often relying on credible third parties to help arrange them.

If you own or work for a small company and feel these issues don't apply to you, remember how global the economy is becoming. Things may change as your company grows and reaches out for new opportunities. In the meantime, the more you understand the customs and sensitivities of different nations, the better equipped you'll be at formulating effective HR policies and procedures if the time arrives.

Forms on the CD

Equal Opportunity Posting Requirements

Sample EEO Posting

Discrimination Guidelines

Americans with Disabilities Act of 1990

Key Provisions of the Family and Medical Leave Act

Title VII of the Civil Rights Act of 1964

Sample Policy Statement on Harassment

Part II
The Right People in the Right Places

In this part . . .

One of the key purposes of the HR function is to help a company build strong teams by locating and attracting the right people to help it grow and prosper. In Part II, I discuss the strategic foundation that supports all your staffing activities. I focus specifically on the hiring process, giving you the background and tools you and your company's line managers need to recruit, interview, select, and orient employees who will be pivotal in making your business a success.

Chapter 3

Building a Staffing Strategy

*P*eople generally assume that when hiring decisions go wrong, the fault lies with bad judgment during the interview process. But companies with successful hiring practices recognize that this explanation is far too simplistic. Hiring is a multistep process, and any missteps that occur early on in the process will invariably catch up with you.

No misstep can do more to torpedo the process than failing to take enough time at the start to form a clear understanding of your overall staffing needs. In this chapter, I examine the critical steps you should be taking as you go through this first phase of the hiring process.

Breaking Out of a Hiring Rut

The traditional hiring notion of "finding the best people to fill job openings" has been replaced by a much more dynamic concept. It's generally referred to as *strategic staffing*, which means putting together a combination of human resources — both internal and external — that are strategically keyed to the needs of the business and the realities of the labor market.

This hiring approach is based on the immediate and long-term needs of the business, as opposed to the specs of a particular job.

Table 3-1 shows the difference between the traditional approach to hiring and the strategic staffing model.

Table 3-1	Paradigms: Old and New
Old Staffing Paradigm	*Strategic Staffing*
Think "job."	Think tasks and responsibilities that are keyed to business goals and enhance a company's ability to compete.
Create a set of job "specs."	Determine which competencies and skills are necessary to produce outstanding performance in any particular function.
Find the person who best "fits" the job.	Determine which combination of resources — internal or external — can get the most mileage out of the tasks and responsibilities that need to be carried out.
Look mainly for technical competence.	Find people who are more than simply "technically" qualified but can carry forward your company's mission and values.
Base the hiring decision primarily on the selection interview.	View the selection interview as only one of a series of tools designed to make the best choice of hiring.
Hire only full-time employees.	Consider a blend of full-time and temporary workers to meet variable workload needs.

True, setting the strategic direction of your company is primarily the responsibility of senior management and not normally an HR function, but you need to look at your company's overall priorities and determine their staffing implications. Equally important, you need to make sure that any staffing decision clearly supports these business priorities. You're not simply "filling jobs." You're constantly seeking to bring to your company the skills and attributes that it needs to meet whatever challenges it may face. To do so, you must look beyond the purely functional requirements of the various positions in your company and focus instead on what skills and attributes employees need to perform those functions exceptionally well.

Chief among the staffing functions are the following:

✔ Working with senior management and line managers to identify staffing needs (see Chapter 4 and the three next sections in this chapter, beginning with "Grasping the Big Picture")

✔ Developing staffing strategies that are keyed to your company's short-term operational requirements and long-term strategic needs (see Chapter 4 and the three next sections in this chapter, beginning with "Grasping the Big Picture")

✔ Overseeing the recruiting process and its many components, including working with recruiters, placing classified ads, and conducting on-campus recruiting (see Chapter 5)

✔ Coordinating applicant evaluation and interviewing activities with line managers — and, in many cases, handling these functions yourself (see Chapter 6 and 7)

✔ Providing the necessary guidance to help managers make the best possible hiring decisions (see Chapter 8)

✔ Coordinating the new hire _onboarding_ process, which includes a logistical, structural, and big-picture orientation to your company; opportunities for peer and senior manager mentoring; a review of job expectations; and other resources to help new employees be successful. (see Chapter 9)

Grasping the Big Picture

Strategic staffing begins with an effort to reassess your department's human resources needs in the context of your firm's business priorities. It's a mindset rather than a process. The idea is to begin thinking in terms of need rather than job, long term rather than short term, and big picture rather than immediate opening. This approach ties directly into the changing role of the HR professional from administrator to strategist, which I discuss in Chapter 1. To succeed, you need to gain a firm understanding of your company's major goals and priorities.

Unless you head an extremely small organization, you can't adopt a strategic staffing approach all by yourself. Make it a priority to introduce the concept to other managers in your organization. You'll need their input to better understand company and departmental priorities — and they'll need your help in guiding them through the process and adopting this mindset as well.

Together, you'll need to identify everything that may affect the efficiency and profitability of your firm's operations — and not just in the short term, either. To get you started, here are some of the key questions that you and other people in your company should answer before you make your next move:

✔ What are your company's long-term strategic goals or those of departments seeking your assistance in hiring employees?

✔ What are the key competitive trends in your industry? (In other words, what factors have the greatest bearing on competitive success?)

✔ What kind of culture currently exists in your company? And what kind of culture do you ultimately want to create? What are the values you want the company to stand for?

✔ What knowledge, skill sets, and attributes (in general) are required to keep pace with those goals and, at the same time, remain true to your company values?

✔ How does the current level of knowledge, skill sets, and attributes among your present employees match up with what will be necessary in the future?

✔ How reasonable is it for you to expect that with the proper support and training, your current employees will be able to develop the skills they're going to need in order for your company to keep pace with the competition?

✔ What combination of resources (rather than specific people) represents the best strategic approach to the staffing needs you face over the near-term and the long-term?

Strategic staffing is not just about hiring more employees. It involves making the best staffing choices available to address the core business needs you and other managers have identified. If a line manager you support is thinking of filling an existing position, encourage him to consider how his group's most critical needs have changed since the last time the job was open, rather than immediately searching for a candidate to fill the vacant position. Is a full-time individual still required in this role? And should a potential replacement have the same skills and experience as her predecessor? Or does the position need to be re-filled at all and the duties handled in other ways?

Ask the hiring manager to analyze his work group's daily activities to better understand how current resources are allocated. Help him identify the frequency and timing of workload peaks and valleys and look for predictable patterns. Discuss the impact of shifts in company priorities and what eventual effect these are likely to have on the work group in question. This discussion allows you to spot any shortfalls in human resources for upcoming initiatives.

Consider a mix of resources

If you identify shortfalls, how will you bridge the gap? By reprioritizing and shifting some duties, can one or more staff members be reassigned to an urgent project when it comes in? The manager may be able to combine some functions or create project teams to focus on critical but temporary activities, with these groups quickly disbanding or reassembling, depending on changing needs.

Redeploying full-time staff may partially address rising demands, but this step alone isn't likely to be the answer to all your company's staffing concerns. If core staff are fully occupied and you have new tasks that must be handled on a long-term basis, it may make sense to hire additional permanent staff. If upcoming projects are of limited duration or you need specialized skills unavailable internally, a mix of full-time and temporary employees may be your best bet. In some cases, *outsourcing,* or turning over an entire function to an outside specialist, may suit your needs best. (See the upcoming section "Outsourcing: The role of HR professionals.")

The point is that by adopting a strategic staffing approach, your options multiply. You gain flexibility. It allows you and other company managers to rapidly expand or contract a well-thought-out mix of talent to meet both current and long-term goals. (In Chapter 13, I discuss more of the specifics of how you can make this concept work.)

Reassess goals annually

Change is the name of the game in business. Company priorities will undoubtedly shift over time as management seeks ways to keep the firm competitive. As a result, you and the managers you support should consider performing your needs assessments on an annual basis to ensure that you're still on track with the assumptions that are guiding your staffing strategy.

Finding New Employees

You can look for new employees in two general places: inside or outside your organization. Looking inside your company is the easier of the two approaches, simply because it's a finite universe. But before you get into the specifics of your hiring strategy, you should have a general idea of what you stand to gain — or lose — when you focus your staffing efforts inside your organization or look outside for new talent.

Inner peace: Filling jobs from within the organization

The rule in successful staffing has always been to do your best to fill new job openings from within before looking for outside candidates. Here are the key reasons:

✔ **Increased efficiency:** Hiring from within usually takes less time and is generally less costly (in the short term, at least) than hiring from the outside. You don't have to wade through reams of resumes. You can cut to the chase more quickly during the interview, and you don't have to worry about the reliability of your reference information. In addition, existing employees are a known quantity. You know what type of performance you can expect from them.

✔ **Increased morale:** Hiring from within sends a message to employees at all levels of your organization that good performance gets rewarded and that employees have a reason (apart from the regular paycheck) to work hard, be reliable, and focus on quality. There's no better way to avoid excessive turnover at junior levels of an organization than to offer excellent advancement opportunities.

✔ **Shorter period of adjustment:** Everything else being equal an existing employee a lot less time to acclimate to the new job than an employee who's never been with your company. Not only are existing employees already familiar with company policies, but they're probably aware of what the new job entails.

Benefiting from a diverse workforce

In recent years, the term *diversity* has entered the business world in a big way. Over the last 15 years, hundreds of articles, papers, studies, and books talk about how diverse the workplace is becoming. Everyone knows that the workplace is no longer dominated by white males, but did you know that, according to the U.S. Bureau of Labor, by 2008, women and minorities will make up 70 percent of all new entrants to the workforce?

Chapter 2 summarizes the laws that have been enacted to bar discrimination in hiring practices. This legislation is often changed or updated, such as the addition of the Internet Applicant final rule of 2006, which requires federal contractors to collect and maintain data for use in enforcing nondiscrimination laws.

When questions arise regarding any component of employment laws, seek legal counsel. While these often-complex laws can make your job more complicated, a pay-off does exist because diversity has had a tremendously positive impact on the business environment. If everyone in your company thinks alike, you miss the opportunity for innovative ideas that often come from individuals from diverse cultures and backgrounds — ideas that can help you improve your products and level of customer service.

Ensuring that you have a wide spectrum of job applicants to choose from requires making outreach efforts to various community groups or running classified ads in newspapers read by specific ethnic groups. Beyond hiring, the term *diversity training* may entail conducting training sessions among employees that teach them to increase sensitivity toward others. When people feel accepted and valued by their colleagues, subordinates, and supervisors, their loyalty and morale increases, and this in turn greatly increases productivity.

New horizons: Looking for staff outside the company

For all its virtues, a staffing strategy that's built almost entirely around pro-moting from within isn't always the best way to go — especially if your company has never taken the time and effort to develop a well-structured employee development program. Here are the basic arguments for looking outside the company to fill certain positions:

✔ **A broader selection of talent:** Basic mathematics shows that if your search is confined solely to your current employees, the pool of likely candidates is going to be a lot smaller than if you're looking outside the company. This constraint may not be a problem for certain jobs, but for critical positions, you may not want to limit your options.

✔ **The "new blood" factor:** Bringing in outside talent can go a long way toward diminishing the "We've always done it that way syndrome," gen-erally known as *organizational inbreeding*. Recruiting from outside the company is usually helpful for companies that have held on to the status quo for too long.

✔ **The diversity factor:** Workforce *diversity* (or the effort to allow and encourage diversity in the workplace) enables a business to draw on the resources, expertise, and creativity of people from the widest possible range of backgrounds: gender, age, color, national origin, ethnicity, and other factors. And filling jobs from the outside may turn out to be the only way you can keep your company within EEOC compliance (see Chapter 2). But remember, having a diverse workforce is not just a matter of satisfying the law. It also makes good business sense. (See the sidebar "Benefiting from a diverse workforce" for more information on this topic.)

Diversity doesn't mean that you have to include employees from every possible background, which is impossible. However, a commitment to diversity means that you create a workplace environment supportive of a wide range of perspectives.

Outsourcing: The role of HR

Outsourcing is the practice of turning over an entire function (shipping, pay-roll, benefits administration, security, computer networking) to an outside specialist. In many cases, the outside firm's employees or consultants work side by side with a company's regular employees. In some cases, a function may be moved to a remote location miles away from your office — even occasionally out of the country. This latter approach, often referred to as *offshoring,* has grabbed headlines and generated much economic and politi-cal debate in recent years.

Of course, outsourcing is hardly a new concept. Small companies and Mom-and-Pop businesses have been outsourcing since the beginning of time. What's new is the emergence of outsourcing as an increasingly useful staffing strategy for companies that have historically used their own personnel.

Companies usually outsource to save time and money, either because of necessity or choice. Necessity is the driving factor when a company's business demands outstrip its ability to handle a particular function without investing heavily in new equipment (or a new facility) or bringing in a large number of new employees. Choice is the driving factor when companies want to focus all their internal energies on those operations that contribute directly to their competitive advantage — and outsource those that may only be necessary for a discreet period of time or specific function.

In your HR role, you need to grasp the implications of outsourcing so that you can help provide strategic counsel throughout any hiring process — and contribute to decisions about whether to use this alternative in the first place. After all, any outsourcing effort inherently carries a demand not just for one discreet hire, but for many people — and your input about how to conduct an effective search for skilled contractors or consultants is extremely valuable.

Another reason to be aware of the outsourcing trend is that it is affects the HR function itself: Companies are increasingly outsourcing some of their HR services. But no matter which business process is involved, your ability to apply hiring principles can play a major role in ensuring that any outsourcing effort is implemented as efficiently as possible.

Chapter 4

Smart Start to Hiring: Kicking Off the Hiring Process

. . . .

In This Chapter

▶ Creating effective job descriptions

▶ Understanding employee classification

. . . .

*I*f you're making good hiring decisions, nearly everything else you do with respect to HR policies and practices becomes easier. You can create new initiatives and institute new practices that reflect your company's mission and its values. And you don't have to lose sleep over whether employees will understand, be receptive to, and be able to follow through on your instructions. If you don't have to spend the bulk of your time each day putting out fires, you can concentrate on the big picture: where you or your senior management want your business to go in the years ahead, and what needs to happen on the HR side to get you there.

That's the benefit of good hiring decisions. A bad hiring decision (which brings to your company someone who can't make a meaningful contribution) produces just the opposite result. You spend more time as a firefighter and less time as a manager and strategic planner.

But you don't need to panic. Most bad hiring decisions are avoidable, assuming that you and others in your company approach the process with respect, understanding, and discipline. This chapter gets you started in the right direction.

The Costs of a Bad Hire

Your company loses more than time, money, and effort by recruiting, interviewing, orienting, and training people who shouldn't have been hired in the first place. You must also deal with all the other havoc that the "wrong" employee can create: the business you may lose when that employee interacts with customers, the costs you incur when you have to repeat procedures that were handled ineptly, and the pressures on other employees who must pick up the slack created by underperformers. And consider the expense and the hassle that arise when you have to cut your losses and dismiss an employee who shouldn't have been hired in the first place. In the long run, it's more difficult for the manager and team to accommodate a poor performer than it is to invest in recruiting quality candidates.

The biggest mistake you can make when you're in the market for new employees is to assume that you can rely on the same tried-and-true methods that you've been using for years. What's different today is, well, everything. Consider the following factors:

- ✔ **A lot more is at stake today than in the past.** Gone are the days when you could minimize the consequences of a bad hiring decision by "finding a place" for that newly hired person who isn't working out in the new job. The pace and pressure in today's workplace are too great. Everybody has to contribute. And to "contribute" means more than simply doing one's own job. It means having a measurable impact on a company's ability to compete. It means maintaining high quality standards, keeping customers happy, and keeping costs under control.

- ✔ **The qualifications for jobs that used to be considered "routine" have begun to escalate.** With fewer layers of management in place in most companies, today's line employees must do their jobs with less supervision than in the past, and not every employee can flourish in this kind of environment.

- ✔ **Technology is having a huge impact as well.** Because just about every task in business has to be done faster than ever, companies of every size are relying on technological advances to streamline day-to-day operating procedures. And few companies can afford to have employees who can't adjust to the new pace and growing demands.

Hiring: Think "Strategy"

Recruiting and hiring good employees is arguably the most critical of all the areas you're responsible for overseeing in your company. After all, if you're not hiring the right people to begin with, your ability to succeed in nearly everything else you do in your staffing practices will be greatly compromised.

As I discuss in Chapter 3 and throughout Part II, hiring is no longer a simple matter of filling job openings. More than ever, successful hiring is a multidimensional process. It is rooted, above all, in your ability to understand your company's strategic needs. When you're helping other people in the company make a hiring decision (something you're going to be doing a lot of if you're the only person handling human resources in the company), you're probably going to have to change the way people view the hiring process. You have to get them to see that in today's workplace, the idea isn't simply to find the "best person" for any given "job." The big challenge today is for you and the hiring managers in your organization to step back and take a long-term view of your specific business needs, and then determine the right combination of resources to help you meet those needs. In effect, you approach staffing from a proactive rather than a reactive perspective.

Building Competency Models

Whether you decide that internal promotions, full-time new hires, part-time workers, temporary project professionals, or a carefully thought-out combination of these roles will best meet your business needs, before you can seek out these individuals, you need to determine what qualities you want them to have. Many firms today are using a process called *competency modeling* to help target the characteristics that distinguish top performers. Companies can then use this information in the hiring process to seek and evaluate prospective employees.

Closely related to — and supportive of — the basic concept of strategic staffing, competency modeling is an increasingly important way to assess your true talent needs. Although this term may sound complicated, the concept itself is actually quite simple and understanding it has very useful implications for you. Competency modeling is merely a matter of determining, as accurately as you can, what particular mix of skills, attributes, and attitudes produce superior performance in those operational functions that have the most bearing on your company's competitive strength. This strategic recipe becomes the basis not only of your hiring decisions but also of your training and development strategies.

Suppose, for example, that your company is in the business of selling home security systems. One way that you market your service is to solicit potential customers by phone. The basic job of a telemarketer, of course, is to generate leads by calling people on the phone. Some telemarketers, however, are clearly much better at this task than others. They're better at engaging the interest of the people they call. They don't allow repeated rejections to wear down their spirits. In other words, they possess certain attributes that contribute to superior performance in this job. And these attributes (as opposed to the actual tasks of the job) are the basis of the competency model.

You can apply the concept of competency modeling to virtually any function in your company. The basic objective is always the same: To determine as precisely as you can what combination of skills and attributes are required to excel at that function. You may not always find the perfect match between the skills and attributes that dominate your competency model for a given function and the skills and attributes of the candidates you're considering for that job. But at least you have a frame of reference from which to work. You can now identify with greater precision any skill deficits — gaps between the requirements of the job and the qualifications of the candidate. And you can frequently close these gaps (assuming that they're not exceptionally wide) through training and coaching.

Some consulting companies specialize in helping businesses develop competency models for key functions or positions. But you don't necessarily need an outside consultant to gain more insight into the types of skills and attributes that form the basis of your hiring criteria. The following suggestions can help you gain insights on your own:

✔ **Interview your own "top" performers.** Assuming that you have a group of people who perform the same job — and assuming that one or two of those people are clearly the "stars" of the group — sitting down with your key people to determine what makes them so successful at what they do is certainly worth your time. Try to answer the following questions:

- What special skills, if any, do these star performers possess that the others don't?

- What type of personality traits do they share?

- What common attitudes and values do they bring to their jobs?

A competency-model consultant would ask these very questions, so don't be shy as you're attempting to find the answers to these same questions. And don't worry about offending anyone or invading anyone's "space" either. Most are likely to find the fact that you're singling them out as exemplary performers quite flattering.

✔ **Talk to your customers.** One of the best — and easiest — ways to find out which employees in your company can provide the basis for your competency modeling is to talk to people with whom your staff interact on a regular basis: your customers. Find out which employees your customers enjoy dealing with the most, and, more important, what those employees do to routinely win the affection of these customers.

The ABCs of Job Descriptions

After you've determined the qualities that are most important to specific functions and positions in your company (see preceding section), you're ready to use these competency models to create hiring criteria. Your first stop is the job description.

The job description has long been the bread-and-butter tool of hiring. And, as any hiring professional can tell you, a high percentage of hiring "mistakes" (not to mention hiring disasters) result from job descriptions that fail to accurately capture the essence of the job in question.

Done correctly, a well thought-out job description delivers the following benefits:

- ✔ Ensures that everyone who has a say in the hiring decision is on the same page with respect to what the job entails.
- ✔ Serves as the basis for key hiring criteria.
- ✔ Ensures that candidates have a clear idea of what to expect if, indeed, you hire them.
- ✔ Serves as a reference tool during the evaluation process.
- ✔ Serves as a benchmark for performance after you hire the candidate.

You can best think of a well-written job description as a "snapshot" of the job. The job description needs to communicate as specifically but concisely as possible what responsibilities and tasks the job entails and to indicate the key qualifications of the job — the basic requirements (specific credentials or skills) — and, if possible, the attributes that underlie superior performance.

Following is a quick look at the categories that make up a well-written job description:

- ✔ Title of the position
- ✔ Department (if applicable)
- ✔ Direct report (to whom the person directly reports)
- ✔ Responsibilities
- ✔ Necessary skills
- ✔ Experience required

Sample job description

The following job description is a good model to follow, regardless of what job you're describing. Notice the following:

- ✔ A distinction is drawn between overall responsibility and specific areas of responsibility.
- ✔ The experience requirement is separated from skills and attributes.
- ✔ The language is easy to understand.

Position title
Senior Mailroom Clerk

Department
Operations

Reports to
Building Services Supervisor

Overall responsibility
Supervise mailroom staff and interface with all levels of management regarding mail and supply deliveries

Key areas of responsibility

- ✔ Maintain established shipping/receiving procedures
- ✔ Sort and distribute all mail on a timely basis
- ✔ Maintain all photocopiers, fax machines, and postage meters
- ✔ Order, store, and distribute supplies
- ✔ Facilitate all off-site storage, inventory, and record management requests
- ✔ Document current policies and procedures in the COS Department as well as implement new procedures for improvement
- ✔ Oversee the use of a company van when needed
- ✔ Ensure that water and paper is available for customers on a continuous basis

Skills and attributes

- ✔ Strong sense of customer service
- ✔ Good organizational skills
- ✔ Ability to lift a minimum of 25 lbs.

Experience requirement

- ✔ Supervisory experience in a corporate mailroom environment
- ✔ Good driving record

See the CD-ROM for a Blank Job Description Form and sample job descriptions.

The following sections describe six guidelines that can help you through the important — but often overlooked — stage of creating a job description.

Look ahead, not behind

The tasks and responsibilities that constitute most people's "jobs" today are a far cry from what they were as recently as ten years ago. What's happened in most companies is that tasks and responsibilities that were formerly regarded as jobs unto themselves are now consolidated with other tasks and responsibilities. The overall result is that many existing job descriptions are pretty much obsolete. Jobs today are generally broader in scope than those of the past; job descriptions, therefore, now need to take into account the expanded skill sets that employees need to handle the greater responsibilities.

The implications for you? Don't rely solely on a job's history as you're putting together a job description for today. Focus instead on what the job should be now and what it may look like in the near future, based on your company's current needs and long-term objectives

Don't confuse tasks with requirements and qualifications

A *task* is what the person or people you hire actually do: take orders over the phone, deliver pizzas, keep your computer network up and running, and so on. *Qualifications* are the skills, attributes, or credentials a person needs to perform each task, such as possess a driver's license, have an upbeat personality, be familiar with computer networking, and so on.

Do your best to avoid the common pitfall of blurring this distinction. Discipline yourself to clarify the actual tasks and responsibilities before you start to think about what special attributes are needed by the person who will be carrying out those tasks and fulfilling those responsibilities.

Set priorities

A well-written job description consists of more than simply a laundry list of the tasks and responsibilities that the job entails. It reflects a sense of priorities. In other words, it differentiates those responsibilities and tasks that are primary from those that are secondary, based on core competencies.

Don't box yourself into a corner

Credentials such as degrees and licenses are formal acknowledgements that a candidate has passed a particular test or completed a specific field of study. Credentials are absolute necessities in some jobs. (The person who delivers pizza for you, for example, must have a driver's license; the appropriate medical boards must license the surgeon you hire.) You can often use credentials as a way to eliminate certain candidates from the running if you have far more applicants for a job than you can reasonably handle. (You may decide, for example, to consider only those who have a bachelor's degree or the equivalent.)

At the same time, stay flexible. What you prefer in a candidate — such as an advanced degree — may not necessarily be what's required for the position, particularly when you take into account a candidate's various work experiences and accomplishments. This advice is particularly true when hiring for middle and senior-level managers. The thing that you want to make sure of most of all is that the credentials you establish have a direct bearing on a candidate's ability to become a top performer.

Don't forget soft skills

While, of course, every job has a set of technical requirements that you typically define in partnership with line managers, don't overlook those broad but telling aspects of a candidate known as *soft skills*. These skills include an aptitude for communicating with people of all levels, skill sets, and backgrounds; the ability to work well in teams (as both leader and team member); and other factors, such as a strong sense of ethics and a talent for efficient and creative problem-solving. Candidates who are weak in these areas — even while having solid hard skills and work experience — may prove unable to grow as your company goes through the inevitable changes that are a part of today's business world.

Consider this: When you read about CEOs who build successful companies, you hear far less about their technical skills — be it finance or marketing, engineering or administration — and much more about their strong people skills. The types of people you want in your company are adept at communicating ideas, providing leadership, collaborating with others, and simply making things happen.

Make sure that the job is doable

Some job descriptions work beautifully until the person you hire actually tries to perform the job. So the job that you describe must truly be doable. Remember, the number of tasks that you may call on a person to perform in a job isn't necessarily what determines the doability of that job. One factor is the compatibility of those tasks. Most people agree, for example, that people who are unusually creative don't usually excel at tasks that require considerable attention to detail. By the same token, people who are at their best when they're working by themselves on complex, analytical tasks tend, as a rule, to be more introverted than extroverted. The lesson here is to make sure that when you're lumping several tasks into the same job description that you're not creating a job that very few people could fill.

Be specific

You don't need to be William Shakespeare to write a solid job description, but you definitely need to appreciate the nuances of the language. And you want to make sure that the words you choose actually spell out what the job entails. Table 4-1 provides a handful of examples of task descriptions that are far too general, coupled with suggested rewrites.

Table 4-1	Good and Bad Task Descriptions
Too general	*Specific*
Handles administrative chores	Receives, sorts, and files monthly personnel action reports
Good communication skills	Ability to communicate technical information to nontechnical audiences
Computer literate	Proficient with Microsoft Word, Excel, and QuickBooks

Set a salary range

Before you start the recruiting process (see Chapter 5) and look at options for how and where you'll find the ideal candidate for the job you're designing, you should establish a salary range for the position. In Chapters 10 and 11, I discuss the details of salary and benefits and what constitutes an effective compensation structure.

What's in a Job Title?

Now that the majority of jobs in most companies involve multitasking, job titles are no longer a reliable indicator of the responsibilities of any particular job and, as such, can be tricky to handle. Even so, you need to give some attention to what you're actually calling the job. An inaccurate or overblown job title can create false expectations and lead to resentment, disappointment, or worse.

It's also important to clarify whether the job is *exempt* or *nonexempt.* Exempt workers receive a flat weekly, monthly, or annual salary, regardless of the number of hours they work over a given period. Nonexempt workers are paid on an hourly basis (though some receive salaries) and are eligible for overtime pay if they work more than 40 hours in a given week. (For more on this topic, see Chapter 10.)

If you're having trouble coming up with a job title, go to the Web site of the U.S. Department of Labor's Dictionary of Occupational Titles (DOT), located at www.wave.net/upg/immigration/dot_index.html. It lists jobs by occupational groups and, within groups, by functions and responsibilities. The DOT assigns each specific job a unique nine-digit code number and defines the principal tasks each job involves. The dictionary is especially useful for describing technical or skilled jobs or if you're trying to translate a veteran's Military Occupational Specialty into a civilian skill.

Apart from everything else, a job description is generally regarded as a legal document. As such, any references to race, color, religion, age, sex, national origin or nationality, or physical or mental disability can expose your company to a possible discrimination suit. (In rare cases, an employer can specify a requirement usually considered discriminatory if it's a bona fide occupational qualification or need. The limiting of recruitment of a live-in counselor in a female residence hall to women is one frequently cited example. You can also find exceptions to the age prohibition. These exceptions are so conditional, however, that the wise employer has a lawyer scrutinize every word.)

Employee Classification: Yes, It Matters

Your customers may not care about the specific arrangements different employees have with your company, but your accountant does, and so do the federal and state agencies that are responsible for collecting payroll taxes. The following sections provide the general classifications, along with a brief description of the main classification criteria. (For more information on the way these classifications affect salary, payroll taxes, and benefits administration, see Chapter 10.)

Full-time employees

General definition: Employees who generally work a full week, regardless of what they do for the company, where they work, or who they work for.

Major implications: Employers are required to pay whatever payroll taxes are required by law and must also withhold applicable state, federal, and local taxes. Full-time employees enjoy full protection under all the federal and state laws and statutes that govern HR administration.

Regular part-time employees

General definition: Employees who generally work less than a full week, but nonetheless have a regular schedule, perform a prescribed set of tasks, and have a fixed place where they do their work.

Major implications: Enjoy many of the same benefits (usually on a prorated scale) and the same federal and state protections as full-time employees.

Temporary workers and contract employees

General definition: Individuals who work on an as-needed (that is, contingency) basis, with no set schedule.

Major implications: Temporary or contract workers, often referred to as *contingent workers,* represent the fastest growing segment of the workforce, and the tasks they perform are no longer primarily administrative or clerical. Indeed, the world of temporary professionals now includes doctors, teachers, and lawyers — even CEOs.

Businesses can hire temporary workers directly. More commonly, though, an outside staffing source provides temporary workers. (Frequently staffing is arranged by a specialist with the company's particular field.) The company pays a fee to the staffing agency, which takes responsibility for the temporary worker's compensation, payroll taxes, and, in many cases, benefits.

Temporary and contract employees also receive the same legal protection against discrimination and sexual harassment as do the full-time workers. (Chapter 13 covers the details of using temporary professionals.)

Independent contractors

General definition: Individuals (frequently professionals such as accountants, lawyers, trainers, graphic artists, and so on) who perform services for a company on a project basis and then bill the company for those services and related expenses.

Major implications: Strictly defined, an independent contractor controls the methods and means of performing the tasks and is responsible to the employer only for the results. Employers have no tax liability and almost no other administrative responsibility other than paying the invoice and reporting payments on 1099 forms.

Note: The IRS may not agree with your interpretation of an independent contractor and may classify the worker as an employee. Be sure that you understand the specific distinctions.

Two significant risks should be considered:

✔ The IRS has a subjective, multifactor test it applies to independent contractor relationships. If an arrangement fails the IRS test, the relationship is recharacterized, and the individual is deemed to be an employee. The employer then becomes liable for back pay, tax withholding, and other statutory payments and penalties that should have been paid on behalf of the employee, which may add up to a lot of money.

✔ Under some Employee Retirement Income Security Act (ERISA) plans, independent contractors who work substantially full time for much of the year may be counted as part of the workforce in determining whether the plan meets ERISA requirements. This classification may result in your plan being disqualified for tax benefits afforded to ERISA plans (see Chapter 13).

Leased workers

General definition: *Leased workers,* like temporary workers, are employees who are provided by an outside agency, known as *professional employment organizations* (PEOs.) The main difference: Leased employees work on a full-time basis.

Major implications: The basic working arrangement — where employees work, what they do, who supervises them, how much they're paid — stays virtually the same. The only difference is that the PEO assumes financial and administrative responsibility for the employees' salaries and benefits. Because PEOs are administering the benefits for very large groups of employees, they can generally offer the same basic salary and benefits package to employees, charge the client company less than the company would otherwise have to pay, and still walk away with a profit.

A Final Note

I refer to the preceding staffing options throughout the book as I describe various aspects of HR management. For now, though, bear in mind two important points:

✔ Companies that meet their staffing needs in the most effective and strategically sound manner aren't locked into any one philosophy or any one staffing option. The idea is to put together the most strategic mix.

✔ The way you classify the people in your organization embodies more than simple operational significance; it also has legal and tax ramifications.

Forms on the CD

Blank Job Description Form and Sample Job Descriptions

Chapter 5

Resourceful Recruiting

. . . .

In This Chapter

▶ Finding talent inside the organization

▶ Writing an effective job ad

▶ Maximizing the Internet as a recruiting tool

▶ Identifying sources you may not have thought of

. . . .

*T*he recruiting stage of the hiring process is a lot like fishing. Your success depends not only on how well you do it, but on where you do it and on what bait you're using. You can go fishing for qualified candidates in any number of ways. You also discover that no one fishing expedition meets the needs of every company in every situation. Some strategies involve more time and cost than others, but in your quest to attract the best possible employees the extra effort is usually worth it. Most of all, the key to effective recruiting is to make sure that whatever options you select are logically and strategically aligned with your priorities.

Recruiting: The Big Picture

The obvious objective of a recruiting effort is to attract as large a pool of qualified candidates as possible. Two considerations, however, are less obvious but no less important. For one thing, the measure of a successful recruiting effort isn't only numbers; it's also about quality. Keep in mind that everything you do as a recruiter — from seeking candidates on the Internet to placing an ad in your local paper to paying a recruiting visit to your local community college — is making a statement about your company, and, in the process, shaping your company's reputation.

To recruit the best talent, you need to represent your company as professionally as possible. When the time comes to choose the person or people who will represent your company at a job fair or a local college campus, forget about seniority and look instead for those who have good people skills and consistently generate positive energy. Pay attention, too, to the presence created on your company's Web site and what happens when applicants call your company for information or show up for interviews. Try to impress on everybody who might interact with a candidate how important it is to be warm and courteous. After all, today's job-seeker may be tomorrow's desired employee or a potential customer. The last thing you need in a tight labor market — or any labor market, for that matter — is a bad reputation.

Getting Started

Clearly, recruiting is probably the most challenging stage of the hiring process. Whenever you post an opening online or place a classified ad, you never know how many responses you're going to get or whether you're going to attract a good group of candidates. When you visit colleges, you have no idea who's going to show up at your recruiting sessions. And even more troubling, no roadmaps are out there to guide your way — no tried and true formulas exist for getting the most mileage out of your recruiting efforts. You must stitch together your own campaign, ensuring that whatever decisions you make take into account those factors that are unique to your company and to the specific position you seek to fill.

The following list covers some of the general guidelines that you want to bear in mind.

✔ **Make recruitment an ongoing process.** Companies known for their ability to attract and hire good employees are always recruiting — even if they have no current openings. If recruiting is indeed an ongoing process, and if you're the person in your company responsible for recruiting talent, you're always on the lookout for people who can contribute to your organization's success — even if they're working somewhere else now and you have no immediate need for them. At the very least, you want to keep an active database of the names and resumes of people whom you've met or who've sent in letters or contacted you online expressing interest in your firm — assuming, of course, that they have the qualities for which you're looking.

Your diversity outreach efforts can also be a way to make recruiting an ongoing process. Booths at ethnic and cultural community fairs or events, for example, can serve both marketing and recruiting purposes.

Continually recruiting for your firm doesn't mean overselling the company to attract more candidates. If you misrepresent your business' scope or capabilities, you'll feed false expectations for employees who decide to join you, leading to later job dissatisfaction once they're on board. Clearly communicate what the company is, as well as what it wants to become and why you need capable, committed employees to help the business reach its goals.

✔ **Create a plan.** You should always have a general idea before you start any recruiting effort of how you intend to conduct and manage the process. For starters, you need some idea of the various candidate sources you're going to seek out, including those you're going to rely on as primary sources — those sources that you're going to be focusing on the most as you move forward in the recruiting process. A good way to start is to set a deadline for when, ideally, you want to see the position filled. After the deadline is set, you can then establish a sequence of steps, each with its own deadline. You may decide, for example, that you're going to look inside your company for a certain period of time — say, two weeks — and if unsuccessful, you intend to either post the opening on the Internet, run a classified ad, or seek the services of an outside staffing firm.

No one plan is right for everyone, so keep your options open at all times. Don't become so locked into one strategy that you become unable to see that it's not working for you.

✔ **Be systematic.** If you don't get your arms around the purely administrative side of recruiting early on in the process, you're asking for trouble. Before you start the search, set up a *protocol* —a predetermined, systematic procedure — for how you intend to process applications, resumes, and cover letters. Try to set aside a certain amount of time each day to focus on the recruiting effort. If you're using an outside recruiter, make sure that someone in the company — either you or the hiring manager — has a direct line to the individual who's handling the search. If you're seeking candidates through the Internet, have secure and streamlined systems in place for taking in, sorting, and tracking the many resumes you'll attract (more on the Internet later in this chapter in the section "The Internet – Powerful, but Be Careful"). If you plan to advertise in a publication, make sure that you're aware of the publication's deadlines. And if you intend to use a variety of publications or Web sites for your classified ads, think about setting up some sort of database of basic information (audience, rates, payment methods, and so on) so you don't need to reeducate yourself every time you decide to run a new ad.

✔ **Keep tabs on your progress.** You should be monitoring your recruiting efforts on a daily basis and evaluating your progress not only on the number of inquiries you receive, but also on the quality of those inquiries. Quality in this context refers to responses originating from applicants who not only meet but also exceed your basic requirements. Depending on your sense of urgency, be prepared to intensify your efforts if you come up empty in the initial stages of the process.

✔ **Be flexible.** In most situations, you can pick up a pretty good idea early on as to how successful you're going to be in attracting quality candidates in sufficient numbers to give you a viable choice in filling the position. But if the initial response to your recruiting efforts ends up a big zero, you need to have a contingency plan on hand. Be prepared to revisit the job description or even explore the possibility of restructuring the job — breaking it into two part-time jobs, perhaps — in an effort to attract more (or better) candidates.

Inside Story: Recruiting from Within

The advantages of recruiting from within your own employee ranks are well-known and well-documented. Promoting from within helps keep morale and motivation levels high. And, assuming that your internal search is successful, you don't need to worry about the employee fitting into your culture. She already knows the territory.

The drawbacks? Only two, really. The most obvious one is that limiting your search to internal candidates limits the candidates to choose from, and you may end up hiring someone who's not up to the challenge of the job. The second drawback is that, whenever you recruit from within, you always run a risk that otherwise important and valuable employees who don't get the job may become resentful and even eventually decide to quit.

Your only real defense against these problems is to be forewarned about them and to go out of your way to ensure that everyone understands the scope and basic duties of the job plus the hiring criteria you're using. You also must make sure that, whatever system you use to alert employees to job opportunities in the company, everyone gets a fair shot at the opening.

Creating a successful internal hiring process

Following are the key procedures that you need to initiate in setting up a successful internal hiring process:

- ✔ **Create a pipeline.** You can communicate internal job opportunities to your employees in several different ways — everything from posting notices on a password-protected part of the company's Web site to a bulletin board in the cafeteria to sending an e-mail about the position, to passing out internal mail circulars. What's important is that everyone knows the system and that you post jobs on a regular basis.

- ✔ **Spell out the criteria.** Wherever it appears, any notice about a job needs to set specific requirements for the job — length of time in current position, the level of seniority needed, and so on. Include the basic rules in every posting notice. If you have specific requirements or rules for a specific job — a college degree or equivalent, a driver's license, the ability to tap dance, and so on — make sure that you clearly note these requirements up front.

✔ **Establish procedures**. If you don't already have one, make sure that you establish a procedure for how employees can apply for a position. Some companies require workers to apply through their department heads, but this approach can be a problem if the department head doesn't want to lose the employee applying for the job. Others enable employees to apply directly to the HR office. It's your call.

Developing an employee skills inventory

If you see yourself hiring internally at some point down the road, an employee skills inventory set up now can be a great help when the time comes. This inventory is exactly what the name implies: a portfolio of the human capital in your company — a catalog of the individual skills, attributes, credentials, and areas of knowledge that currently exist. The idea itself is not that new: Most companies have traditionally maintained a "personnel file" or "job history" file for each employee. The difference lies in how the information is categorized. Conventional job histories tend to focus on accomplishments. An employee skills inventory focuses on the skills and attributes that led to those accomplishments.

You may assume that this practice is one that is suitable for only big companies, such as Microsoft, General Electric Company, and Procter & Gamble. And you may assume, too, that the process is more bother than it's worth. Neither assumption is entirely warranted.

Even if your company is relatively small — 100 employees or fewer — it still may be worth the time and effort to develop an employee skills inventory. The chief benefit is that, instead of picking your way through reams of folders to compile a list of people who may be logical candidates for an opening in your company, you simply search the database of your employee-skills inventory to identify the employees in your company who come closest to the requirements of that particular position.

Setting up the categories

The key to developing a practical, user-friendly employee skills inventory lies in how you organize various categories of information. Given the versatility and power of most databases today, you face no limit to the number of categories that you can incorporate into your inventory. But try to keep the number of fields to a reasonable minimum and make sure that they're job-related. (In other words, you don't need to document a candidate's favorite rock star or astrological sign.) Each field that you set up in the database should have some administrative or strategic importance.

A typical employee skills inventory form may incorporate the following fields, including conventional job history data:

- ✔ **Skills/knowledge areas:** Business-related functions or activities in which the employee has either special knowledge or a proven record of proficiency.

- ✔ **Second language skills:** Anything other than English. ("While-U-Drive French" doesn't count.)

- ✔ **Special preferences:** Requests that employees have made about their own career aspirations, other jobs in the company they'd like to pursue, or areas of the country (or world) to which they may be interested in relocating.

- ✔ **Educational background:** Schools, degrees, and subjects in which the employee majored and minored.

- ✔ **Job history at your company:** Include the title, the department, the organizational unit, and the actual functions each employee performs.

- ✔ **Previous job history:** Include the same general information as for the preceding category.

- ✔ **Training courses and seminars:** List the program, the topics covered, and the number of days spent in training.

- ✔ **Test results:** Key results, if applicable, of any company-sanctioned tests or other types of measurement activities that employees have formally undergone during their tenure at the company.

- ✔ **Licenses, credentials, and affiliations:** Obviously, these categories should all be work-related and should be logically linked to the tasks and responsibilities of the job. (A warehouse employee who is going to operate a forklift, for example, doesn't need a certificate from a stunt-driving school, and the person you hire to supervise the kitchen of your company cafeteria doesn't need to belong to an international wine society.)

The preceding list is meant to be a set of recommendations, nothing more. You can incorporate into your own employee skills inventory anything that you consider relevant. Just be careful, however, that, as you develop your employee skills inventory, you don't inadvertently violate any EEO laws. If you have any question about whether including a particular category may leave you vulnerable to an EEO suit, check with legal counsel.

For a Sample Skills Inventory Form and a blank form to tailor to your needs, see the CD-ROM.

Gathering the information

The best way to gather most of the information that you need to build and maintain an employee skills inventory is to create a simple questionnaire and distribute it to your employees. The most efficient method is to gather this information electronically through e-mail that sends employees to a customized, password-protected Skills Bank Web site. The more in touch you are with the existing talents, skills, and attributes of those within your company, the easier time you'll have getting the most out of your employees' expertise. To paraphrase an old saying, many companies today spend so much time looking for the diamonds in the horizon that they often overlook the "pearls" in their midst. Your employee skills inventory is a valuable jewel case.

Writing a Good Job Ad

Whether you plan to post a job ad in the newspaper, on your company Web site, or on a job board, you're not going to have much luck if it doesn't concisely convey what you're offering potential applicants. Writing a good job ad is a critical step in the hiring process, but the task is often more difficult than many people think. What you need to remember is that you're not trying to win a literary prize. You're trying to attract job candidates — and the right candidates at that.

Keep in mind the following two considerations in writing a job ad:

- **The goal of a job ad is not only to generate responses from qualified applicants, but also to prevent candidates who are clearly unqualified from applying for the position.** You're better off getting only five responses, each from a person who clearly deserves an interview, than getting 100 responses from people you'd never dream of hiring.

- **Think "sell."** You're advertising a product — your company. Every aspect of your ad must seek to foster a favorable impression of the organization.

Your next step is to actually compose the ad. If you've done a good job of writing the job description (see Chapter 4 for more about developing a quality job description), then you've already accomplished this task. In fact, you actually want to think of the ad as a synopsis of the existing job description.

As for the ad itself, the following list describes the elements you need to think about as you compose the ad:

- **Headline:** The headline almost always is the job title.

- **Job information:** A line or two about the general duties and responsibilities of the job.

Don't forget the look of it

Before you start to actually compose any ad, keep in mind that an advertisement, regardless of whether it's on the Internet or in a newspaper, needs to look as good as it reads. Several purely visual factors — the headline, type size, placement, and graphic element — can influence the responses as much as the wording. If the position is important or difficult to fill, you may want to spring for a larger headline and type and maybe even your company's logo in a box.

✔ If something's special about the job or company, spell it out. ("WebWidget is the largest widget store on the Net.")

✔ State responsibilities and qualifications accurately. Include sufficient hiring criteria to discourage the obviously unqualified.

✔ Make replying easy for applicants. You can even create a special e-mail address for candidate replies. Ask for only enough information to make an initial evaluation; this information usually includes a cover letter, a resume, and possibly salary requirements. The more difficulty applicants face in responding to your ad, the fewer responses you're going to get.

✔ **Company information:** Always include a few words on what your company does.

✔ **Qualifications and hiring criteria:** Specify the level of education and experience and relevant attributes and skills (per your competency model) required to do the job.

✔ **Respond method:** Let applicants know the best way to get in touch with you: e-mail, regular mail, fax, or phone. Also let them know certain ground rules, such as whether you prefer to receive online resumes as an attachment or embedded in the e-mail itself.

Bear in mind, too, the following key points:

✔ You want to convey some sense of your organizational culture and values with a few phrases (fast-paced, results-oriented, client-centered).

✔ Use active voice and action words throughout the ad. Make the ad move — not just sit passively on the page.

✔ Create a buzz, a sense of enthusiasm; arouse applicants' interest. A dull ad assuredly draws dull candidates.

Following is an example of an ad that takes into consideration the preceding criteria.

ADMINISTRATIVE ASSISTANT, LAW OFFICE

Busy, growing law office specializing in entertainment and intellectual property seeks well-organized individual to support staff of five lawyers and two paralegals. Responsibilities include processing correspondence, maintaining attorney schedules and client files, and updating publications. High school diploma or GED required; AA (associate of arts) degree preferred. Must be familiar with Microsoft Office. Competitive salary and benefits. AAjob@lawfirm.com or Hollywood Law, P.O. Box 999, Los Angeles, CA 99999.

The Internet: Powerful, but Be Careful

I promise this section isn't a long treatise on all the ways the Internet has changed the world. It's my goal here to zero in on the Web's relevance strictly for your HR endeavors.

You'd have to go back to the dawn of newspaper advertising to find something that's revolutionized the recruiting process more than the Internet. It has created countless new opportunities for employers and job seekers alike. Job boards abound, and today even the smallest of companies frequently have a Web site describing what they do and, often, the advantages of working for them. In fact, a 2005 study by the Society of Human Resource Management found that 92.4 percent of candidates will visit a company's Web site at some point during a job search.

No doubt, you're already familiar with many of the benefits of the Internet as a recruiting tool: access to a much larger potential candidate base and a relatively low-cost way to manage the process of hiring and continually attracting future employees. Literally thousands of job boards cover virtually every industry, profession, educational background, experience level, ethnic group, and much more. Dice.com, for example, is a popular job search site for information technology professionals. LawCrossing.com focuses on legal positions — not just lawyers but paralegals, assistants, and other legal professionals. Jobsinthemoney.com is dedicated to corporate finance, accounting, and commercial banking jobs.

A miraculous tool, but there's no free lunch

The Internet is unquestionably a godsend, but along with the opportunities it creates come a number of significant implications — both practical and legal — that you need to understand and properly manage in order to maximize the effectiveness of this incredibly powerful tool.

One of the Web's huge appeals is its ability to help you locate qualified candidates at extremely low costs. More candidates for less money? Sounds like a hiring manager's dream. But hang on. It can also become a nightmare if not managed properly. For starters, the Internet has the potential of dramatically increasing the number of responses to your job ads. Many HR managers report they have great difficulty even keeping track of submissions. Even small companies can receive hundreds of resumes from a single ad, depending on the position and job market. Some HR professionals, or their staff members, still manually read through or at least scan each resume.

If your budget allows, however, you can reduce problems caused by this sheer volume by creating computer protocols that flag certain qualifications to help you narrow down resumes. These electronic codes enable your computer to rapidly sort through resumes by designating certain terms, words, credentials, or any other information. You can set a filter for an accounting position, for example, to eliminate candidates who lack a CPA credential.

Keep in mind, though, that you should create these protocols carefully, taking time to talk extensively with line managers about the experience and credentials that really matter for a position. Otherwise you may inadvertently eliminate viable candidates.

Computer protocols can help, but they're not a cure-all. In many businesses, electronic filtering may not provide you with the information you really need to determine who is worthy of an interview. Managers hiring for many service-oriented jobs — retail, delivery, and certain administrative positions, for example — frequently care much more about the enthusiasm and work ethic people bring to the job than any particular set of technical skills or experiences. These qualities are, of course, best assessed during a personal interview, but manually processing resumes by reading each one may pick up indications about personal attributes a machine would miss.

You also encounter potential problems with e-mailed resumes that you don't encounter with paper submissions mailed or faxed to you. Sometimes e-mailed resumes or applications include attachments that you can't read or, worse, contain computer viruses. You can sidestep these issues by including a request in your job ad asking applicants to cut and paste resumes directly into the message field instead of sending as an attachment.

You must also consider an alphabet soup of laws affecting the handling of online job ads and candidate responses. Any time you post a job opening, you must be sure not to imply that candidates can apply for the job electronically only. Title VII of the Civil Rights Act of 1964 (Title VII), the Americans with Disabilities Act (ADA), and the Age Discrimination in Employment Act (ADEA) stipulate that employers can't discriminate in any aspect of the employment process. This ruling, of course, includes interactions via the Internet. In other words, you must make sure that you offer avenues to candidates who do not own computers or have access to e-mail to apply for an open job. And you must spend as much time reviewing these resumes as you do those that come in electronically. This requirement is particularly important given the fact that some candidates may not only send you resumes electronically but also direct you to home pages that extensively showcase their accomplishments and qualifications. You must keep in mind that those without access to such online tools deserve an equal chance to be considered for a position as those who do have access.

Another key factor is the way in which you *respond* to candidates who apply via the Internet. Consider creating a template of automated, carefully worded, neutral e-mail replies that merely let each candidate know that you've received his application or resume and that you will be in touch as the search progresses. My reasoning is three-fold:

✔ First, if you, like many HR managers in small to midsize companies, list your own e-mail in the job ad, it can take a lot of time to carry on an online dialogue with numerous candidates. Prior to the Internet, you would never have spent your time talking on the phone with applicants at this stage of the hiring process.

✔ Second, you run the risk of even the most casual comment boomeranging into a legal problem. I recently heard the tale of an HR professional who wrote back to a candidate she'd worked with at another company asking about her children. When the candidate didn't get the job, she in turn accused the company of discrimination because she was a parent and perhaps unable to work the long hours this company typically demands of its employees. An automated response lets you avoid online discussions entirely until they become necessary.

✔ Third, and perhaps most important, being responsive to job applicants is simply a good business practice. After all, anyone who comes in contact with your company forms a perception that can influence the firm's reputation. A simple, straightforward message sent to all applicants is a good way to showcase your organization's professionalism.

For a good sample of an Acknowledgement of Receipt of Resume/Job Application Form, see the CD-ROM.

Quality in, quality out

In a marketplace with so many possibilities, you want to make sure that your job ads attract the best and brightest candidates. You've got to design ads that stand out, and, as a medium, the Internet is certainly no exception to this rule. Think carefully about how any job posting you write and design is packaged. For example, does the posting explain what makes your company an exciting place to work? Does it make the job attractive, showcasing its growth potential, the chance to use certain skills or other compelling opportunities such as travel? If you write the ad generically — "Real estate firm seeking administrative assistant" — you'll attract generic, undistinguished candidates. But if you make it dynamic — "Orange County's leading mortgage broker seeks administrative assistant to help senior executives manage new opportunities" — then you're likely to get more people enthused about working for your organization.

You're only as good as your Web site

There was a time when ambitious candidates would try and "study up" on the company they were applying to by requesting company literature — annual reports, sales literature, marketing brochures — or even go to a library and conduct various forms of research. Much as employers appreciated the diligence of candidates who made that effort, the information they'd gathered was rarely relevant to the interview process.

The Internet has dramatically changed the quality of applicants' research, however. Just as you're now able to find out more about candidates who may be applying from all over the world, job seekers in turn can uncover in-depth assessments and facts about your company. While the savvy ones review a variety of sources — articles, discussion groups, industry analyst reports, and so on — your Web site is a great place to communicate your unique culture and most appealing characteristics. Well executed, your site can give job seekers a glimpse into the employee experience — what it's like to work in your company.

In addition, many people who've grown up using computers also engage in active *social networking*. Jobseekers age 25 and younger, in particular, have an incredibly large network of friends who they'll contact through instant messaging and e-mail to get their thoughts on various jobs and companies.

The implications of these changes for HR professionals are two-fold:

✔ With information now so much more accessible then ever, you want to make sure (to the extent that you can) that your company's Web site accurately showcases your firm's strengths and range of capabilities. After all, you want the best people to be drawn to your company, and a Web site that's outdated, difficult to read, or lacking relevant information can reduce your chances of luring top-notch candidates.

✔ Don't be surprised at how well prepared candidates are today when you get to the interview process. You'll also need to be prepared and raise your expectations for the discussion. The topics you cover can relate more specifically to business priorities and issues affecting your industry and company. (I discuss interviewing in detail in Chapter 7.)

Classified Ads Remain a Factor

At one time, classified ads were the most widely used recruiting method in business. Despite the opportunity created by the Internet, classified ads still have their advantages. First, they're legally sound. Anyone can have access to a newspaper. Second, they attract potential candidates who may not be necessarily focused on searching for a job (as most people are who access job sites on the Internet), but may well find themselves intrigued should they come across your ad while reading the Sunday paper.

An executive I know who was perfectly happy in her job used to make a weekly habit of scanning job postings each Sunday just to stay on top of various market and hiring trends in her city. One day, though, she saw an ad for a position with a company that had always intrigued her. The next day she sent a cover letter and resume. Three weeks later, she was offered a new job. Classified ads also help keep your firm visible and let people know that since your company is hiring, it's also probably thriving.

Another advantage is that advertising in newspapers — especially ethnic or cultural publications — may be your only way of ensuring that you reach all minorities and age groups, a key aim of your diversity efforts.

The downside, of course, is that classified ads cost money and also can attract hundreds of unqualified candidates or even just random job seekers whose resumes you have to sort out. Still, they have their place and remain a useful tool.

A word about blind ads

Some companies choose to place *blind ads* — an online posting or classified ad that doesn't identify the company and typically directs replies to a P.O. box number. Sometimes, you have sound reasons for placing a blind ad. Your company may not want anyone to know — for competitive or internal morale reasons — that you have an opening for a critical job. Senior management may be seeking to replace a current employee or a key worker or executive who's indicated a desire to leave. Or perhaps the company has an image problem that may discourage candidates.

The only problem with blind ads is that they're a turnoff to many potential candidates — particularly those who are already employed, but looking. Because the company isn't identified, they worry that their response to a blind ad could cause them to inadvertently apply at their current employer, who they may not want to know they're job hunting. (One trade journal has a policy of allowing applicants responding to blind ads to advise the magazine of any employers to whom they do not want their replies forwarded.) Even by those not currently employed, blind job postings may harm a company's credibility and reputation.

Bottom line: Unless you have a compelling reason to do otherwise, avoid blind ads.

Establish a system to keep track of your recruiting success for classified ads and Internet channels. How many candidates did each source produce? How qualified and skilled was each applicant? These metrics can help you determine the return on your investment in a variety of recruiting channels.

Using Recruiters

Recruiters can be an invaluable part of your search arsenal. And if you know how to maximize their services, recruiters can more than pay for themselves. Using outside recruiters has several key advantages — namely, the following:

✔ Outside recruiters generally have access to a large pool of applicants — after all, it's their job to continually locate quality candidates.

✔ They handle such cumbersome administrative details of recruiting as placing ads, skills evaluation, and preliminary interviews.

As I describe in Chapter 8, you play a key role in checking the references of potential employees. In the course of their evaluation process, staffing firms typically check selected references from their candidates' past employers to gather skill proficiency information and job performance history, but employers should perform their own reference checks as well. This is because a preliminary check may or may not reveal all the information you want to consider in making your final decision as to whether to bring an individual into your company.

✔ They're often a valuable source of staffing advice. A recruiter who knows her stuff can often help you identify whether you need a temporary or full-time employee or a generalist or specialist and provide feedback on what the market looks like right now to find the applicant you need.

Who does what?

If you at times have difficulty determining what makes a *headhunter* different from a *recruiter* and an *employment agency* different from a *search firm*, you're not alone. The names can be confusing. All these sources fulfill the same basic function: They find job candidates for client firms for a fee. The difference between the various specialists in this large and growing industry is primarily how they charge and on which segment of the labor market they focus.

The following list offers you a rundown on how these players differ on the recruiting field.

✔ **Employment agencies, staffing firms,** and **contingency search firms** are companies you engage to find job candidates for specific positions. What they all have in common is that you pay them a fee — but only after they find you someone you eventually hire. These firms recruit candidates in virtually every industry, and companies call on them to fill positions at all levels of the corporate ladder. They typically charge you a percentage of the new employee's first year's salary. It can range from 15 percent to 30 percent, depending on the level of the position you're filling and the skills required.

Employment agencies, staffing firms, and contingency search firms typically differ in the types of positions they help you fill. In most cases, employment agencies are generalists and focus on entry- and mid-level jobs in a range of industries, whereas staffing or contingency search firms focus on mid- to upper-level positions usually in a particular field or profession — finance or marketing, for example. (For more information on selecting and working with staffing firms, see Chapter 13.)

The trend toward specialization is good news for you because those firms that specialize generally have a strong sense of the marketplace in a given field. Among other things, they make sure that the package you're offering is competitive. Many of the larger staffing firms offer an expanded variety of services, including preliminary reference checks, as well as refunds or replacement guarantees if the new employee doesn't work out.

✔ **Executive search firms, or headhunters,** focus on higher level executives, up to and including CEOs. Unlike employment agencies, most search firms charge a retainer whether they produce results or not. You can also expect to pay, in addition to expenses, a commission of 25 percent — or even a third — of the executive's annual salary if the firm's successful in its search.

Why, then, go to an executive search specialist? The main value comes into play if you're seeking someone for a high-level job that's most likely to be filled by an executive who's already working for another company. A good search specialist usually has the contacts and the expertise to handle very targeted, high-level searches.

Should you use recruiters?

Most companies that rely on outside recruiters to fill positions do so for one of two reasons:

✔ They don't have the time or the expertise to recruit effectively on their own.

✔ The recruiting efforts they've put forward to date have yet to yield results.

True, using an outside recruiter involves an extra cost, but you need to keep in mind, too, that, if you handle recruiting yourself, you're still paying for such out-of-pocket expenses as classified ads, as well as diverting your employees' time and resources from their core expertise. Composing an Internet posting or classified ad may be a routine task for somebody with a background in human resources, but it can be an onerous and timely task for somebody who has never written one before. The same principle holds true for other basic recruiting functions, such as reviewing resumes, which has become exceptionally labor intensive because of the Internet. Routine though they may seem to you, these tasks can take others in your company an inordinate amount of time.

Finding the "right" recruiter

You choose a recruiter the same way that you choose any professional services specialist: You take a look at what services are available. You ask colleagues for recommendations. You talk to different recruiters. And you leave it up to the recruiters to convince you why your best interests lie in having them operate on your behalf. Ultimately, you want a recruiter whom you feel confident will be able to articulate your company's mission, values, and culture to job prospects effectively. The following list provides some reminders that can help you make a wise choice:

- **Check them out personally.** However busy you may be, make visiting any recruiter who may be representing your company part of your business. Make sure that you feel comfortable about the way the recruiter runs and maintains its office. (A good question to ask yourself as you visit a recruiter: Would I, as a job candidate, like to work with this recruiter?) Don't hesitate, either, in asking for references.

- **Be explicit about your needs.** The cardinal rule in dealing with recruiters is to be as candid and as specific as possible about your needs. Make sure that the firm understands your business, your company culture, and what, exactly, you're looking for in a candidate. Extra bonus: A savvy recruiter can often tell you, simply by looking at the job description, how likely you are to find someone to fill the position.

- **Clarify fee arrangements.** Make sure that you have a clear understanding — before you enter into a business agreement — of how your recruiter charges and make sure that any arrangement you make is in writing. If you don't understand something, ask for clarification — a reputable firm is always happy to explain its fee structure. (No professional wants a hassle with a client over money.)

- **Ask about replacement guarantees.** Most of the leading recruitment firms today offer a replacement guarantee if a new employee doesn't work out after a reasonable period of time. Just make sure that you understand the conditions under which the guarantee applies.

✔ **Express your concerns openly.** If you aren't happy about any aspect of the arrangement you've struck with a recruiter, speak up. Tell the recruiter exactly what your concerns are. If you don't feel comfortable expressing your concerns with the recruiter you've chosen, you're probably dealing with the wrong company.

As in any industry, recruiting has its bad apples. Fortunately, the industry has done a very good job in recent years of policing itself, but you still need to be wary of any recruiter who exhibits any of the following traits:

✔ Is evasive about providing a list of satisfied clients it has worked with or unwilling to provide information about its procedures.

✔ Is reluctant to provide progress reports or is vague about fees and billing arrangements. ("Don't worry about it. We're friends.")

✔ Charges applicants for services (preparing resumes, testing fees, and so on).

✔ Has no business track record or has a record of consumer complaints.

Back to School: Recruiting on Campus

College campuses have long been a fertile hunting ground for companies in search of entry-level talent. Smaller firms without well-organized college recruiting programs have always been at something of a disadvantage. If you're one of the "smaller guys," the following list tells you how to level the playing field.

✔ **Get to know the folks in the placement office.** Campus recruiting is usually coordinated by the college placement office. As long as your company has a reasonably good reputation, the people in the placement office are going to be receptive to your recruiting overtures and are likely to steer good candidates your way. A big part of their job, after all, is getting good jobs for their graduates. The best way to build a strong relationship with placement office personnel is to pay them a personal visit — or better still, invite them to your company to see what you have to offer.

✔ **Be prepared to sell your company.** The image projected by you (or anyone else in your company who goes on a campus recruiting mission) goes a long way to determine how successful you are at attracting the top candidates at the school. Make things simple for yourself. Put together a PowerPoint presentation that you can use repeatedly.

Things to watch out for when recruiting on campus

Consider the following three points before taking part in any campus recruiting activities.

✔ **Be prepared to be challenged on your policies.** Don't be surprised if you're closely queried on policies ranging from diversity to domestic partner benefits, to ecology or any number of social issues. You might spend a little time with your corporate communications department clarifying the best way to smoothly answer these questions.

✔ **Get a good night's sleep.** Placement offices tend to stack interviews, often every 30 minutes. You may wind up interviewing 16 students in a single day. That's why students often complain that interviewers frequently seem perfunctory. (**Note:** Savvy students are aware of this problem and vie for appointments in the morning.)

✔ **Keep your energy up.** Burning out after a day of interviews is all too easy to do. After all, you must repeat the same information over and over, and you must be equally enthusiastic at 10 a.m. and at 4:30 p.m. (And that's not to mention the food in the college cafeteria.)

✔ **Speak their language.** By speaking "their" language, I don't mean "like totally," "I'm so sure," "awesome," and terms that crop up every day among students and other young people. Think instead "opportunity," "growth," and "learn." Yes, money still talks for most college students today, but the latest generations of students are expressing increased interest in the nature of the job and the culture of the company.

Other Recruiting Sources Worth a Look

Aside from some of the traditional recruiting options that I discussed earlier in this chapter, the following resources may help you in your search for qualified candidates.

All in the family: Employee referrals

Employee referrals were formerly considered a somewhat risky practice — an invitation to nepotism and favoritism. But, in reality, employee referrals may represent one of the most reliable recruiting sources: Most employees would rather walk across a bed of hot coals than recommend a friend or relative who may turn out to be a source of embarrassment. The evidence suggests, too, that the turnover rate among those employees whom other employees recommend is lower than that the rate among employees you recruit from other sources.

No surprise, then, that more and more companies today have instituted employee referral programs, with rewards (extra vacation days, trips, cash bonuses, and so on) for employees who recommend a person whom you eventually hire and who stays with the company for a specific period.

Before you launch any employee referral program, make sure that you consider all the ramifications and establish a systematic process for administering it. Some questions you need to answer are as follows:

- ✔ What incentives are you going to offer to the employee who refers someone, and are you going to vary the incentives based on the importance of the job?

- ✔ How long does any referred employee need to remain with your company before the person who makes the referral becomes eligible for the incentive? (The norm in most companies is between three and six months.)

- ✔ What procedure must any employee who's making a referral follow?

After you set up an employee referral program, don't keep it a secret. Publicize it in every way that you can: through posters, e-mail, and newsletters, for example. Remember, your objective is to generate as many quality referrals as possible. Reminders always help. And make sure that everyone knows whenever an employee receives a bonus for a referral.

Job fairs

Job fairs are recruiting events that bring together employers and job-seekers in one location. They're generally sponsored by professional associations, community organizations, or educational institutions and are often held by regional groups, such as a state teachers association. The sponsoring group hires a hall, invites potential employers to set up recruiting and/or information booths and tables, and handles all the administrative and publicity arrangements. Sometimes the sponsors charge admission fees to defray expenses. Most job fairs are held on a single day or over a weekend, but some fairs can run as long as a week.

Most job fairs focus on a particular industry or professional group — computer engineers, teachers, or perhaps recent college graduates. Properly run job fairs resemble trade shows or conventions and have the same lively atmosphere and buzz.

The main downside of job fairs is their competitive aspect. Because job fairs are usually regional and industry-specific — computer professionals from the New England states, for example — they tend to attract firms from your region who are looking for the same folks you're looking for, so you may well end up with your company's booth located just down the aisle from your main local competitor. This proximity means that potential job applicants can directly compare your company with your nearest competitors simply by walking across the room. It also means that you have to make the strongest impression possible. Here are some suggestions:

- ✔ **Put your best foot forward.** Whether you're going to be greeting applicants at a booth or at a table, you want to make sure that the general impression you're conveying is one of quality and professionalism. The promotional information you distribute doesn't necessarily have to be expensively designed and printed — and you don't have to invest vast sums in elaborate posters or audiovisuals. Just make sure that everything you do with respect to your booth or table is neat, substantive, and well organized.

- ✔ **Send good company ambassadors.** The people staffing your booth or table should not only be able to handle all the questions attendees are likely to ask about your company, they should also be enthusiastic and personable — the kind of people potential employees will enjoy meeting. Remember, too, that having senior people as part of your recruiting team tells applicants that your company takes potential candidates and the job fair seriously. Having a high-quality recruiting team on campus is also key.

- ✔ **Keep the paperwork down.** Rather than force applicants to fill out lengthy applications, put together a simple form that takes only a minute or two to complete. You will have the opportunity later in the recruiting process to gather more detailed information.

Open houses: Our house is your house

Open houses are most commonly held by companies in industries — mass market retailing or fast food restaurants, for example — that experience high turnover and thus have an almost constant need for new employees. But open houses can also be an effective recruiting strategy for companies that are about to expand into a new region.

Conducting a successful open house hinges on several keys. One key, certainly, is getting the word out by using a variety of media (flyers and store posters, notices to local schools and colleges, and even commercials on local cable and radio outlets) to stir up interest. Yet another key is to set up an effective, well-organized, and nondiscriminatory process that makes applicants feel welcome, but also enables you to eliminate from the running those individuals who are clearly unsuitable.

Some other considerations:

- ✔ **Choose the place carefully.** You can hold open houses at either your own premises or at some outside location, such as a hotel ballroom, or conference room, and each location has pros and cons. Holding the event on company premises gives attendees a first-hand look at what you have to offer, but perhaps your facilities — because of their location, configuration, or security considerations — may not lend themselves to this kind of an event.

- ✔ **Think about timing.** Open houses are typically held after working hours and on weekends so that you can attract potential applicants who are currently employed. Before you select the date, double-check to make sure that your open house doesn't conflict with other events that can hold down attendance, such as a local football game or religious holiday.

- ✔ **Be friendly and informal.** Every person who attends your open house may not be a potential candidate, but each of them will come away from the event with an impression that they will communicate to friends, relatives, and acquaintances. It's to your advantage — especially in a tight labor market — that the impression be as favorable as possible.

Professional associations and unions

Most professional associations have some sort of job referral service, publish a newsletter listing available positions, or maintain a resume bank. The Internet, of course, has made this process even easier, in essence creating an online community that lets members exchange information and ideas. Any of these sources can be a good starting point for a focused candidate search, especially if you're looking for a technical or professional specialty. And advertising your opening on these services is usually free. These associations also give you a chance to meet potential candidates, formally or informally, at meetings and conventions, where you can circulate or, perhaps, host a hospitality suite or information booth.

Direct applications (walk-ins)

Some people view walk-in applicants as a nuisance, but consider the following: Anyone who has the energy and the gumption to make a cold, face-to-face call is someone whose resume probably deserves a review. So at the very least, have a policy in place to deal with such applicants. Invite the person to either leave behind or send you a resume, along with a cover letter.

Government employment services

Since the Great Depression of the 1930s, every state has operated a public employment service in conjunction with the Department of Labor (DOL). Employer-paid unemployment taxes fund these offices — in other words, you foot the bill. These agencies exist primarily to offer services to job seekers. They register the unemployed, determine and pay unemployment benefits, offer counseling and training, and provide labor-market information.

In the past, state employment agencies have generally been considered a source for unskilled labor and lower-level clerical and industrial jobs. This perception, however, is not necessarily the case any more: Technicians and professionals are registering with these agencies, too, and, as is true of many other aspects of the government, their operations are becoming less bureaucratic and more client-oriented. Your local agency is always worth a try; after all, you pay for it.

The downside: Although all government agencies are subject to federal standards and guidelines, the quality and usefulness of the services they offer can vary widely from state to state.

The DOL, working with the state agencies, has launched an online resume and job listing service, America's Job Bank (at www.ajb.dni.us). To use your local state employment service, you first need to determine the DOL job code for your position; often, the service staff helps you do so. You then submit a job order to the agency, which matches the order to its pool of candidates. Suitable candidates are then evaluated, according to DOL guidelines, and applicants are sent to your organization for interviews.

Forms on the CD

A Sample Skills Inventory Form and a Blank Form

Acknowledgement of Receipt of Resume/Job Application Form

Chapter 6

Narrowing Down the Field

● ●

In This Chapter

▶ Setting up an evaluation and interviewing system

▶ Knowing the employer responsibilities during the evaluation process

▶ Developing job applications

▶ Narrowing the field of resumes

● ●

*J*ust about everybody agrees that the job interview is the most important element of the hiring process. But what many otherwise savvy business people often forget is that one of the keys to effective interviewing is effectively evaluating candidates.

If you don't have an efficient process in place for evaluating candidates, two things are likely to happen, neither of them good for you or your business: First, you may inadvertently "weed out" candidates who clearly deserve a second look. Just as bad, your process may fail to accomplish its fundamental purpose: making sure that you're not wasting your time and effort on candidates who are clearly unqualified for the position you're seeking to fill. This chapter can help you avoid this common — but very avoidable — staffing pitfall.

Job Applications: Are They Obsolete?

Job applications were at one time the primary method of evaluating candidates in most companies. Thanks to the resume, however, applications no longer figure as prominently in the hiring process, which isn't surprising. One reason is that the typical resume today contains most of, if not all, the information normally asked for on a typical job application.

A bigger issue, however, is Equal Employment Opportunity (EEO) legislation. EEO legislation now prohibits many questions that routinely appeared on traditional job applications years ago — items relating to gender, age, marital status, and even birthplace. Some states also have specific regulations regarding what you can or cannot ask.

How the Internet Is changing the definition of a job applicant

The Internet's exponential expansion since the late 1990s has dramatically changed the world of recruiting and job-seeking (see Chapter 5). While submitting and processing resumes and applications online is a boon for both employers and job hunters, it has also complicated the process of record-keeping and compliance with employment nondiscrimination laws.

The Internet Applicant final rule of 2006, issued by the Office of Federal Contract Compliance Programs (OFCCP), addresses recordkeeping by federal contractors doing more than $10,000 in government business in one year. The law requires these firms to collect and maintain specific records about hiring done with the assistance of the Internet or related technologies, such as e-mail, applicant tracking systems, and a variety of databases containing information on job seekers.

While these requirements don't currently apply to companies that are not federal contractors, given the continuing growth of the Internet, HR professionals should keep abreast of new developments in this area. In the near future, similar rules may apply to public and private companies as well.

Employers using or seeking to use technology to sort job applicants may want to create an Internet hiring policy, anticipating these and other requirements. At a minimum, ensure that your job descriptions are very clear as to applicant qualifications and take special care in designing and phrasing questions meant to identify candidates who meet the requirements for the job. Later in this chapter, I talk more about the kinds of questions that are appropriate and inappropriate when evaluating applicants.

The one big advantage of a job application form over a resume is that it simplifies the task of keeping a file on unhired candidates whom you want to consider for future job openings. In addition, if you design the application form to match your business needs, it generally works better than a resume does as a candidate evaluation tool, because the same information appears in the same place, regardless of the candidate. And because job applications force candidates to supply you with certain information (along with dates), they don't leave the candidate room to "weasel out" of answering key questions

Setting up the application

Many business-supply companies offer inexpensive preprinted application forms, and their services are worth looking into. If you decide to create your own, however, give yourself some time to think about how much information you really need.

As a general rule, less is more.

Second general rule: You want to make absolutely sure that the questions you ask are not discriminatory and are in line with federal and state laws. Don't shoot yourself in the foot by including questions in the application that relate to any of the following areas:

- ✔ Race

- ✔ Religion

- ✔ Sex or sexual orientation

- ✔ Age

- ✔ Ancestry or national origin (but you can ask whether a candidate is eligible to work in the United States)

- ✔ Marital status

- ✔ Arrests

- ✔ Military service

- ✔ Height or weight (unless directly related to job performance)

- ✔ Political preference or membership in social organizations

- ✔ Handicaps or disabilities

The following list describes other things you shouldn't do during the preliminary stages of the hiring process:

- ✔ **Say cheese.** You can't request the applicant to provide a photograph before employment.

- ✔ **Name game.** You can ask an applicant's name but not a maiden name or a spouse's maiden name. Why? Such a question may be interpreted as another way of asking about the candidate's marital status.

- ✔ **House rules.** You can ask an applicant's address but not whether the applicant owns or rents the residence or how long the applicant has lived there.

- ✔ **Class act.** Most education qualifications are fair game, but some states prohibit you from asking for high school or college graduation dates. It's a dead tip-off for age.

Final rule: If you don't need it, don't ask it.

Be careful to seek legal counsel to review your company's job applications. Among other things, you want to make absolutely sure that the forms are not in any way discriminatory.

You always need to require applicants to sign the application and affirm the accuracy of the information they furnish. This step doesn't necessarily guarantee that the information is true, but it gives you some protection if, after you hire an applicant, he doesn't work out and you discover that he made misrepresentations on his job application.

Using the application as an evaluation tool

Some application forms are *weighted,* meaning that you give each element in the form a certain value, putting more emphasis, or weight, on qualifications you feel may more heavily influence later performance on the job. In other words, weighting the application questions can help you figure out how likely a person with a certain type of experience or skill is to turn out to be the right employee for this particular job. You can usually recognize a weighted application form if you see a section on the side that reads, "Do not write in this section," along with some mysteriously numbered boxes.

The trick, of course, is figuring out how to weigh the criteria. The basic idea is to determine how accurately a specific criterion might predict superior job performance. The problem, however, is that no one has developed any sort of weighting scale flexible enough to cover everything that can affect job performance. Educational levels, for example, may closely link to success in a certain job in a company filled with people with advanced degrees, in which case you would assign it a higher weighting value relative to other criteria. But education credentials may not be as important in a company with less educated employees. And if you assign values to work experience, licenses held, and so on, you have to be careful that the criteria you're using relate to actual job performance. Again, if you don't really need the skill, you shouldn't list it as a criterion.

Is the entire process scientific? Hardly. But a weighted system can weed out obviously unqualified employees and give you at least a preliminary idea of who the top candidates are for the job.

One way to add validity to a weighted application form is to do your own tracking. Score applicants for a while and then recheck the scores of those you hire. You're looking for relationships between good performance and objective qualifications. The criteria used in an interview to assess related fit for a job should be the same criteria used for the performance evaluation of the person in that job. If you can determine the attributes and qualifications that make successful employees, you may find that you can structure a weighted application form that allows you to identify applicants with these qualities. This procedure is useful if you do a lot of hiring; if you hire only a few people a year, on the other hand, you may just create more work for yourself without any worthwhile results.

Setting Up a System for Evaluating Candidates

No set rules exist for evaluating job applicants — other than common sense. The important thing is to have some kind of system or protocol in place before resumes begin to arrive.

No matter who is in charge of the process — an HR specialist, line manager, or owner — it should include a set of hard criteria to use as the basis of your decisions. Otherwise, there's a good chance you'll end up making choices based on factors that may have no bearing on desired work performance, such as courses taken at a university you admire or a particularly impressive skill that would be virtually useless in tackling the responsibilities of your job opening. You need to keep in mind the following three key questions at all times:

- ✔ **What are the prerequisites for the position?** These should track with the qualifications listed in the job description, as long as your description is targeted and carefully thought through, as I describe in Chapter 4.

- ✔ **What are the special requirements in your organization, such as certifications or special education?** If you own a public accounting firm, for example, you would most likely consider only applicants with a valid CPA credential.

- ✔ **What qualifications and attributes are critical to high performance in this particular position?** Think of the competency models I outline in Chapter 4. If your business depends on telemarketing, for instance, some people will be better than others at engaging the interest of the people they call. What attributes make them better? One is certainly their ability to not allow repeated rejections to wear down their spirits. There may be other characteristics as well. Identify those attributes that you feel will produce superior performance in functions critical to your company's competitive strength and look for these attributes in prospective employees.

If you haven't answered these three questions, you're not ready to start.

Here's an overview of the evaluation process:

1. **Scan applications or resumes first for basic qualifications.**

   If you do a good job of communicating the job's qualifications to your recruiter or in the ad you write, you shouldn't get too many replies or resumes from unqualified candidates. Keep in mind, however, that some applicants apply to virtually any job opening, whether they're qualified or not. Their attitude is "Hey, you never know." For example, if you're seeking to hire a medical technician who will be working on equipment that requires a license, eliminate applicants without this license.

2. **Look for key criteria.**

   After you eliminate unqualified candidates, you can focus on more specific hiring criteria, such as good organizational skills, supervisory experience, or good driving record. Here again, your task is considerably easier if you do a thorough job of identifying these requirements at the time you put together the job description. But no matter how much time you spent identifying criteria, you can't rush this step. Some resumes clearly reflect the skills and experience you're looking for; others may come close but just don't do the trick.

   Begin the evaluation process by setting a high standard (for example, the resume must meet a certain high percentage of the criteria), but if your reject pile is growing and you haven't "cleared" anyone, you may need to lower the bar somewhat.

3. **Set up a process to flag and identify your top candidates.**

   At this point, you probably want to separate the wheat from the chaff, which means establishing a separate file for each of the applicants who pass the initial review. Some HR professionals like to develop a *flow sheet* — a document that you attach to the outside of a folder that lists the steps in the evaluation process with spaces for the date and initials of the person completing the step. Nothing's really complicated about such a sheet. It's simply a form that enables you to tell at a glance what stage of the process the candidate has reached.

   Instead of this manual method, many HR organizations use an *applicant tracking system* or a *candidate management system,* which are software applications that can post job openings on various Web sites, automate resume scanning, generate letters, and perform other functions.

4. **Extend an invitation.**

   Your next move depends on how many applicants remain. If you have only a few, you may want to invite them all to come in for an interview. If you have more applicants than you can handle, you may want to add yet another level of evaluation. Possibilities for the latter include a phone conversation or a visit to your office, where they can complete your company's own application form. (For more information, see the sections "Job Applications: Are They Obsolete?" and "Phone Interviews: Narrowing Your List" in this chapter.)

Resume Roulette: Reading Behind the Lines

Based on resumes alone, you'd think that all your candidates are such outstanding prospects that you could hire them sight unseen. And no wonder. Anyone who does any research at all into how to look for a job knows, at this point, how to write a resume that puts him in the best light. And those who don't know how to write a great resume can now hire people who do know.

Why, then, take resumes seriously? Because resumes, regardless of how "professional" they are, can still reveal a wealth of information about the candidate — after you crack the code.

Mastering the basics

Here's what you probably know already: Basically, job candidates submit only two types of resumes:

- ✔ **Chronological,** where all the work-related information appears in a time-line sequence
- ✔ **Functional,** where the information appears in various categories (skills, achievements, qualifications, and so on).

In the past, the general rule was that candidates trying to hide something, such as gaps in their work history, wrote functional resumes. But because a well-rounded background (in conjunction with one's specialty area) can prove an asset in today's job market, the functional resume is now more acceptable. The key point to keep in mind: Don't automatically turn off to either type of resume.

Some applicants use a combination of the two formats, presenting a capsule of what they believe are their most important qualifications and accomplishments, together with a chronological work history. If a resume is short on work history, look for skills that may be transferable to your position. Identifying these skills will be much easier if, as I discuss earlier in this chapter, you've weighted the application questions to tie certain types of experience or skills with success in the job.

Before diving into that pile of resumes, consider the following observations:

✔ No job applicant in his right mind is going to put derogatory or detracting information in his own resume.

✔ Many resumes are professionally prepared, designed to create a winning, but not necessarily accurate, impression.

✔ Reviewing resumes is tedious, no matter what. You may need to sift through the stack several times. Have plenty of aspirin handy.

✔ If you don't review resumes yourself or delegate it to the wrong person, you're likely to miss that diamond-in-the-rough, that ideal employee who unfortunately has poor resume-drafting skills.

Reading between the lines

Now that more and more people are using outside specialists or software packages to prepare their resumes, getting an accurate reading of a candidate's strengths simply by reading his resume is more difficult than ever. Even so, here are some of the resume characteristics that generally (although not always) describe a candidate worth interviewing:

✔ **Lots of details:** Though applicants are generally advised to avoid wordiness, the more detailed they are in their descriptions of what they did and accomplished in previous jobs, the more reliable (as a rule) the information is.

✔ **A history of stability and advancement:** The applicant's work history should show a steady progression into greater responsibility and more important positions. But don't go by job titles alone; look at what the candidate did. Assess how important the work was to the company involved. Generally, too, you should be wary of candidates who have bounced from one company to the next, although here again, you should be open to the possibility that she had good reasons for the career moves.

✔ **A strong, well-written cover letter:** Assuming that the candidate wrote the letter, the cover letter is generally a good indication of his overall communication skills.

Watching out for red flags

Resume writing is a good example of the Law of Unintended Consequences. Sometimes what's not in a resume or what's done through carelessness or mistake can reveal quite a bit about a candidate. Following are some things to watch out for:

✔ **Sloppy overall appearance:** This is a fairly reliable sign that the candidate is lacking in professionalism and business experience.

✔ **Unexplained chronological gaps:** Such gaps in an employment history may mean one of two things: The candidate was unemployed during these gaps, or the candidate is deliberately concealing certain information. But before jumping to conclusions, check to see whether periods of schooling or military service cover the gap. A well-designed application form or probing interview questions can uncover "hidden" work history gaps — for example, if a candidate says that he left one job and started another in the same year but actually left the first job in February and didn't start his new one until late December.

✔ **Static career pattern:** A sequence of jobs that doesn't indicate increasing responsibility may indicate a problem — the person wasn't deemed fit for a promotion or demonstrated a lack of ambition. Exceptions occur, however, especially for those types of workers in highly specialized fields.

✔ **Typos and misspellings:** Generally speaking, typos in cover letters and resumes may signify carelessness or a cavalier attitude. In a Robert Half International survey, 76 percent of U.S. executives said that they wouldn't hire a candidate with even one or two typographical errors in his resume. Although not all jobs require candidates to have strong spelling skills, most do call for attention to detail. Not proofreading a resume or not having someone else do it may be a sign that the candidate isn't conscientious.

✔ **Vaguely worded job descriptions:** Perhaps the applicant didn't quite understand what his job was. Or perhaps the job responsibilities didn't match the title. Before you go any further, you probably want to find out what a "coordinator of special projects" actually does. You want to see job descriptions that indicate how crucial the job is to his company's success.

✔ **Weasel wording:** Phrasing such as "participated in," "familiar with," "in association," and so on can indicate that the applicant may not have the actual experience he's claiming. Did the applicant actually work on that vital project, or did he merely run errands for someone who did? A sentence doesn't need to be untruthful to be misleading.

✔ **Job hopping:** While cradle-to-grave employment is by no means the norm today, a series of many jobs held for short periods of time may signal an unstable or problem employee or a chronic "job-hopper." Be sure to look at the whole picture of employment history. People do leave jobs for good reasons and should be prepared — and willing — to tell you about it.

✔ **Overemphasis on hobbies or interests outside of work:** This kind of emphasis may indicate an applicant who's unwilling to work extra hours or put in an extra effort. Someone who considers his job a side interest may be best employed by your competitor.

For a sample of a "thanks, but no thanks" (rejection) letter to an unsuccessful candidate, see the CD-ROM.

Testing: Knowing What Works and What's Legal

Pre-employment testing is probably the most controversial of all the candidate evaluation options in use today. Everybody agrees with the basic rationale that test results can often alert you to attributes and potential problems that you can't infer from a resume and that don't necessarily surface during an interview. No one, however, has yet to prove in a scientifically conclusive way that testing leads to foolproof or even better hires. In addition, many types of tests are subject to legal restrictions.

So why do testing? Because if you use them correctly and in the right situations, many tests can help you evaluate job candidates. Correctly and fairly administered tests objectively measure basic skills (such as software proficiency), assess acquired knowledge and qualifications, and gauge aptitudes for certain jobs. The quality and sophistication of tests have improved markedly in recent years, and many organizations, including some of the largest in the nation, are returning to certain types of testing as a valuable predictive tool. Thousands of tests are now commercially available.

Businesses often conduct some types of tests prior to selecting candidates for an interview. These are the kind of tests I describe in this section. Some companies also administer more comprehensive, extensive, and costly tests and checks *after* the candidate's first or second interview when managers are closer to making a final decision (background checks, for example), and I discuss these in Chapter 8. Some tests, such as drug tests, may come at either point in the hiring process, so I talk about these in both this chapter as well as Chapter 8.

If you do test your candidates, keep in mind that individuals can't be singled out to be tested. Tests must be job-related and applied consistently to all candidates for a position or, in some cases, for all positions within a particular department or business unit. You can require a forklift ability test, for example, of anyone applying for a position as a forklift operator, but all applicants must take the same test. Likewise, you can establish a policy that says any accounting department candidate who will handle cash needs to have a credit check. Bottom line: You can tailor your testing policy to a specific situation (and not company-wide), as long as the business rules are clear, documented, job-related and consistently practiced.

No matter what type of test you select, all tests must meet, at a minimum, the following requirements:

✔ They must assess the skills a candidate must possess to perform the job functions.

✔ They must show a positive correlation with job performance.

✔ They must be free of *disparate impact* (actions you take not intending to discriminate but which have the effect of doing so anyway. See Chapter 2).

✔ They must not present an unfair barrier to the disabled.

Tests that fail these requirements may violate the antidiscrimination laws and regulations governing your company.

Finding the right test for your situation

Tests are simply tools meant to measure specific aspects or qualities of applicants' skills, knowledge, experience, intellect or—more controversially—personality (or psychological makeup). Figure out what you want to find out about a candidate and then choose the appropriate test.

Finding the right test for your situation probably won't be a problem because your choices abound. Dozens of commercial test publishers collectively produce more than 2,000 different tests. You can find out about these tests by looking in two reference books — *Tests in Print*, Volume Two, and *The Mental Measurement Yearbook,* both published by the Buros Institute, University of Nebraska-Lincoln (www.unl.edu/buros).

Other sources are regional government or nonprofit employment agencies, which may even conduct some of the testing for you. The business centers of your local colleges also may provide test materials or at least point you in the right direction (or connect you with an expert who can lead you by the hand through the testing thicket). A recruiter often handles testing in such areas as computer software skills.

Employment tests come in all sizes and shapes, so the following sections provide a rundown of what they are, what they do, and how to use them.

Proficiency tests
What do they do? Measure how skillful an applicant is at a particular task (word processing, for example) or how knowledgeable he is in a particular field.

Why would you use them? Proficiency tests measure skills that applicants need for successful job performance and are useful if a baseline of particular (usually trade-related) skills is essential.

How reliable are they? Generally quite good. This sort of testing has a good track record of validity in the business and industrial world.

Aptitude and ability tests

What do they do? Measure an applicant's capability to learn and perform a particular job and his capability to learn or potential to acquire job-related skills or tasks. These tests fall into the following three basic categories:

- Mental abilities: These types are tests of intelligence, verbal reasoning, perceptual speed, and so on, and are sometimes called *cognitive tests*. Classic example: The SAT taken each year by college hopefuls.

- Mechanical abilities: These tests measure the ability to recognize and visualize a mechanical relationship. Tests of this type often ask applicants to distinguish between pulley and lever systems.

- Psychomotor abilities: These varieties test an individual's skill and/or ability to make certain body movements or use certain senses. The U.S. Navy, for example, tests every recruit's ability to hear differences between tones. High scorers are urged to apply for sonar school.

Why would you use them? Aptitude and ability tests show a readiness to learn or perform a certain task. Whether you use them alone or in batteries of tests, they help many organizations, including governments, select the most likely applicants for specific jobs. The U.S. Employment Service has developed the General Aptitude Test Battery, which it makes available to employers.

How reliable are they? Generally excellent to adequate as long as they don't violate antidiscrimination laws. (You need to make sure that hiring decisions based on the results of such tests do not work to the disadvantage of groups covered by EEO legislation.)

Personality and psychological tests

What do they do? Measure certain personality characteristics, such as assertiveness, resiliency, temperament, or stability. This group of tests also includes interest inventories, which claim to show how close an individual's interests match those of a particular occupational group. These tests are generally lengthy and sometimes involve elaborate and complex scoring keys to predict different personality profiles and traits. There are a number of aptitude/style indicators available, ranging from the Myers Briggs Type Indicator (MBTI) and NEO Personality Inventory to the Hogan Personality Inventory and many more that are available online. Be careful when selecting a personality indicator, or any other kind of test, for that matter, to make sure that the one you choose is both legal and appropriate for hiring.

Why would you use them? This sort of testing is designed to uncover personality traits that make good employees — or those that make bad employees. Because personality is a component of job performance, finding out all that you can about an applicant's personality can help predict his performance.

How reliable are they? Depends on whom you ask. These tests were originally designed to diagnose mental disorders, and even for that purpose — and in the hands of trained professionals — they often leave much to be desired. A main problem is that the results aren't always crystal-clear and sometimes need professional interpretation. If this kind of information is necessary to your evaluation process — for example, you're looking for people who can fit into a certain work team or have certain personality traits that are important to the job — you may feel you should use personality tests. Be aware, however, that the subjective nature of the evaluation process creates a legal risk for any company that chooses to use them in the selection process. Consider consulting a lawyer.

How reliable are they? Yet to be empirically proven and is only as good as the handwriting analyst.

Physical tests

What do they do? Measure an individual's health and physical condition or the ability to perform a certain task.

Why would you use them? To establish fitness to perform job-related tasks. Be forewarned, however, that requiring a physical or medical examination before employment is illegal under federal law. You can't ask about an applicant's height or weight because you may use this information to discriminate unless height (or weight) is a bona fide occupational requirement. You can test for physical agility or ability if it's a legitimate job requirement, but you must administer exactly the same test to every applicant for the same position. (An example is testing for the ability to lift packages of a certain weight if lifting such weights is vital to job performance.) Before you decide that some physical attribute or ability is necessary for the job, however, keep in mind that a number of fire departments around the country have been successfully sued because of their physical tests. Talk to a lawyer first.

How reliable are they? Depends on who does the exam but usually quite good.

Drug tests

What do they do? Measure the presence of illegal drugs or controlled substances in an applicant's urine.

Why would you use them? Substance abuse costs money in lost time, impaired performance, and potential employee theft. Drug tests to check candidates for current substance abuse are legal and can help eliminate applicants with these problems from the running. For some positions, pre-employment drug tests are mandatory. Certain classes of employees — school bus drivers, for example — must submit to testing for drugs and alcohol under the law. In fact, pre-employment drug testing has become so common in some industries that it causes hardly a ripple. Keep in mind, however, that you must give all applicants advance written notice that you intend to test for drugs. You can't observe the test itself, and you must hold test results confidential. You must give applicants notice of a positive result. You can also test only for what you say you're testing for. Privacy concerns make this a legal minefield. Talk with a lawyer before you start testing.

How reliable are they? If conducted by a competent, reputable lab, very accurate. Shrewd and/or experienced abusers can sometimes slip by, however, either by abstaining long enough to eliminate drug traces from the system or by the use of other substances to mask drug traces.

See more about drug tests in Chapter 8.

Integrity tests

What do they do? Measure an individual's personal honesty and sense of integrity. These tests generally include questions on situations of ethical choice — an employee sees a coworker steal company property; what should he do? Or they include questions that can reveal personal standards of behavior — whether the candidate can follow simple procedures and keep company information confidential.

Why would you use them? An employer needs to determine how an applicant may behave in a position of trust — handling cash or safeguarding property, for example. A test of this nature is designed to uncover people who may be too unreliable to trust with the company cookie jar. Most employers understand that honest people make the best employees. Keep in mind, however, that integrity tests must be job-related. You can't ask questions about an applicant's level of debt or credit rating (a violation of the Fair Credit Reporting Act). Tests must remain free of biases based on race, sex, and age. As is the case with personality and psychological testing, these tests are very risky legally, with many privacy issues to consider. Talk to a lawyer before embarking on this form of testing.

How reliable are they? Depends on the exact test. Research has shown that some of these tests can produce reliable, unbiased information, while others aren't very accurate at all.

Polygraph (lie-detector) tests

What do they do? Measure stress-related physiological changes, such as blood pressure, sweating, temperature, and so on, to detect untrue statements.

Why would you use them? Employers need to ensure that people who are being hired for jobs with critical security implications are telling the truth about their backgrounds.

How reliable are they? Depends on whom you ask and, especially, on the tester. Most experts agree that a competent polygraph operator can usually detect falsehoods from the average individual, provided that person hasn't taken any number of drugs that can modify the reactions the machine measures. The problem is the sociopath with no concept of right or wrong who slides right by. People mistrust polygraphs enough that their results are inadmissible as evidence in any U.S. court. Be aware that the passage of the Employee Polygraph Protection Act of 1988 prohibits private employers — except under certain conditions — from conducting polygraph tests either on employees or on job applicants. (The same holds true, incidentally, for other devices that purport to measure honesty, such as voice stress analyzers.) Under this law, you can't even ask an applicant to take a polygraph test.

Staying out of test trouble

The following tips may keep you out of testing hot water:

- ✔ Establish what traits or information the test is to evaluate and make sure that a relationship exists between these traits and the hiring criteria.
- ✔ Check carefully into the credentials and reputation of any test vendor. Ask to see validation data.
- ✔ Double-check that the test isn't biased, even unintentionally, against any group.
- ✔ Verify that the test is certified by an established reputable group.
- ✔ Network. Talk to colleagues, associates, and people in other companies who may be conducting testing to determine their levels of success.
- ✔ Local colleges or other organizations sometimes offer skills assessment assistance or programs. Check them out.
- ✔ Federal, state, and local laws limit testing. You should get legal advice before adopting any form of test.

A final word of advice on testing: Remember that your company is ultimately responsible for any testing that you conduct. Recognize that EEOC guidelines treat online testing in the same manner as paper and pencil tests. You must be prepared to demonstrate how any test you use is job-related and necessary for business operations.

For more on testing and other measures for evaluating candidates, see Chapter 8.

Phone Interviews: Narrowing Your List Further

After you've sorted through resumes and selected the most promising candidates, conducting a telephone interview can help you narrow down the list of individuals to call in for an interview. In a recent Robert Half International survey of executives, 58 percent of respondents said interviewing prospective employees by telephone prior to meeting them was more important than other stages in the hiring process.

Before calling a candidate, review the resume and cover letter carefully, noting questions to ask. You'll likely see a pattern emerge among the applicants who are a good fit for your firm. Here are a few good questions to ask:

- ✔ "Tell me a little about yourself and your work history."
- ✔ "What interests you about this job?"
- ✔ "What skills can you bring to the job?"
- ✔ "What sort of work environment brings out your best performance?"

Estimate how long you'll need to effectively conduct a telephone interview with job applicants. It typically can take from 15 to 30 minutes: 15 minutes for a basic interview and 30 minutes if you want to ask deeper questions for a more comprehensive initial assessment of match and fit to your company.

Without a guideline, you may spend too much or too little time on a phone interview. The key is to be consistent with your questions so that you can fairly compare job hopefuls.

If the candidate isn't available and you need to leave a message, suggest a timeframe (morning, between 2 and 5 p.m., and so on) for when she should return your call the next day. This request can be a good test of initiative — candidates who fail to return the call or who do not make a reasonable effort to contact you to make alternative arrangements demonstrate either a lack of interest or a lack of commitment.

Forms on the CD

Rejection Letter

Chapter 7

One on One: Getting the Most Out of Interviewing

Conducting a job interview looks easier than it is. And that's the problem. The vast majority of managers and small business owners who conduct job interviews day in and day out appear to be under the impression that, after you get a few Larry King shows under your belt, you know pretty much all you need to know about this critical and often mishandled component of the staffing process. As a result, most managers take interviewing for granted. They don't invest the time, effort, and concentration that effective job interviewing requires. And, above all, they don't prepare enough for interviews. Instead, they "wing it." (I guess you could say they're "ducking" their responsibilities.)

The results of this misguided mindset speak for themselves. More often than not, little correlation exists between the "positive reports" that emerge from the typical job interview and the job performance of the candidates who receive those glowing reports. That's the bad news. The good news is that this correlation goes up dramatically whenever interviewing becomes a structured, well-planned process — one that's well integrated into a company's overall staffing practices.

This chapter takes an in-depth look at interviewing, with a focus on the things you need to know and do to get the most out of the interviewing process.

Interviewing: The Basics

Job interviews enable you to perform the following four tasks that, combined with other steps you take, are essential to making a sound hiring decision:

- ✔ Obtain firsthand information about the candidate's background, work experience and skill level that clarifies what you need to confirm from the resume or previous interviews.

- ✔ Get a general sense of the candidate's overall intelligence, aptitude, enthusiasm, and attitudes, with particular respect to how those attributes match up to the requirements of the job.

- ✔ Gain insight — to the extent possible — into the candidate's basic personality traits and her motivation to tackle the responsibilities of the job and become a part of the company.

- ✔ Estimate the candidate's ability to adapt to your company's work environment.

That's pretty much it. What occurs during a job interview doesn't tell you — not directly, at any rate — how effectively candidates may perform on the job if, indeed, you hire them. Nor does the image of the candidate that emerges during the interview necessarily represent an accurate image of who the candidate really is and how he's likely to react in actual job situations.

Today's interview-savvy candidates

Following are a few observations about people you'll be interviewing in today's business environment:

- ✔ **"Funny you should ask that."** More and more candidates these days are well-schooled in the art of making you believe, by virtue of their interview performance, that they're the answer to all your hiring prayers. Unless you're disciplined and vigilant, you're likely to fall in love with the wrong candidate — who has all the right answers.

- ✔ **Sour grapes, legal scrapes.** Now that more candidates than ever are well-versed in antidiscrimination legislation, candidates who don't get the job are more likely than ever to claim, justifiably or not, that your company's interviewing practices are discriminatory. Your best protection is to make sure that you and everybody else conducting job interviews steer clear of any subject or any line of questioning that may leave your company open to a discrimination claim.

The Five Deadly Sins of Job Interviewing

The following list takes a look at some of the all-too-common practices that create a surefire recipe for hiring mistakes.

✔ **"We're too busy to take our time."** Failing to give the interviewing process the time and effort it deserves is, by far, the main reason that interviews produce such mediocre results. You can probably under-stand, of course, why managers frequently neglect to take the necessary steps to prepare for interviews, conduct them diligently, and evaluate the results in a thoughtful manner: You're busy. Everybody's busy. Time is at a premium. But your job is to make every interview you conduct count and encourage line managers who make their own hiring deci-sions to do the same.

✔ **"I get bored if I do it the same way every time."** One major difference between interviewers who have a knack for picking winners and those who don't is nothing more complicated than simple discipline. Skillful interviewers think through the process and tend to follow that same method each time — albeit with variations that they tailor to individual situations. Unsuccessful interviewers tend to "wing it," creating a differ-ent routine for each interview and entering unprepared. The hidden danger of winging it: You deprive yourself of the one thing you need the most as you're comparing candidates — an objective standard on which to base your conclusions. Without structure, you have no way of know-ing whether the impressions you gather from the interview would be dif-ferent if your approach and other aspects of the interview were consistent for each candidate. If you "wing it," you're also not giving the candidate a very good impression of your company.

✔ **"The candidate was brilliant — he agreed with everything I had to say."** If you're talking more than 20 percent of the time during a job inter-view, you're talking too much. Savvy candidates are usually adept at get-ting their interviewers to do most of the talking. They've figured out that the more interviewers talk, the easier they, the candidates, can deter-mine what answers are going to carry the most weight. Probing through active listening (for example, letting the candidate's comments spark related questions) is a critical interviewing skill because it allows you to gain valuable information you'd miss if you did most of the talking. Notice how Larry King, Oprah, and all the other talk show hosts do it, and you'll see what I mean. You can — and should — react, comment on, and build on the answers that candidates give in a job interview. Just bear in mind: The only thing you discover about a candidate during any session where you're doing most of the talking is that the candidate knows how to listen.

✔ **The halo effect: "I loved his Armani suit."** The *halo effect* is the phrase managers generally use to describe a common phenomenon in hiring. You may become so enraptured by one particular aspect of the candidate — appearance, credentials, interests, and so on — that it colors all your other judgments. Then again, you're only human. You can't always help yourself from placing too much significance on one particular aspect of the candidate's overall presentation. At the very least, however, be aware of your halo effect tendencies and do your best to keep them in check.

✔ **"I taught Sigmund everything he knew."** The ability to "read" people can be an enormously valuable skill for anyone who interviews job candidates. But unless you're formally trained as a psychologist or psychiatrist, leave your couch at home and try not to seek out the subconscious meaning behind everything the candidate says and does. If you have strong evidence that ties certain psychological factors to a person's ability to handle a particular job, great. Bring in an outside professional to help you develop questions that can capitalize on that knowledge.

Setting the Stage

Your ability to get the most out of the interviews you conduct invariably depends on how well prepared you are. Here's a checklist of things that you should do before you pop the first interview question:

✔ **Thoroughly familiarize yourself with the job description, especially its hiring criteria.** Do so even if you draw up the criteria yourself.

✔ **Review everything the candidate has submitted to date:** resume, job description, cover letter, and so on. Note any areas needing clarification or explanation, such as quirky job titles, gaps in work history, or hobbies that may reveal aspects of the candidate's personality that can have a bearing on job performance.

✔ **Set up a general structure for the interview.** Create a basic schedule for the interview so that, as the meeting progresses, you reserve enough time to cover all the key areas you want to address. Having a rough schedule to adhere to will help you begin and end the session on time, allowing you to be more efficient and showing that you respect the candidate's time.

✔ **Write the questions you intend to ask.** Base your questions on the areas of the candidate's background that deserve the most attention (based on the job description and your hiring criteria). Keep the list in front of you throughout the interview.

✔ **Make arrangements (if practical) to hold the interview in a room that's private and reasonably comfortable.** (Generally speaking, a conference room is a better place to conduct an interview than your office, but if your office is your only option, try to create a reasonably calm environment.) Clear your desk, close the door, and either set your phone so all calls go to voice mail or have your calls forwarded somewhere else.

Try not to schedule job interviews in the middle of the day. The reason: You're not likely to be as relaxed and as focused as you need to be, and you may have a tough time fighting off interruptions and distractions. The ideal time to interview candidates is early morning, before the workday starts. You're fresher then, and so is the candidate. If you have no choice, give yourself a buffer of at least half an hour before the interview so that you can switch gears and prepare for the interview in the right manner.

The Introduction: Warming Up

Your priority in meeting a candidate face-to-face for the first time is to put her at ease. Disregard any advice anyone has given you about doing things to create stress just to see how the individual responds. Those techniques are rarely productive, and they put both you and your company in a bad light. Instead, view the first minutes of the meeting as an opportunity to build rapport with the candidate. The more comfortable she is, the more engaging the interview will be, and the more you'll learn about her.

Multiple and panel interviews

It's not unusual for more than one company employee to interview a candidate to provide a variety of opinions on the individual, especially if she will play a key role in the organization. In fact, sometimes these meetings are carried out simultaneously through the use of an interviewing panel made up of the hiring manager plus other members of the management team or work group, usually no more than three to five people.

Panel interviews are beneficial when you want to quickly get a promising hire through multiple interviews in a timely manner. It's best for the hiring manager to conduct one-on-one interviews with applicants first, however, choosing only a few finalists for panel interviews. This saves panelists' time and ensures that the hiring manager is presenting only those candidates she may ultimately hire. Panel interviews are most successful when the hiring manager distributes job criteria to the interview team in advance along with specific questions. This ensures panel members will be able to compare candidates in a consistent fashion using like criteria.

If you're seated at your desk as the candidate walks in, a common courtesy is to stand and meet the individual halfway, shake hands, and let him know that you're happy to meet him. (Basic stuff, but easy to forget.) You don't need to cut to the chase right away with penetrating questions. Skilled job interviewers usually begin with small talk — a general comment about the weather, transportation difficulties, and so on — but they keep it to a minimum.

The same guidelines for appropriate questioning and comments that apply to the formal interview apply also to casual discussions and chit chat.

After the small talk is out of the way, your next step is to give the candidate a very basic overview of what you're expecting to get from the interview and how long you estimate it to last. Be careful not to give too much information, though. Saying too much about the skills and characteristics you're looking for turns a savvy interviewee into a "parrot" who can repeat the same key words she just heard. Don't give away the keys to the kingdom!

Q & A: Mastering the Art

The Q&A is the main part of the interview. How you phrase questions, when you ask them, how you follow up — each of these aspects of interviewing can go a long way toward affecting the quality and usability of the answers you get. The following sections describe the key practices that differentiate people who've mastered the art of questioning from those who haven't.

For an Interview Q&A form, see the CD-ROM.

Have a focus

Even before you start to ask questions, you want to have a reasonably specific idea of what information or insights you're expecting to gain from the interview based on your research and the hiring criteria you develop in your job description. You may uncover two or three items on the candidate's resume that can use clarification. Or you may have a specific question about one particular aspect of the candidate's personality. Whatever the need, decide ahead of time what you want to know more about and build your interview strategy around that goal.

Make every question count

Every question you ask during a job interview must have a specific purpose. That purpose may be to elicit specific information, produce some insight into the candidate's personality, or simply put the candidate at ease. The general rule: If the question has no strategic significance, think twice before asking it. Again, tie questions to the job criteria defined in the job description.

Pay attention

Listening attentively is a difficult challenge under the best of circumstances, but it's often an even tougher challenge during a job interview. That's because your tendency in a job interview is to draw conclusions before the candidate has completed the answer. Yet another tendency is to begin rehearsing in your mind the next question you intend to ask while the candidate is still answering the earlier question. Fight that tendency. Consider writing down your questions before the interview begins and then pour the full measure of your concentration on the candidate and what he's saying.

Don't hesitate to probe

Whenever a candidate offers an answer that doesn't address the specific information you're seeking, nothing's wrong with asking additional questions to draw out more specific answers. If a candidate talks about the money he saved his department, ask how much and how, specifically, the savings were realized. Too many interviewers let candidates "off the hook" in the interest of being "nice." That practice, however, can prove counterproductive — he may give you valuable background on specific abilities if your questions are more penetrating.

Give candidates ample time to respond

The fact that a question you ask doesn't produce an immediate answer from the candidate doesn't mean that you need to rush in with another question to fill the silence. Give the candidate time to come up with a thoughtful answer. If the silence persists for more than, say, ten seconds, ask the candidate if he wants you to clarify the question. Otherwise, don't rush things. Use the silence to observe the candidate and to take stock of where you are in the interview. Remember that the interview is a time for you to listen, not talk.

Tread carefully whenever you come across a candidate who seems flat and disinterested during the job interview. If a candidate can't demonstrate any real enthusiasm during the interview, don't expect him to muster any enthusiasm after you hire him.

Suspend judgments

Reserving judgment isn't easy, but try to keep your attention on the answers you're getting instead of making interpretations or judgments. You're going to have plenty of time after the interview to evaluate what you see and hear. What you don't want to do is prejudice yourself in the beginning of the interview so that you fail to accurately process information that comes later.

Take notes

Memories can do tricky things, leading people to ignore what actually happens during an interview and to rely instead on general impressions. Taking notes helps you avoid this common pitfall. Just make sure that you do so unobtrusively so that the candidate doesn't feel like she has to pause for you to keep pace. It's a good practice to ask the candidate if he is comfortable with you taking notes. Few individuals are likely to object, but most will appreciate being asked. Keep all notes factual and within ethical and nondiscriminatory boundaries. Also make sure that you give yourself a few moments after the interview to review your notes and put them into some kind of order.

Vary the style of questions

You can usually divide questions into four categories, based on the kinds of answers you're trying to elicit.

Closed-ended

Definition: Questions that call for a simple, informational answer — usually a yes or no.

Examples: "How many years did you work for the circus?" "Did you enjoy it?" "What cities did you tour?"

When to use them: Closed-ended questions work best if you're trying to elicit specific information or set the stage for more complex questions.

Pitfall to avoid: Asking too many of them in rapid-fire succession and failing to tie them back to the job criteria, thus making candidates feel as though they're being interrogated.

Open-ended

Definition: Questions that require thought and oblige the candidate to reveal attitudes or opinions.

Examples: "Describe for me how you handle stress on the job." "Can you give me an illustration of how you improved productivity at your last job?"

When to use them: Most of the time, but interspersed with closed-ended questions. Using open-ended questions related to candidates' past experiences on the job is known as *behavioral interviewing*. Because this approach requires candidates to describe how they've handled real tasks and problems, it can be very useful and revealing.

Pitfalls to avoid: Not being specific enough as you phrase the question and not interceding if the candidate's answer starts to veer off track.

Hypothetical

Definition: Questions that invite the candidate to resolve an imaginary situation or react to a given situation.

Examples: "If you were the purchasing manager, would you institute an automated purchase-order system?" "If you were to take over this department, what's the first thing you'd do to improve productivity?"

When to use them: Useful if framed in the context of actual job situations.

Pitfall to avoid: Putting too much stock in the candidate's hypothetical answer. (You're usually better off asking questions that force a candidate to use an actual experience as the basis for an answer.)

Leading

Definition: Questions asked in such a way that the answer you're looking for is obvious.

Examples: "You rarely fought with your last boss, right?" "You know a lot about team-building, don't you?" "You wouldn't dream of falsifying your expense accounts, would you?"

When to use them: Rarely, if ever. You're not likely to get an honest answer — just the answer you want to hear. And you run the risk of appearing unprofessional.

Record at your own risk

If you want to record an interview (and most interviews aren't recorded), check first with a lawyer for any local restrictions. Even if recording the interview is legal, you're wise to advise the candidate that he's being taped. Most people resent being recorded secretly. Usually the interviewer tells the candidate that the interview is being taped to ensure an accurate record for the protection of both parties. The big problem with recording is that most people are less forthcoming and candid if they're aware that they're being recorded.

A Crash Course in Nondiscriminatory Questioning

As I mention earlier in this chapter under the sidebar "Today's Interview-Savvy Candidates," the questions you or others in your company ask during a job interview can result in legal problems for the company if you fail to follow certain guidelines. Even the most innocent of questions can result in a discrimination suit at some point. Antidiscrimination and consumer-protection legislation passed since the 1960s restricts the type and scope of pre-employment questions that you can ask. Moreover, court decisions and administrative rulings have refined what you can and can't ask, and, to make matters even more confusing, standards can vary from state to state.

Here are some current pitfalls:

- **Be sensitive to age discrimination issues.** Remember that any question that may indicate the candidate's age may be interpreted as discriminatory. In other words, don't ask a question such as "When did you graduate high school?"

- **Beware of double-edged questions.** Caution all the interviewers in your company to keep their innocent curiosity (as evidenced in a question such as "What kind of a name is that?") from exposing your company to charges of discrimination.

- **Don't confuse before and after.** Questions considered illegal before hiring may be acceptable after the individual is on the payroll. Age is a good example. You can't ask a person's age before hiring, but you may do so after hiring when the information will be needed for health insurance and pension purposes.

For more detailed information on how to avoid discrimination when you're asking interview questions, see the Employment Inquiries Fact Sheet on the CD-ROM.

The following sections provide a rundown of which questions are permitted before hiring and which are not. Check with your attorney for any local restrictions or new rulings and keep in mind that all questions must directly relate to a bona fide job requirement.

Even questions that seem okay to ask under the following guidelines may be discriminatory if they're asked only in circumstances that support a discriminatory intent. For example, you ask only female employees who reveal they have children if they have any reasons why they could not work overtime or days other than Monday through Friday.

Keep your questions focused on the job requirements and away from the candidate's personal life.

National origin

Okay to ask: None.

Risky ground: Questions related to the candidate's national origin, ancestry, native language or that of family members, or place of birth of applicant or applicant's parents.

Discriminatory: What sort of an accent is that? Where were you born? Where were your parents born?

Citizenship status

Okay to ask: If hired, will you be able to prove that you have the right to remain and work in the U.S.?

Risky ground: Questions that may oblige a candidate to indicate national origin.

Discriminatory: Are you a U.S. citizen?

Address

Okay to ask: Where do you live? How long have you lived here?

Risky ground: Questions about housing aimed at revealing financial status. (May be considered discriminatory against minorities.)

Discriminatory: Are you renting, or do you own?

Age

Okay to ask: None.

Risky ground: Questions regarding age when age is not a bona fide job requirement.

Discriminatory: How old are you? What year were you born? When did you graduate high school?

Family status

Okay to ask: Can you relocate? (If relevant to the job.)

Risky ground: All questions regarding marital or family status.

Discriminatory: Are you pregnant? (Even if the candidate is obviously pregnant.)

Religion

Okay to ask: Can you work overtime on days other than Monday through Friday?

Risky ground: Any question whose answers may indicate religious beliefs or affiliation.

Discriminatory: In college, what fraternity (or sorority) were you in? What religious holidays do you observe?

Health and physical condition

Okay to ask: Here are the expected functions of the job. Can you perform them with or without reasonable accommodation?

Risky ground: Questions that aren't directly related to a bona fide job requirement and, in addition, aren't being asked of all candidates.

Discriminatory: Do you have a hearing impairment? Have you ever filed a workers' compensation claim?

Name

Okay to ask: Have you ever used another name or nickname?

Risky ground: Whether the applicant has ever changed her name; maiden name.

Discriminatory: What kind of name is that?

Language

Okay to ask: What language do you speak, read, and/or write? (Permissible if relevant to the job.)

Risky ground: Questions that reveal the applicant's national origin or ancestry.

Discriminatory: What language do you speak at home? Is English your first language?

Fifteen Solid Questions to Ask and How to Interpret the Answers

What makes an interview question "good"? The answer, simply, is that a "good question" does two things:

- ✔ It gives you the specific information you need to make a sound hiring decision.
- ✔ It helps you gain insight into how the candidate's mind and emotions work.

Avoid timeworn, cliché questions, such as "What are your strengths and weaknesses?" or "Where do you see yourself in the next five years?" or "If you were an animal, which one would it be?" Instead develop a list of questions designed to elicit responses that will be most helpful in evaluating a candidate's suitability for your position and organization. You can ask hundreds of such questions, but following are 15 to get you started, along with ideas on what to look for in the answers.

- ✔ **Can you tell me a little about yourself?** Most interview strategy books describe this one as the "killer question." You can bet the farm that a well-prepared candidate has a well-rehearsed answer. A confident applicant can give a brief summary of his strengths, significant achievements, and career goals. Your main job? To make sure that the answers are consistent with the applicant's resume. A rambling answer with few specifics may indicate a poorly focused or incompetent candidate.

- ✔ **What interests you about this job, and what skills and strengths can you bring to it?** Nothing tricky here, but it's a solid question all the same. Note that the question is not "What are your skills and strengths?" but "What skills and strengths can you bring to the job?" The answer is yet another way to gauge how much interest the applicant has in the job and how well prepared she is for the interview. Stronger candidates should be able to correlate their skills with specific job requirements: "I think my experience as a foreign correspondent will be of great help in marketing products to overseas customers." They will answer the question in the context of contributions they can make to the company.

- ✔ **Can you tell me a little about your current job?** Strong candidates should be able to give you a short and precise summary of duties and responsibilities. How they answer this question can help you determine their passion and enthusiasm for their work and their sense of personal accountability. Be wary of applicants who bad-mouth or blame their employers. If they're not loyal to their current employer, how can you expect them to be loyal to you? ("They wouldn't let me bring my pet iguana to work. Can you believe it?")

- ✔ **In a way that anyone could understand, can you describe a professional success you are proud of?** This question is especially good when you're interviewing someone for a technical position, such as a systems analyst or tax accountant. The answer shows the applicant's ability to explain what they do so that anyone can understand it. Do they avoid jargon in their description? Do they get their points across clearly? Failure to do so may be a sign that the individuals can't step out of their "world" sufficiently to work with people in other departments, which is a growing necessity in many organizations today.

- ✔ **How have you changed the nature of your current job?** A convincing answer here shows adaptability and a willingness to "take the bull by the horns," if necessary. An individual who chose to do a job differently from other people also shows creativity and resourcefulness. The question gives candidates a chance to talk about such contributions as efficiencies they brought about or cost savings they achieved. If a candidate says he didn't change the nature of the job, that response can tell you something as well.

✔ **What was the most difficult decision you ever had to make on the job?** Notice the intentionally vague aspect of this question. It's not hypothetical. It's real. What you're looking for is the person's decision-making style and how it fits into your company culture. Someone who admits that firing a subordinate was difficult demonstrates compassion, and those who successfully decided to approach a coworker over a conflict may turn out to be great team players. Individuals who admit a mistake they've made exhibit honesty and open-mindedness.

Also listen how people went about making the decision. Seeking the advice of others, for example, may mean that they are team-centered. This question is an especially important one if you're interviewing a candidate for a middle- or senior-level management position.

✔ **Why did you decide to pursue a new job?** This question is just a different way of asking, "What are you looking for in a job?" Some candidates come so well rehearsed they are never at a loss for an answer. Sometimes by phrasing the question in a different way, you can cause them to go "off script."

✔ **I see that you've been unemployed for the past months. Why did you leave your last job, and what have you been doing since then?** This question is important, but don't let it seem accusatory. Generally speaking, people don't leave jobs voluntarily without another one waiting in the wings, but it happens. It isn't really unusual for highly competent people to find themselves unemployed through no fault of their own. Keep an open mind. But try to get specific, factual answers that you can verify later. Candidates with a spotty employment history, at the very least, ought to be able to account for all extended periods of unemployment and to demonstrate whether they used that time productively — getting an advanced degree, for example.

✔ **Who was your best boss ever and why? Who was the worst, and looking back, what could you have done to make that relationship better?** These two are more penetrating questions than you may think. Among other things, the answers give you insight into how the candidate views and responds to supervision. A reflective, responsive answer to the second part of the question may indicate a loyal employee capable of rising above an unpleasant supervisory situation and/or learning from past mistakes, both highly desirable qualities. A bitter, critical answer may indicate someone who holds grudges or simply can't get along with certain personality types. Yes, personality clashes occur all the time, but in today's team-oriented workplace, you want employees who try to minimize these clashes and not use them as excuses.

- **Which do you enjoy the most: working alone with information or working with other people?** The ideal answer here is "both." People who say they like working with information are obviously a good choice for technical positions, but it may be a red flag if they don't also mention their like for communicating and collaborating with other individuals, which is increasingly a function of even technical jobs. An excellent candidate might say the different perspectives within a group produce more innovative ideas than one person working alone can, but without information, a team can't get very far.

- **What sort of things do you think your current (past) company could do to be more successful?** This one is a great "big picture" question. You're probing to find out whether the candidate has a clear understanding of his current or past employer's missions and goals and whether he thinks in terms of those goals. Candidates who can't answer this question well are demonstrating a lack of depth and interest, which can quite likely carry over into your organization. Sometimes the answer to this question also reveals hidden bitterness or anger at an employer. But make clear to the candidate that you're not looking for proprietary or specific information.

- **Can you describe a typical day at work in your last job?** Strong candidates can give you specific details that you can later verify, but the main point of this question is to see how the applicant's current (or most recent) routine compares with the requirements of the job in question. How interviewees describe their duties can prove highly revealing. Do you sense any real enthusiasm or interest? Do the details match the information you already have? You're looking for enthusiasm and some indication that the applicant connects his current duties with company goals.

- **What sort of work environment do you prefer? What brings out your best performance?** Probe for specifics. You want to find out whether this person is going to fit into your company. If your corporate culture is collegial and team-centered, you don't want someone who answers, "I like to be left alone to do my work." You may also uncover unrealistic expectations or potential future clashes. ("My plan is to spend a couple months in the mail room and then apply for the presidency of the company.") People rarely, if ever, work at their best in all situations. Candidates who say otherwise aren't being honest with themselves or with you.

- **How do you handle conflict? Can you give me an example of how you handled a workplace conflict in the past?** You want candidates who try to be reasonable but nonetheless stand up for what's right. Unfortunately, most candidates say the right things, which is why you want some specifics. Be suspicious if the answer is too predictable. While some people may be naturally easygoing, candidates who say that they never get into conflict situations are either dishonest or delusional.

✔ **How would you respond if you were put in a situation you felt presented a conflict of interest or was unethical? Have you ever had this experience in previous positions?** Given the publicity surrounding the collapse of Enron and other corporate scandals, no rational candidate today is going to say that sometimes it's okay to be unethical. But how individuals approach this question and anecdotes they relay can offer valuable insights as to how they may respond if faced with such a situation.

In addition to an opportunity to showcase their qualifications, savvy candidates also use the interview to find out as much as they can about the position and company, so don't be surprised if they come prepared with questions of their own. Don't interpret questions as disruptive to your agenda: They're a show of interest and professionalism. In fact, you can address many of their concerns by proactively "selling" your company during the interview. Just as candidates try to show how their skills are a match with the position, you can also point out programs and policies that fit the needs of promising applicants and promote your firm as a great place to work.

End Game: Closing on the Right Note

With only a few minutes to go, you can bring the session to a graceful close by following these steps:

1. **Offer the candidate a broad-brushstroke summary of the interview.**

   Sum up what the candidate has said about his fit for the position, reasons for wanting the job, and so on. This summary demonstrates that you were a sincere listener and that you care about the candidate as a person — leaving a good impression. It also gives the candidate an opportunity to clarify any misunderstandings.

2. **Let the candidate ask questions.**

   Provide an opportunity for the individual to ask any questions he may have on his mind after the interview.

3. **Let the candidate know what comes next.**

   Advise the candidate how and when you're going to contact him and whether any further steps need to be taken — forms, tests, and so on. This practice not only is a common courtesy, but also creates a businesslike impression.

4. **End the interview on a formal, but sincere note.**

   Thank the candidate for her time and repeat your commitment to follow up. Either stand or shake hands again. This action formally ends the session and provides a signal for the candidate to leave. Walk the applicant out of the office to the elevator lobby or front door.

And one last suggestion: As soon as possible after the candidate's departure, take a couple of moments to collect your thoughts and write your impressions and a summary of your notes. You don't need to make any definitive decisions at this point, but recording your impressions while they're still fresh in your mind will help you immeasurably if the final choice should boil down to several candidates, all of whose qualifications are comparable.

The CD-ROM contains a Blank Candidate Interview Evaluation form so that you can record your impressions of job candidates.

Forms on the CD

Interview Q & A form

Employment Inquiries Fact Sheet

Blank Candidate Interview Evaluation Form

Sample and Blank Interview Evaluation Forms

Interview Q & A form

Chapter 8

The Home Stretch: Making the Final Decision

In This Chapter

▶ Identifying decision-making resources

▶ Developing a logical "system" for selecting the best candidate

▶ Checking references

▶ Deciding about background checks

▶ Presenting and negotiating the "offer"

▶ Negotiating salary

Now comes the moment of truth in the hiring process: choosing who will get the job. Because hiring mistakes can be costly, a lot is riding on your ability to select the best people for your available positions. If you find yourself constantly second-guessing your hiring decisions, you may want to take a close look at the process you're using in making your final choices. This chapter can help get you started with such a review.

This is another one of those legally sensitive chapters. Much of the information contained here is the result of a collaborative effort with the law firm of O'Melveny & Myers LLP. But again, don't be your own lawyer. Legally complex (and potentially costly) issues require a case-by-case evaluation by your own attorney. Not only do laws limit what factors can and cannot be considered in making hiring decisions, but negligent hiring lawsuits are on the rise, which hold employers liable for hiring someone with a history of violent or criminal acts. I discuss this and other issues surrounding background checks later in this chapter.

Coming to Grips with the Decision-Making Process

Stripped to its essentials, the decision-making process in the final stages of hiring is no different than buying a car or deciding your vacation destination. You look at your options, weigh the pros and cons of each, and then you make a choice.

Many people differ in their basic approaches to this challenge. Some tend to base decisions on intuition or "a gut feeling." Others are highly systematic. Some people rely entirely on their own judgment and assessments. Others seek outside guidance. You can never be absolutely certain that the decision you make is going to yield the desired result — unless, of course, you can predict the future. You can improve your chances significantly, however, if you manage the decision-making process in a reasonably disciplined, intelligent way, which means that you consistently focus on the key hiring criteria you established at the outset of the process and perform the following tasks:

✔ If you did a thorough job early on in the hiring process of identifying your needs and drawing up a job description that pinpoints the combination of skills, attributes, and credentials that a particular position requires. In other words, you don't aim at a target with your eyes closed (see Chapters 3 and 4).

✔ You gather enough information about each candidate — through interviewing, testing, and observation — so that you have a reasonably good idea of the candidates' capabilities, personalities, strengths, and weaknesses (see Chapters 6 and 7).

For help evaluating a candidate, see the Candidate Rating form on the CD-ROM.

✔ You remain objective in evaluating candidates. Your personal biases don't steer your focus away from your hiring criteria (the "halo" and "cloning" effects I describe later in this chapter).

✔ You develop methods to evaluate your strategies, such as using a particular recruiter or running a classified ad, so that, the next time around, you can repeat practices that produce good results and modify those that lead to hiring mistakes.

The simplest method is to think back on the process that led to the hiring of your top employees and compare that process with how you handled things with candidates whom you eventually had to let go.

✔ You "sell" the candidates on the job, and they're enthusiastic about the position.

If this entire process sounds like a tall order, you're right. Some may feel it involves a great deal of guesswork, but that doesn't have to be the case. Through the activities I discuss in Chapters 3, 4, and 7 (defining a hiring process, establishing specific job criteria, effective interviewing, and so on), the guesswork in making the final decision is greatly diminished.

But it's not as complicated as you may think. You do follow a certain logic in the hiring process. Yes, much of the process involves guesswork, but it's usually educated guesswork. And the more educated you are about the hiring process as a whole, the more accurate your guesses are likely to become.

Utilizing the "Tools" of the Trade

Your available resources in making hiring decisions are usually fairly limited. Only a handful of information sources can serve as grist for your decision mill. The following list takes a brief look at those tools and what you need to keep in mind as you're tapping each one. Then, I discuss them in more detail later in the chapter.

- ✔ **Past experience:** A long-time truism in successful hiring is the concept that the best indicator of a candidate's future performance is his past performance. If a candidate was hard working, highly motivated, and team-oriented in his last job, the same is likely to hold true in the new job. Similarly, the candidate who was a complete washout in his last position isn't likely to become a ball of fire in his next one. People do change, of course, but only in fairy tales do frogs turn into princes.

  The only caveat to this usually reliable principle: The conditions that prevailed in the candidate's last job need to closely parallel the conditions in the job he's seeking. Otherwise, you have no real basis for comparison. No two business environments are identical. For all you know, certain systems or people in place in the candidate's previous job may have been instrumental in his success (or failure) — and you can rarely replicate such factors in your company (and may not, in fact, even want to).

- ✔ **Interview impressions:** Impressions you pick up during an interview almost always carry a great deal of weight in hiring decisions — and understandably. People naturally place more trust in what they actually see and hear than in information from third-party sources. The problem with interview impressions is that they're just that —impressions. You're listening to answers and observing behavior, but your own preconceived perceptions and experience almost always influence your judgments.

As I stress in Chapter 7, no one has yet shown that any correlation exists between a candidate's ability to make a strong impression during an interview and his ability to become a top performer on the job. This observation doesn't mean, however, that you should disregard your interview impressions — only that you keep them in their proper perspective with test results, references, and other information you've collected to evaluate a prospective hire.

✔ **Test results:** Some people regard test results as the only truly reliable predictor of future success. The argument goes as follows: Test results are quantifiable. In most tests, results aren't subject to personal interpretation. With a large enough sample, you can compare test scores to job-performance ratings and, eventually, use test scores as a predictor of future performance.

The only problem: Some candidates simply don't test well. They freeze up, which means that they're penalized in their scores. Other candidates, however, may be clever enough to figure out what most tests are actually testing for and tailor their responses accordingly. So if you're going to use test results in your decision-making process, ensure the validity of the tests (whether they do, indeed, predict the quality of future job performance) and their legality (whether their use complies with all state and federal laws and doesn't result in discrimination). See Chapter 6 and also "Discovering the Truth About Background Checks," later in this chapter.

✔ **First-hand observation:** Call it the proof-in-the-pudding principle. Watching candidates actually perform some of the tasks for which you're considering hiring them is clearly the most reliable way to judge their competence. That's why more and more companies these days, as part of their hiring procedure, ask candidates to complete some sort of project (usually for pay) to help determine whether they can handle the job. Still another key trend in hiring today is the practice of starting out an applicant as an interim employee, with the idea that, if the person works out, the job becomes full time.

In the past, some companies have instituted *probationary periods* to gain first-hand knowledge about candidates. Today, firms should stay away from the term "probation" because it may create an implied contract of employment. Some courts assume that after an employee is no longer on probation, the employer then must have good cause to terminate the employee.

Selecting Your Candidate: You Need a "System"

The easiest way to make a hiring decision is to weigh the options and simply go with what your intuition tells you to do. Easy — but risky. So-called "gut" decisions, whether they originate from one person or a group of people, are almost always biased in the following respect: Their roots tend to be firmly planted in wishful thinking. These decisions often are a reflection of what you'd ideally like to see happen, as opposed to what's most likely to happen based on the evidence.

Decision-makers in companies with good track records of making successful hires don't give themselves the luxury of relying solely on intuition. They use — and generally trust — their intuition, but they don't use intuition as the sole basis for their judgments. The following list describes what such decision makers rely on. We discuss each item later in this chapter:

✔ **They have in place some sort of *system*** — a well-thought-out protocol for assessing the strengths and weaknesses of candidates and applying those assessments to the hiring criteria. They always make it a point, for example, to precede any face-to-face interview with a phone conversation. And they have established a set of steps that they follow routinely after they've interviewed a candidate.

✔ **The system that they use, regardless of how simple or elaborate, is weighted** — that is, it presupposes that certain skills and attributes bear more on job performance than do others and takes those differences into account. They know, for example, that the personal qualities that underlie effective performance in sales aren't necessarily the same ones that underlie effective performance in, say, administrative jobs.

✔ **They constantly monitor and evaluate the effectiveness of the system** — always with an eye toward sharpening their own ability and the ability of others to link any data they obtain during the recruiting and interviewing process to the on-the-job performance of new hires. If a particular type of testing mechanism is used in the selection process, the validity of the test (how closely the test results correlate with successful on-the-job performance) is monitored on a regular basis.

Decision-making tips

Your success as a hiring manager depends largely on your ability to make sound strategic decisions. Here are some additional tips:

✔ **Gather all the facts.** Don't let time constraints or the urge to move ahead too quickly keep you from collecting enough data to make an intelligent, informed choice. The more data you gather, the better your ability to let objectivity trump subjectivity in your decision.

✔ **Brainstorm options.** After you have sufficient information, generate several possible courses of action. You may perform this step alone — as in an emergency situation when fast action is of the essence — or in consultation with your colleagues.

✔ **Ask the right questions.** After you determine several possible courses of action, ask the following questions about each one:

Are the risks involved acceptable? Are the costs in line with, or do they outweigh, the potential benefits? Will this option have the support of others?

✔ **Take action.** Don't become so paralyzed by the prospect of unforeseen consequences of your decision that you fail to make one at all. Procrastination leads to decision-making by default — so much time elapses that the choices are narrowed to the point where only one course of action is viable.

✔ **Evaluate your decisions.** After you've made a choice, remember to objectively assess the results. If it turns out that you made a less than optimal decision, don't despair. You can turn negative outcomes into learning opportunities that can actually strengthen your decision-making skills and enable you to make better choices in the future.

Setting up your own protocol

Some companies invest millions of dollars in developing elaborate selection procedures, the express purpose of which is to make the candidate-evaluation process more objective and accurate. Whether you want to go that route is up to you, but the following sections describe the fundamental steps you must go through with all such processes, regardless of cost.

1. **Isolate key hiring criteria.**

   By this point in the hiring process, you should know what combination of skills and attributes a candidate needs to perform the job well and fit your company's pace and culture. If you don't, you need to refer to Chapters 4 and 5.

2. Set priorities.

You can safely assume that some of your hiring criteria are more important than others. To take these differences into account, set up a scale that reflects the relative importance of any particular skill or attribute. One good way to ensure that you're being reasonably accurate in assigning these numerical values is to ask yourself the following question: If the candidate didn't have this skill or quality, how would it affect his job performance? The greater the effect, the higher you need to make its rating.

3. Evaluate candidates on the basis of the weighted scale you established in Step 2.

This segment of the process is the tricky part. Instead of simply looking at the candidate as a whole, you look at each of the criteria you set down, and you rate the candidate on the basis of how he measures up in that particular category.

This weighted system of evaluation takes into account the performance priorities unique to each of the key hiring criteria. It helps ensure that the requirements of the job reasonably align with the strengths and weaknesses of the candidate.

Say, for example, that one of the candidate's strengths is the ability to work as part of a team. The candidate's rating on that particular attribute may be a five, but the relative importance of teamwork to the task at hand may be anywhere from 1 to 5, which means that the overall ranking may end up as low as 5 (5 times 1) or as high as 25 (5 times 5).

All in all, a weighted system gives you an opportunity to see how well candidates measure up against one another and how closely their skills and attributes match the job requirements. You must be careful, however. The effectiveness of this system depends on two crucial factors: the validity of your hiring criteria and the objectivity of the judgments that underlie any ratings you assign to each candidate in each area.

Tables 8-1 and 8-2 demonstrate how a weighted evaluation system works. Notice that the candidate under evaluation in Table 8-1 is relatively weak in two hiring criteria — previous experience and computer skills — but is much stronger in the criteria that carry more weight. The candidate's aggregate score, therefore, is higher than that of a candidate who meets the technical requirements of the job alone.

Table 8-1	How Candidate No. 1 Shapes Up		
Performance Category	*Weighted*	*Candidate rating (1-5)*	*Score importance (1-5)*
Previous customer service experience	3	1	3
Computer skills	2	3	6
Communication skills	5	4	20
Reliability/work ethic	5	4	20
Ability to cope with stress	4	4	16
Empathy	4	4	16
Total			**81**

Table 8-2	How Candidate No. 2 Shapes Up		
Performance Category	*Weighted*	*Candidate rating (1-5)*	*Score importance (1-5)*
Previous customer service experience	3	5	15
Computer skills	2	5	10
Communication skills	5	2	10
Reliability/work ethic	5	3	15
Ability to cope with stress	4	4	16
Empathy	4	1	4
Total			**70**

Factoring in the intangibles

The really tough part of any evaluation procedure is attaching numerical ratings to the "intangibles" — those attributes that you can measure only through your observations. The following sections cover those intangible factors that you commonly find in the criteria for most jobs, along with suggestions on how to tell whether the candidate measures up.

Industriousness and motivation

Definition: Candidates' work ethic — how hard they're willing to work and how important they feel it is to perform to the best of their ability.

When important: All the time.

How to measure: Verifiable accomplishments in their last jobs. Evaluation of past employers and coworkers. Track record of successful jobs that goes back to college or even earlier.

Intelligence

Definition: Mental alertness, thinking ability, capability to process abstract information.

When important: Any job that requires the ability to make decisions (and not just follow instructions).

How to measure: Evidence of good decision-making ability in previous jobs. Also through testing. (Make sure, however, that the tests aren't in any way discriminatory. See Chapters 2, 6 and "Discovering the Truth about Background Checks," later in this chapter.)

Temperament and ability to cope with stress

Definition: General demeanor — whether the candidate is calm and level-headed or hyper or hot-headed.

When important: In any job where the stress level is high or in any work environment where people must interact and rely on one another.

How to measure: Personality testing can sometimes prove reliable, but the best way to measure these criteria is to ask during the interview about stress levels in candidates' previous jobs and how they feel they performed.

Creativity and resourcefulness

Definition: The ability to think *outside the box* — to come up with innovative solutions to problems.

When important: In jobs that require imagination or problem-solving skills that don't rely on set procedures.

How to measure: Examples of previous work (graphic-design work, writing samples, and so on). Specific examples of situations in which the candidate has come up with an innovative solution to a problem. Previous accomplishments or awards. Outside interests.

Teamwork abilities

Definition: The ability to work harmoniously with others and share responsibility for achieving the same goal.

When important: Any task with a strong need for employees to work closely and collaboratively.

How to measure: Previous work experience. (Did candidates work on their own or with groups?) Team successes mentioned during the interview. Evidence of ability to work within project team rules, protocols, and work practices. Support for coworkers. Willingness to ask for help.

Hiring Right

Bad hiring decisions rarely happen by accident. In retrospect, you can usually discover that you didn't do something you should have. The following list covers the key principles to follow in order to hire the right person.

✔ **Anchor yourself to the hiring criteria.** The hiring criteria that you establish from the beginning should serve as your guiding force throughout the evaluation process. If, in looking ahead, you decide to change the criteria, fine. Just make sure that you're not changing criteria simply because you're enamored with one particular candidate and decide to change the ground rules to accommodate that candidate. Anchoring yourself to hiring criteria helps to prevent three of the most common pitfalls in hiring:

  • The *halo effect* (becoming so enraptured by one particular aspect of the candidate — appearance, credentials, interests, and so on — that you let that aspect influence all your other judgments.)

  • The *cloning effect* (hiring someone in your image even though someone with your particular mix of skills and attributes clearly isn't qualified for that particular job)

  • How much you "like" the candidate

✔ **Take your time.** The more pressure that you're under, the greater the likelihood of rushing the decision and ending up with an employee who not only isn't your best choice but someone you're probably going to end up firing — with all the disruption that firing someone entails. Keep in mind the main pitfall of acting out of urgency: Doing so induces you to overestimate the qualities of candidates who may be only marginally qualified to fill the job. The better alternative: See whether you can bring in a temporary replacement as you continue the search.

✔ **Cross-verify whenever possible.** Whatever else they may disagree on, most hiring experts contend that you can never have enough information from enough different sources. So try not to rely solely on any one source of information, whether interview impressions, resume data, reference checks, testing, and so on. Spread a wide net and pay careful attention to discrepancies.

✔ **Get help, but avoid the "too many cooks" syndrome.** A smart practice — particularly when filling a key position — is to get input from others before you make a final choice. Involving too many people in the final decision, however, is a mistake. If too many people have a say, the likely outcome is a compromise choice. Instead of getting the best employee, you end up with the candidate who's the least objectionable to everyone. Try to restrict your circle of decision-makers to 3-5 people who understand the job, your company's culture, and the personality and working style of the hiree's manager. As I discuss in Chapter 7, you can gain these additional perspectives on candidates by holding multiple and panel interviews. When it comes time for the final decision, these same people can help you choose the best applicant.

✔ **Don't force the issue.** The recruiting process sometimes uncovers a "dream" employee — except for one problem: The candidate's skills and attributes don't match the hiring criteria of a particular job. The best thing to do if you find yourself in this situation is to see whether you can find another job in the company that better suits this particular candidate. The worst thing that you can do is try to put a "good" employee in the "wrong" job.

✔ **Avoid the "top-of-mind" syndrome.** Do your best to stay alert to any extraneous factors that may distort the selection process. Studies indicate, for example, that employers tend to choose some candidates over others not because those candidates are more qualified but because they're interviewed later in the hiring process and are fresher in the minds of the interviewer. The best way to avoid this pitfall is to keep your focus on the hiring criteria, no matter what.

Getting a Broader View

References and other third-party observations are useful and necessary components of the hiring process. Selected references from past employers help you separate those with good employment records from others who have a less positive job performance history. Not taking these steps can increase your risk of making a hiring mistake and putting your organization at a disadvantage. If you succeed in matching up the candidate and the credentials she has presented to you, however, there's a much better chance that she will prove to be a productive and valuable member of your team. It's best if you conduct reference checks or other checks yourself if you'll be the one working with the employee.

Checking hard-to-check references

Getting a candid reference from an employer is tougher than ever these days. Because employers know that both saying too much and saying too little can have legal consequences, they are increasingly wary of being specific about past employees and their work histories. While companies have been sued for not disclosing enough information about former workers, others have paid enormous settlements because they provided negative references — whether true or false.

Obtaining the most candid references

Because of these difficulties, rushing through the reference checking process — or bypassing it altogether — in order to make a quick hire may be tempting. While it's important not to delay this step and risk losing the candidate to someone else, getting reliable information from a former supervisor is an important step to take before selecting someone as an employee of your company. Here are some tips on approaching this often difficult process. Like much of the advice in this book, these tips apply to you directly if you're the hiring manager and, if you're not, they're for you to communicate to line managers who are spearheading the hiring process in their organizations:

- ✔ **Let the candidate know you check references.** Be clear with candidates at the outset that your company will be checking their references. Checking references is perfectly legal as long as the information being verified is job-related and does not violate discrimination laws. Informing applicants that you're checking usually helps ensure that the answers they give you during the interview are truthful, especially when you start the interview by saying, "If we're interested in you, and you're interested in us, we'll be checking your references."

- ✔ **Don't delegate it.** If the employee will report directly to you, *you* should check the references. No matter how thorough a delegate or deputy may be, the hiring manager will have corollary questions that may not occur to others. Also, calling someone at your same level may establish greater camaraderie that will prompt a more honest and detailed reference. If that weren't enough, checking references yourself is a great way to gain insight from a former supervisor on how to best manage the individual. If you lack the time to do the complete job, then compromise by assigning just part of the reference checking to a capable coworkers in your group. Handle one, preferably two, yourself.

- ✔ **Use responses from the interview.** Asking candidates during the job interview what their former employers are likely to say about them can provide you with a good starting point if you can actually get the former employer to talk openly. You can start out by saying something such as, "Joe tells me that you think he's the greatest thing since sliced bread" and have the employer take it from there. You may not get a totally frank answer, but you can get valuable comments and insights. After all, the candidate must assume that you're going to check out his answers.

Contacting potential references

Remember not to rely on written references presented to you by candidates. They're of limited value. Many are prepared at the time of termination and, because firing a person is a sensitive task, the employer may have focused on the positive and few, if any, negatives. (How many bad letters of reference have you ever seen?)

Sending letters or e-mail messages to companies is usually ineffective as well. References aren't likely to be as candid in writing as they would be verbally, if they respond at all. Companies that do respond aren't likely to be very timely, increasing the likelihood that you'll lose a good potential employee.

The best way to communicate with references is via the telephone. Calling gives you an opportunity to ask spontaneous questions based upon what was said in response to one of your primary questions. You can often detect enthusiasm, or lack of it, if you pay attention to the tone of the voice.

Using your own network for checking

You don't need to limit your search for reference information to former employers. You may find people in your own circle of friends or acquaintances — your lawyer, banker, accountant, or dog trainer, for example — with firsthand knowledge of the candidate who probably aren't as reluctant as a former employer may be to level with you. Try to be fair, however. If you get information that puts the candidate in a bad light, try to get verification from another source, just to make sure that what you're hearing isn't sour grapes from one specific individual. Ask the candidate's references for names of other individuals you may contact for information.

Online reference checking: Proceed with caution

Advances in technology and more sophisticated online search capabilities have increased the popularity of reference checking via the Internet. The practice will undoubtedly grow as more record holders create databases that employers can easily access. The Society for Human Resources Management (SHRM) reports that education verification information is becoming more quickly available due to advances in record keeping among academic and other credential-awarding bodies. Another reason for the increase in technology-driven reference checking is the integration of online search processes into existing human resource and personnel management systems. As Internet-based checks become more standardized, this integration is likely to make turnaround time even faster. (See also "Discovering the Truth About Background Checks" in the next section of this chapter.)

By now, almost everyone with a computer has heard of the practice of "Googling" a person's name to see what comes up. Some employers also access blogs and Web sites like Friendster and Facebook to gain information on candidates. My message here: Proceed carefully. While this approach can reduce costs and sometimes yield faster results, you must also understand that much of the information on a candidate you discover can be either erroneous or irrelevant. A person's *digital footprint* can also reveal facts that are illegal to consider in a hiring decision. The same legal constraints that govern interviewing apply to reference checking. Online reference checking should be viewed as a complement, not a replacement, for traditional methods. A Web search is no substitute for personal assessments of the work quality and professionalism of candidates that carefully selected individuals can offer. As I explain in the next section, inaccuracies exist in many online data records, and some forms of investigation require written permission from the applicant and are subject to other legal limitations.

See the CD-ROM for a sample Reference Check Letter to send to past employers of the candidate. Also included are various disclosure authorization forms.

Discovering the Truth about Background Checks

Many companies, increasingly aware of the pitfalls of failing to adequately evaluate applicants before bringing them on board, are conducting background checks on candidates. *Background checks* take reference checks a step further, and businesses use them because they feel they're a way to gain more assurance that the people they hire are what these candidates represent themselves to be. In other words, where reference checks allow you to verify with former employers a potential hire's accomplishments and personal attributes (see preceding section), background checks attempt to delve into additional aspects of a candidate's activities and behavior.

Background checks can take many forms, depending on the position and what the employer considers most important in evaluating job candidates. The principal measures in use today include

- Criminal background checks
- Education records/academic degree verification
- Certifications and licenses (such as CPA)
- Credit checks

- ✔ Driving histories
- ✔ Medical exams
- ✔ Drug tests
- ✔ Workers' compensation reports

A growing number of online services advertise their ability to perform background checks for businesses in a very short timeframe. These services can be tempting — especially to smaller businesses that lack the budgets to conduct checks on their own.

But there's one problem.

Even though many of the firms offering these services make it sound easy and inexpensive, performing a meaningful background check is, in fact, rarely an uncomplicated undertaking. Many of these providers present an overly simplistic picture of what these searches entail and downplay the potential for obtaining incomplete or inaccurate reports and test results.

Many factors contribute to the complexity of background checks:

- ✔ **No central information source:** It may come as a surprise to you that no single, national source of information exists for most types of background checks. Criminal records, for example, are generally maintained by individual states or counties, many of which do not store them electronically.

- ✔ **Possibility of flawed data:** Another issue is reliability. Even the most comprehensive checks yield flawed or incomplete records with greater frequency than some employers realize. When researchers at the University of Maryland studied criminal recidivism rates, they hired a first-rate investigative agency to search the records of 120 convicted criminals in a Virginia county to see what information would be uncovered. The investigative agency found no criminal records at all for 64 of the 120 convicted criminals chosen for the study!

- ✔ **Need for retesting:** The frequency with which you conduct background checks must also be a factor in deciding whether to use these methods for evaluating prospective new hires. Academic credentials must be verified only once, but a drug test or criminal background check can become out of date almost as soon as it is conducted.

- ✔ **Legal restrictions:** Further adding to the complexity of conducting background checks on job candidates are federal laws governing them, as well as state laws that can vary considerably from state to state. As a result, you may want to consider seeking legal advice before you even request some types of checks.

✔ **Technology not keeping up:** While technology makes background checks easier to some degree, obtaining reliable information can be much more difficult than most people recognize. The apparent ease of accessing information via online background checks obscures the fact that the quality and completeness of the underlying information may not have kept pace with the technology. Many records are simply not available electronically and are accessible via paper-based systems only. And many of the databases that do exist are not updated frequently.

To do or not to do? That is the question!

As you can see, conducting background checks is frequently not a simple matter. But that doesn't mean that they're not useful tools when pursued appropriately. Whether to conduct a background check depends most on the nature of your business and the position for which you're hiring. In limited cases, you don't have a choice because federal and state laws require background checks for certain jobs. But for most positions, the employer determines the need for investigation.

You need to weigh many other questions, including:

✔ Is the job highly visible, such as a senior executive or someone who will be in the public spotlight?

✔ Does the position involve working with children or the public?

✔ Do you have a specific suspicion about a candidate?

The list goes on, but the point is that no formulas or universal criteria dictate whether background checks are necessary or appropriate for a position or an organization. Unless a check is required by law, only you can determine what is right for your business. Similarly, you should not assume that staffing companies perform background checks. Most staffing firms don't routinely conduct background checks. If a background check is required, the staffing company will likely have you work directly with a firm that specializes in this area. After all, while staffing companies are very good at what they do, they don't specialize in this type of investigation. Given the complexities, you want a firm that *does* specialize in background checks.

The logistical and legal complexities alone should not determine whether you conduct a background check. While risk is involved (in addition to the time and expense) if businesses conduct checks and obtain erroneous information, firms can also invite problems if they fail to adequately evaluate appropriate candidates. The decision is always yours to make.

So what's the bottom line?

Because of their complexity, background checks require unique expertise. If, after weighing all the factors, you decide to conduct a background check on a job applicant, employ the services of a third-party investigative agency. Not only is it difficult for a non-expert to conduct a thorough search, but you will likely need assistance in navigating the legal restrictions, which aren't always obvious or commonly known. Laws, for example, govern how information obtained during a background check can and cannot be used in your hiring decision. The best choice is to retain a firm that specializes in performing these services.

The point is that you should go in with your eyes open. If performed properly, background checks can be much more complex than many realize. Conducting rudimentary searches just to "cover all bases" is unlikely to yield accurate and useful information. That is why your decision to conduct a background check should be targeted and based on the unique needs of the position and your business.

Making Offers They Can't Refuse

After you make your final choice, you may think that you and the other decision-makers can just sit back and relax. Not just yet, I'm afraid. You still must make the offer official, and you still need to remember that if you fail to handle this phase of the hiring process carefully, one of two things can happen: You can lose the candidate, or, even if the candidate comes aboard, you can start the relationship off on a bumpy note. The following sections tell you what to bear in mind.

Don't delay

After you make up your mind about a candidate, make the offer immediately, especially if you're in a tight labor market. Remember, even a day or two delay can cost you the employee of choice. If your company has procedures that can slow down the process — for example, no one gets hired unless the president interviews him personally — look for ways to streamline the process.

Put your offer on the table

At this stage in the process, you have no reason to be coy. Call the person you want to hire and give her all the details about pay, benefits, and anything extra. If you don't have these details nailed down yet, you're not ready to make the offer. Most companies make job offers verbally by phone and then follow up with an official letter. Making the offer by phone rather than waiting to get the candidate back into your office will avoid having too much time elapse between the interview and the offer.

You should establish a salary range for the position before you begin recruiting (see Chapter 4). This parameter can help you stay within your budget should you need to negotiate. (In Chapters 10 and 11, I discuss the details of salary and benefits and what constitutes an effective compensation structure.)

Never back down on anything you promise at any stage in the recruiting or hiring process. ("You misunderstood. I didn't say, 'We're giving you a car,' I asked whether you 'had' a car.") That's a sure way to scare off an employee, and it may land you in legal trouble as well.

In addition, make sure that you have a standard job offer letter as a template that you can customize and that you clear the template with legal counsel.

Also use this meeting to remind the individual of the benefits of joining your firm. Augment the discussion about the financial aspects of the offer by high-lighting positives, such as a supportive work environment and exposure to a variety of assignments.

See the Offer Letter to Prospective Employee on the CD-ROM.

Set a deadline

Give candidates a reasonable amount of time to decide whether to accept the offer. What's "reasonable" generally depends on the type of job. The time frame for an entry-level job may be a few days, but for a middle or senior-level candidate in a competitive market or for a position that involves relocation, a week isn't excessive.

Stay connected

While a candidate is considering an offer, you or the hiring manager should stay in touch with him or have individuals from the interview team contact him if you're using multiple or panel interviews. The purpose is for you to reinforce your excitement about the candidate potentially joining your team.

Know how to negotiate salary

After receiving a candidate's response to your offer, you must be prepared to negotiate. Job seekers today have access to an abundance of information on salary negotiation through Web sites and books, so most will enter the meeting knowledgeable on the topic. To reach a fair deal, you need to be equally prepared.

Decide how far you're willing to go

The first step is not unlike that in any other sort of bargaining. If the candidate suggests a higher figure than you've offered, you can choose to raise the amount of your proposal, waiting for the candidate to respond or counteroffer, and, ideally, arriving at an agreement that's within the salary range you've set for the position.

If the candidate keeps pushing, whether you want to exceed the established range generally depends on two factors: one, how badly you want the individual; and two, the policies and precedents in your company. Two questions to ask yourself before you bring in the heavy artillery:

- ✔ **Are other, equally qualified candidates available if the applicant says no?** If the answer is yes, the leverage to make accommodations rests with the company.

- ✔ **Has the job been particularly hard to fill, or are market conditions making finding and recruiting suitable candidates difficult?** If the answer is yes, the leverage rests with the candidate.

- ✔ **Will a stronger offer be significantly out of line with existing pay levels for comparable positions in your company or hiring manager's department?** As I discuss in Chapter 10, the lack of a reasonable degree of internal equity in compensation levels diminishes the spirit of teamwork and fairness.

Recognize that if you decide to go beyond the firm's pay scale to win a really stellar candidate, you risk poor morale among existing staff should they learn that a new hire in the same role is being paid at a higher rate. And the best-kept secrets often do get out.

Think creatively

If you're not able to match a candidate's salary request, consider expanding other components of the package. Applicants are often willing to compromise on base compensation if concessions are made in other areas.

Flexible scheduling is one candidate-pleasing option that will cost you little to nothing. Providing additional time off or opportunities to telecommute may also be acceptable to a candidate in lieu of higher wages. Also consider a signing bonus (see sidebar) or a performance-based bonus after a specified period of time. (Chapter 10 discusses the latter.)

Signing bonuses

A *signing bonus* is a sum of money that is offered as an extra inducement to the candidate to join the company. They were formerly the sole province of professional athletes, but according to the 2005/2006 U.S. Compensation Planning Survey from Mercer Human Resource Consulting, signing bonuses have become a prevalent form of rewarding employees, used by 55 percent of survey respondents. How much do they usually consist of? It varies widely by position, job market, and skills that are sought, but CareerJournal.com estimates that a typical signing bonus for middle managers and professionals runs 5 to 10 percent of base salary.

The signing bonus is exactly what it seems: an up-front cash payment that you give to an employee at the start of employment, independent of salary. The benefit to employees? Cash in their pockets. The benefit to employers? In a tight labor market, it may help you secure the employee you want without distorting your salary structure. If you use signing bonuses, however, it's a good idea to make them contingent upon a specified period of employment. For example, the new manager will receive a signing bonus of $10,000 as long as he or she is employed with your company for a period of at least one year.

Know when to draw the line

Some HR experts insist that you shouldn't push too hard if a candidate isn't interested. Probing a bit in order to find out why he's being hesitant isn't a bad idea, though. Try to identify the source of the problem and make reasonable accommodations.

But don't get so caught up in negotiations that you lose sight of what is appropriate for your organization. Sometimes you just have to walk away. If your attempts to woo a reluctant candidate fall short, the best thing to do in many cases is to cut your losses and look somewhere else. It may well be that the candidate knows something about himself that you don't know, so don't push too hard. The goal at this point should be to end the process so that the candidate leaves with a feeling of being treated fairly and with dignity.

Clarify acceptance details

If a promising candidate accepts your final offer, congratulate yourself! You're helping build a strong team that can carry your business forward. But before you break out the champagne, you still need to take care of some details.

Some companies are now asking candidates to sign a duplicate copy of the job-offer letter as an indication of acceptance. The signature confirms that the candidate understands the basic terms of the offer. If you're making a job offer contingent on reference checking or a physical examination and/or drug and alcohol testing, or background checks make sure that the candidate understands and accepts this restriction.

Stay in touch

Even after a candidate accepts your offer and you agree on a starting date, keeping in touch with the new employee is still a good idea. Two to three weeks is the customary time between an acceptance and start date. Most people who are changing jobs give a standard two-week notice to their former employer. For those who want to take a few days off before starting their new job, a three-week interval is not unusual. Use the transition period to mail off all those informational brochures and employment forms and to schedule a lunch or two, if appropriate. You want to subtly help the new employee transfer loyalty from his old employer to you and to make dismissing any other offers that may surface from prior interviews easier for the person you now want on your team.

Employment contracts: Should you or shouldn't you?

Once a rarity, employment contracts are increasingly prevalent in the United States — as protection for both employers and new employees. An *employment contract* is an agreement between an employer and an employee stating the level of compensation and other benefits the employee will receive in exchange for specific work performed.

These contracts are usually (but not always) made for executive or senior-level positions. In highly competitive industries and in those that handle issues of intellectual property, employment contracts can help employers by contractually prohibiting employees at any level from working for a competitor and revealing trade secrets. You have to be careful, however, that you don't word the contract in such a way that guarantees employment.

An employment contract doesn't need to be a 20-page legal document. It can take the form of a one-page letter that specifies the job title, duties, responsibilities and obligations, conditions of employment, and, most important, severance arrangements if things don't work out. (See the sample Employment Agreement on the CD-ROM.)

Forms on the CD

Candidate Rating Form

Reference Check Letter

Employment Inquiry Release

Consent to Criminal Background Check

Background Check Permission (Comprehensive) for Prospective Employee

Disclosure and Authorization Regarding Procurement of Consumer Report for Employment Purposes

A Summary of Your Rights Under the Fair Credit Reporting Act

Confirmation of Receipt of the Summary of Your Rights Under the Fair Credit Reporting Act and the Copy of Consumer or Investigative Report

Disclosure of Adverse Action Based on Information in a Consumer or Investigative Report

Offer Letter to Prospective Employee

Employment Agreement

Chapter 9

Starting Off on the Right Foot

· ·

In This Chapter

▶ Taking a broader view of orientation

▶ Empathizing with new employees

▶ Easing the transition with mentoring

· ·

*O*ne of the running themes of Clint Eastwood's *Dirty Harry* movies is that the main character, San Francisco police inspector Harry Callahan, has a new partner in each film. Someone always warns each partner that when you work with Callahan, you stand a good chance of getting killed or injured, and Callahan himself makes clear from the beginning that the partner must watch him in action to learn the ropes. By mid-movie, after a series of adventures, both Callahan and his partner are working effectively as a team.

Although working in corporate America is a lot less treacherous than the plot of a police drama, your new employees are similar to Dirty Harry's new partners in one key respect: They're uncertain of what's expected, apprehensive of what's going to happen, unsure of what to do — and looking to the HR department and others for the answers.

The initial weeks or months on the job are especially pivotal for newcomers in establishing attitudes about their duties, their colleagues, and your company. Activities planned for this early period must not only provide job-related information but also foster a clear understanding of your firm's philosophy and core values.

You're likely familiar with many of the logistical aspects of helping a new hire adjust to the company, ranging from completing forms and learning about office technology to parking and security procedures. But the big picture goal of this chapter is to help you create a rigorous, ongoing process that truly helps new employees thrive. In this chapter, you discover ways to ensure that newcomers thoroughly grasp their responsibilities, become productive, and feel they're part of the team.

Onboarding: Going Beyond Orientation

Historically, the process to help just-hired employees acclimate to a new environment has been known as *orientation*. An introduction to the work area and basic building or factory facilities is normally taken care of on the first day of work. But soon after, a formal or informal orientation typically communicates company policies, operating procedures, and other administrative details.

Today, however, orientation is not a stand-alone event but part of a bigger process, often called *onboarding*. Some view onboarding as just a new buzzword for orientation, but it's actually your opportunity to do far more to ensure that new employees become productive and satisfied members of your staff. The process is also known by other names among HR professionals, such as alignment, assimilation, integration, and transition. Though you can probably spend a few hours talking with other HR colleagues parsing each term's differences, what they all have in common is an attempt to go beyond, while still including, the old concept of employee orientation.

An effective onboarding program consists of supplemental efforts taken early in a new employee's tenure to help him build a better understanding of your organization's culture, his job responsibilities, and how they tie into company and departmental priorities. This more holistic approach to orientation is consistent with your strategic HR role. Onboarding goes beyond mere practicality and acknowledges that what new employees learn in their first few weeks has long-term effects on their ability to tackle the challenges of today's faster paced business environment. In other words, starting out on the right foot is even more important than employers ever thought.

Depending on your company's size and the complexity of the work, an onboarding program can last from several weeks to several months. It covers matters related to training, scheduled milestones, mentoring programs, and interactive meetings where employees can ask questions about corporate or departmental initiatives.

Above all, onboarding is an opportunity. Virtually all new employees are enthralled about the experience they're about to have. This period is the time to capitalize on that excitement and begin building strong bonds between new hires and the organization.

While you set up overall onboarding events and policies, the line manager handles specific job-related parts of the process. But here, too, you're responsible for offering advice and guidance to supervisors, especially those who are new to management, and play an important role as a value-added resource for both the manager and the new employee. The policies and procedures you establish about how to onboard new employees greatly shape how managers and employees interact with one another. It's your place to ensure managers understand these guidelines and the importance of adhering to them. And you'll also want to make yourself available throughout the new employee's early days to address any concerns or questions.

Three Unproductive Approaches

The key to successful onboarding is to get the right results. No one formula works for everyone. Every company and every new employee is different. Some ways do exist, however, of getting your new employees up to speed that are clearly *un*productive. The following sections cover three examples that unfortunately occur all too often.

Osmosis

How the method works: No formal orientation event or adjustment process exists for new employees. You leave each employee alone to learn the ropes simply by observing and asking questions on a spontaneous, as-needed basis.

Faulty rationale: If employees are smart enough to get hired, they can probably figure out for themselves what they need to know about the job, the company, and the facilities.

Why this method doesn't work: Relying on osmosis fails to take into account how difficult it is for new employees to grasp the nuances of a company and simultaneously learn what's expected in a new job. Worse yet, this method conveys a general attitude of indifference that can very easily carry over into employee performance. Another problem is that new employees are often shy about asking questions, which means that they don't get the answers or guidance they need until after they begin to make costly mistakes.

"Just follow Joe around"

How the method works: "Joe" can be "Jill," "Frank," "Melanie," or anybody who has been with your company for more than a few years. The idea is to pair the newly hired employee with one of your "veterans" — but without giving the experienced employee specific instructions on how to manage the process.

Faulty rationale: If you have the newcomers simply follow around more tenured employees for a couple days, they pick up the basics. And this approach is simple and inexpensive.

Why this method doesn't work: Joe and the newcomer may have nothing whatsoever in common, making communication strained. By the time the first day of shadowing is over, you may have a veteran employee convinced that the company is now scraping the bottom of the barrel and a newcomer who wonders whatever possessed him to join this company in the first place. Another problem is that Joe's idea of communicating with the new employee may be for the newcomer simply to watch as Joe does his job, regardless of what the newcomer's job may be. In addition, the newcomer may pick up more than just Joe's skills — for example, any negative feelings Joe may have toward the company. Without clear instructions and careful selection of which person the new hire "follows around," you may unwittingly be undermining your efforts.

Watch the video

How the method works: You hire a hot-shot production company to produce slick video content in CD-ROM, DVD, or other format that tells new employees everything they need to know about your company in a 12- to 15-minute session. The program consists of seating new employees in front of a monitor and having them watch the CD. You don't serve popcorn. Or worse yet, you hand it to new employees, telling them to watch it on their computers whenever they have the time.

Faulty rationale: Everybody loves videos, right? Besides, you don't need to waste any time with person-to-person contact or training.

Why this method doesn't work: Videos, no matter how cutting edge the delivery format, can't answer questions, and you have no guarantee that the newcomer is actually paying attention and not daydreaming. Nor do they offer concrete insights into that specific individual's job. By simply using a piece of technology with little or no input from you and other key managers, you also run the risk of employees assuming that you view helping new employees adapt to the company as little more than a formality, like getting your driver's license renewed. That's not a good message to send.

Doing It Right: A Little Empathy Goes a Long Way

You don't need a Ph.D. in clinical psychology to appreciate what's going on inside the heads of new employees the first day that they walk through the door. The first few days and weeks on a new job can be exciting — and often stressful. As the new kid on the block, the most recent addition to your staff will encounter unfamiliar people, policies, and procedures. Everything from your first-day welcome to the remainder of your onboarding process should address those concerns.

Think about what *you* would want and need if you were going through the process of joining a new company. Your concerns or areas of interest would likely include new employee anxieties, job tasks and goal-setting, company operations and culture, as well as basic policies and procedures. These topics are areas to focus on — and encourage line managers to focus on — regardless of how formally or informally you want to approach the onboarding process.

After the number of new employees joining your company reaches a certain threshold — and you must determine when the company reaches this point — you probably want to formalize your approach, creating a series of onboarding activities that you repeat whenever a new employee or group of new employees joins your company. The following sections should help ensure that any program you develop is as effective as possible.

Your onboarding program can be as elaborate as a six-week combination training and boot camp or as simple as a series of scheduled one-on-one conversations between the new employee and a manager or HR staffer, or something in between. Whatever form you take, however, you want to give it structure. You need to provide a schedule, and everyone involved needs clearly defined roles. You want the individual elements of the program *weighted*. In other words, a logical and strategic connection between the importance of a particular issue or topic and how much time you devote to that issue or topic must exist.

The First Day: Ease Anxieties

Even though new employees have likely been on your company premises previously during the interview phase, their experiences on the first day of work will leave a lasting impression, even from the minute they walk into the building or onto the job site. You need to offer a first-day welcome to begin the process of making them feel at home. Following are tips for you — or the individuals' bosses if you're not supervising the new hires — to remember:

- ✔ Alert the receptionist or security guard (if you have one) that a new employee is arriving and make sure that this person greets the newcomer warmly.

- ✔ Arrange for someone (you, if possible) to personally escort the new hire to his work station or office.

✔ Personally introduce the newcomer to other members of the working team.

✔ Give the new employee a company roster with names and phone numbers of people to contact, along with their job titles.

✔ Encourage current employees who haven't been formally introduced to the new hire to introduce themselves and offer to help in any way they can.

✔ At some point during the day, meet with the employee to take up where the last interview left off. Let him know how glad you are to have him on board and that you will be providing a comprehensive introduction to the company and the job within the next few days.

✔ Schedule a lunch with the new employee and his manager on the first day.

The First Week: Discover More about the Company and the Job

You probably gave the new employee plenty of information about your company while recruiting and interviewing. Even so, the first few days on the job are the best time to reinforce that information and build identification with the company. At the very least, a new employee should know the following:

✔ Your company's basic products or services

✔ Size and general organization of the company

✔ An overview of your industry — and where your company fits into the overall picture (Who's your chief competition?)

✔ Your company's mission statement (if you have one) and values

✔ Department goals and strategic objectives

✔ The corporate culture

Provide the rules of the road

If your company has a procedures manual or handbook, make sure that the employee gets one on his first day and give him time to look it over, just to make sure that he has no misunderstandings. (For more information on policy manuals, see the section on policy and procedures later in this chapter.) Make sure, in particular, that new employees are aware of policies regarding their immediate work areas (that is, whether you allow personal photographs, digital music players, and so on). If your company has unusual rules in this regard, take the time to explain the rationale — for example, "The last employee we had liked to play Wagner operas at full blast."

Don't take anything for granted, particularly about basic considerations such as where employees park and how they sign in. Make sure that the newcomer knows whom to call — and how — for questions and emergencies. Provide keypad door codes and advise employees of any security procedures. Other locations that you want to show new employees as soon as possible include the following:

- ✔ Restrooms, break rooms, lunch areas, and employee lounges
- ✔ Fire exits, evacuation points, and emergency assembly areas
- ✔ Immediate supervisor's office
- ✔ Departmental facilities (copy room, supply lockers, and so on)
- ✔ Health facilities, nurse's office, first aid kit, and so on
- ✔ Security office
- ✔ Parking lot and any assigned parking space

If your company has specific security procedures or policies regarding personal phone calls or e-mail, make sure you communicate these policies on the first day of work.

See the CD-ROM for an example Onboarding Checklist.

Keep orientation practical

Because new employees join your company at varying intervals, scheduling formal sessions can sometimes present a problem. On the one hand, an orientation event should be conducted as soon as possible. Of course if you're frequently adding new employees, holding a formal session on each new hire's first or second day may be impractical. The best option is a combined approach — a formal event that takes place on a weekly or monthly basis (depending on how many employees you're hiring), preceded by an informal, first-day, personalized orientation that covers the mandatory administrative and operational aspects of the job. (See "The First Day: Ease Anxieties," earlier in this chapter.)

Involve senior management

Formal orientation sessions should always include an appearance (and, ideally, a brief message of welcome) from some key member of senior management — the CEO or president, if possible. Some companies launch these sessions with a digital video message from the head of the company — which is acceptable as long as the video is of high quality and up to date. Generally speaking, however, having members of senior management appear during a session gives more credibility and importance to the entire process.

Hold large-group sessions in a suitable location

If you're running large group orientation sessions with video and oral presentations and so on, you need a room large enough to accommodate the audience comfortably. Unattractive, cramped surroundings sabotage your ability to communicate and send the wrong message to new employees. An attractive environment tells new employees that the company is organized, professional, and cares about its workers. If you don't have suitable facilities for holding these sessions on premises, consider renting a hotel conference room for the purpose.

Make group presentations user-friendly

Keep in mind that the orientation event is often the first formally structured experience an employee has on the inside of the company. With that in mind, you want everything that occurs that day to be consistent with the message that you conveyed during the recruitment process. To put it simply, everything should reflect how the company presents itself to the business world. You can convey information in several different ways — verbally; in written form, such as in a workbook; or through audiovisual materials. Each does a different job. The following list gives you a look at which option works best with varying types of information:

- ✔ **Verbal information:** This type of information is okay for the simple and most obvious stuff — the location of the lunchroom and restrooms, how to use the door keypad, the best places to eat lunch in the area, and so on.

- ✔ **Audiovisual presentation:** This type of presentation is most effective if you're seeking to create an emotional effect, as in the case of the company mission and goals.

- ✔ **Written documentation:** Use written documentation for anything complex or legally mandated, such as the company's Equal Employment Opportunity policy, sexual harassment polices, policies regarding disciplinary action, and so on.

Deciding on the mix of oral, audiovisual, and written information to include in an orientation event depends primarily on how often you need to conduct a session and how many employees you're working with at any given time. You don't need to go overboard. Unless you're typically hiring large groups of new employees at the same time, a company video is a luxury you can probably do without. Rely instead on a PowerPoint or similar presentation. Whatever you do, however, make sure that you provide new employees with information on key policies and benefits in writing. (Suggestion: If you contract out your benefits administration, vendors usually provide brochures, forms, and so on.) One last point: Have everything ready before new employees walk in the door.

Provide an orientation agenda

A written agenda for orientation events serves three main purposes: It eases a new employee's anxiety by mapping out what's going to happen during the day (or days); it enables you to adhere to a formal structure; and it shows newcomers that you take the matter of orientation quite seriously as opposed to feeling you can just "wing it." By creating a well-organized and businesslike agenda, you also let employees see how your company likes to conduct business. The document needn't be fancy. A single sheet of paper works fine.

Space things out

One consistent criticism shared by new employees is that too much information gets thrown at them too quickly. So try to space things out. Break up orientation sessions during the first week or move parts of them into the second or third week to give your new team members a chance to absorb what they're learning. Another benefit of this approach is that subsequent information is likely to make more sense to employees after they have several days of experience working with your company under their belts.

See the CD-ROM for sample policies on e-mail and a drug-free workplace.

Give a clear sense of tasks and set concrete goals

At some point during the first week of work, newly hired employees need to sit down with their supervisors for an in-depth discussion about job responsibilities and goal setting. The role of the HR practitioner is to ensure not only that this meeting happens, but that the manager is well prepared for the meeting and understands its importance. The new employee should come away from this discussion with a crystal-clear understanding of expectations, tasks, and priorities. In the process, the employee and supervisor will clarify the job's objectives and, most importantly, together set specific, concrete goals for the newcomer. The following list provides several suggestions for this meeting:

- ✔ Tell new employees about how the department operates, including information on expectations about quality standards.

- ✔ Make sure that each employee has a written copy of the job description.

- ✔ Review each item in the job description and make sure that the employee understands the nature of the task, its importance, and how it fits into broader corporate objectives.

- ✔ Define the factors that will shape the new employee's evaluation.

- ✔ Together, set short- and long-term goals. Involving employees in defining their objectives makes it more likely that they will work harder toward achieving them. Goals should include not only specific job tasks and results, but also training and development activities.

- ✔ Build a timetable for reaching goals over the next 30 to 60 days, as well as longer range objectives.

Sample agenda for a one-day orientation program

The following agenda can serve as the basis of a one-day orientation program. Notice that for each activity, you provide a location and the name of the person who's handling the task. I emphasize: This agenda is only a basic example. As I describe in "Space things out" in this chapter, you may want to break your orientation into several sessions.

9:00 a.m.	Welcome by Patricia Welcome of Human Resources
9:15 a.m.	Remarks by Ray Joinus, President and CEO. Conference Room 124
9:45 a.m.	Coffee break with Mr. Joinus
10:00 a.m.	Company overview. Conference Room 124. Bill Smiley, HR Manager
10:45 a.m.	Walking tour of key facilities. Patricia Welcome
11:15 a.m.	Benefits briefing and completion of forms. Conference Room 124. HR staff
12 noon	Lunch
1:00 p.m.	Distribution of company manuals and presentation of key rules and policies. Conference Room 124. Bill Smiley
2:15 p.m.	Tour of office with manager
3:00 p.m.	Security office: ID photos and parking permits
3:30 p.m.	Work area familiarization with manager

Second Week and Beyond

A key part of the onboarding process is early followup. You or supervising line managers should meet with employees at predetermined points: two weeks after the first day on the job, a month after, two months, or at intervals that work best for each job's complexity and changeability. These times are when you check in with new team members to find out how things are going for them. How well do they understand the company and their roles? Do they have any questions that have not been answered? Inquire especially as to the value of training programs. Are they helpful? Do they address the right areas? Are they worth the time being spent on them? What future developmental experiences would employees like to see?

These followup meetings are also a good time to hear their assessment of the onboarding process thus far. (See the section "Feedback: How good is your program?" later in this chapter.)

Develop a checklist

To make sure that you're covering all bases during employees' first 90 days on the job, create a checklist of everything they need to know — every place they need to see, every form they need to fill out, and everyone they need to meet. If possible, sort everything by time and priority. Make both the new employee and manager responsible for completing all items and submitting the completed checklist.

Ensure goals continue to cascade

Change is the name of the game in today's companies. Though goal-setting should be part of the initial onboarding process, employee objectives must also be periodically revised as time goes on to ensure that they remain aligned with current company strategies and departmental priorities. It is counterproductive for an employee to be focused on a set of tasks that aren't quite in sync with a new overall company direction. You, line managers, and employees need to keep goals cascading and attuned to the visions articulated by senior management.

Cascading goals: Aligning individual goals with corporate strategy

In the most successful organizations, employees don't set their goals in a vacuum. HR professionals ensure that line managers fully understand the company's strategic goals and are properly prepared to help their employees create individual objectives that support this higher level vision. Sometimes called *cascading goals,* this approach allows the broader perspectives of senior management to cascade, like falling water, into more specific goals at all levels of the company.

In the case of a food company, for example, senior management might share a new direction, such as "connect more with the desires of local families." This vision in turn takes on several meanings as it "cascades" through the organization and individuals in each department. For product development, the focus may be on creating more family-friendly food items. For marketing, it may mean researching the attitudes of local families toward eating. This method also allows employees to set their objectives in line with their managers' goals, all of which are part of the "cascade" throughout the organization. Simply stated, cascading goals put everyone "on the same page."

The net result of cascading goals is a better company performance. When employees are aware of what they're being evaluated for and what's expected, they tend to do a better job. And when they're encouraged to create goals that are in sync with something larger, workers tend to feel more of a sense of purpose and importance, which leads to increased morale and productivity.

Don't let your message die

The company values and best practices you stressed during the orientation period should come through loud and clear month after month — through the actions of role models such as supervisors and mentors, as well as through internal communications, such as employee publications and your company intranet. In ongoing training activities, continue to make it plain that values such as respect for colleagues, commitment to quality service, and doing what is right rather than what is easy or convenient are not just first-day lip service, but integral to your philosophy of doing business.

Use mentoring to build a solid foundation

Mentoring programs have become a popular way for firms to assist new employees during the initial months on the job. By being paired with appropriate *mentors* — more experienced employees who act as a new hire's guide to your workplace — newcomers gain valuable, real-world experience and skills that are difficult to transmit in classroom settings or workshops.

Mentoring relationships are a key part of the onboarding process, although they often continue beyond an employee's initial period with the company as well. These pairings augment other elements of onboarding, helping fill in the gaps that even the best thought-out programs invariably contain. After all, no matter how many steps you to take to ensure a smooth adjustment to the company's culture, a few areas invariably require additional clarification. And a mentor and an employee can discuss certain "unofficial" topics in a way that's not possible in a structured setting or with an immediate supervisor.

The one-on-one nature of the mentoring relationship can help a new hire integrate quickly into your firm's culture and become a productive member of the staff. Mentors can show new employees the ropes, introduce them to individuals in other work areas, and serve as a sounding board for thoughts, ideas, and concerns. Good mentor-protégé relationships also nurture an inviting culture, demonstrating to newcomers the benefits of an open environment where people are constantly sharing knowledge, generating ideas, and are mutually committed to building a successful company.

But keep in mind that mentoring is not a one-way street. Individuals who become mentors stand to gain as well. For example, serving as a mentor can help even the most accomplished long-term employee improve his management skills. In addition, new employees often bring with them fresh perspectives than can benefit a tenured mentor in return.

Mentoring is also a valuable recruiting and retention tool. When evaluating a firm as a potential employer, many job candidates consider a formal mentoring program an attractive asset. It indicates that the company is committed to the professional development of all its employees.

Mentors are different from supervisors. They don't typically oversee the new employee's day-to-day work performance. Their true function is to act as an additional source of support during an employee's early period with your company (although, again, these relationships can continue indefinitely).

Sometimes you'll hear the term coaching used in place of mentoring. In the field of HR, however, they have different, but related, meanings. In general, *coaching* tends to be more situational and peer-to-peer or trainer-to-peer. A coach, who can be either external or internal to the company, helps an employee improve in specific areas. Mentoring, on the other hand, typically implies a more long-term relationship, most often between a senior or more experienced company manager who is quite familiar with an organization's overall structure, policies, and culture, and a less experienced individual. Mentoring is often, but not always, a one-to-one relationship.

The key to an effective mentoring program is to choose mentors who are temperamentally suited to the task. They don't necessarily need to be your most senior managers. They should, however, be naturally empathetic and enjoy the role of helping, listening and sharing information with others.

Following are suggestions on how to find those people in the company best suited to fill the role:

- **Get recommendations.** Ask your managers to recommend members of their own staff who have the personality to act as effective mentors. Make sure that whomever they recommend has the time to devote to the task.

- **Find common ground.** Look for things — same school, similar hobbies, past experience in certain industries — that can create a rapport between the mentor and the new employee.

- **Choose good role models.** Pick employees whose attitudes you'd ideally want the new employee to emulate — flexible, agile, creative, enthusiastic.

- **Provide training**. If this is their first time serving as a mentor, employees need to understand what you expect of them and what *they* can expect. Emphasize the fine line between being a valuable source of insight and "hovering" to the point where the employee feels smothered.

If the mentor and newcomer clearly aren't hitting things off, end the relationship diplomatically but quickly. Without prejudging, try to get to the root of the problem. Maybe the mentor found out something that you should have discovered during the recruiting process. Or perhaps the new employee felt that the mentor was acting more as a boss — giving instructions — than a thoughtful sounding board. The best mentors know that, in large part, talking is less important than listening.

Feedback: How good is your program?

Whether through surveys or meetings, you need to get feedback on how your onboarding program is perceived so that you can make improvements for future new hires. Following are some questions that can form the basis of any feedback mechanism you develop for new employees immediately after the initial orientation:

- What elements of the initial orientation event(s) were most useful?
- What elements were least useful?
- What information should be included in future programs?
- How well did the session relate to your job?

But, of course, your work isn't done after you've received initial feedback. I also suggest that you gather assessments from employees several months after they're hired. After they've been part of your organization for a while, they'll likely have a broader perspective about what helped them effectively adjust to the company and what was less valuable — and perhaps offer suggestions for improvement.

Here are additional questions you can ask employees after several months into the job:

✔ What were the things you most wanted to know when you first joined the company?

✔ Were those issues and concerns adequately covered during your first month on the job?

✔ Were you given enough time to acclimate yourself?

✔ Were other employees helpful when you asked questions?

✔ Were the printed materials you received useful? What could be improved?

✔ And a final key question: What do you know about your job and this company now that you would have benefited from knowing during the first few days you were on the job?

Policy and Procedures Manual: Yes, You Need One

Even if your company has only a handful of employees, keeping your basic procedures and policies well documented is always a good practice. Whatever effort may be required to get basic company information in print and on a password-protected part of your intranet can save you time and grief down the road.

The following list gives advice for creating a procedures manual:

✔ **Separate company policies from job-specific procedures.** Try to make a distinction in your employee manual between policies that apply to everyone in the company (general hours, payroll, vacation, and so on) and procedures that relate specifically to how people do their individual jobs. Keep these distinctions separate. You may find that you need to publish one specific document that lists companywide policies and procedures and separate manuals — if you want to take this extra step — for specific job procedures.

✔ **Keep it simple.** Employee manuals don't need to be literary works, but they do need to be clear and concise. Use plain English and try to avoid overly formal, bureaucratic wording and phrasing. You may want to consider hiring a professional writer to polish your final draft.

✔ **Pay attention to legalities.** Here's some scary news: Anything that you put in writing about your company's policies or procedures automatically becomes a legal document, and someone may use it against you in a wrongful dismissal suit. Numerous cases have occurred over the past decade in which discharged employees received large settlements because they proved in court that either they were following procedures published in the company manual or that the company itself didn't follow these procedures. Play things safe. Make sure that an expert in employment law reviews the manual before you publish it.

✔ **Control the distribution.** Every employee who receives a manual should sign a document that acknowledges his receipt of the manual and that he understands its contents. Keep the signed form in the employee's personnel file. You may need it in the event of a disciplinary proceeding or lawsuit. You don't want the manual to circulate outside the company — and the manual needs to contain a clear statement to this effect. Some companies require departing employees to turn in their company manuals before they leave. You may want to consider this policy as well, especially if your manual details your operational procedures, contains trade secrets, or includes confidential or proprietary information.

Paying attention to presentation

A policies and procedures manual doesn't need to be a visual masterpiece, but you want the layout to be attractive and to enhance rather than interfere with the reader's ability to grasp its contents. If someone on your staff has a graphic-design background, have that person create a basic template. You don't need an expensive graphics package: You can probably make do with an advanced word-processing application or an office suite package containing presentation software. The following list provides some layout pointers for your consideration:

✔ **Be consistent.** Use the same design and typeface throughout the manual. The most common body types are Times, New Century Schoolbook, and Bookman. The fewer typefaces that you use, the better the manual looks

✔ **Use bullets, not paragraphs.** Set off important points in lists, just as I'm doing here.

✔ **Avoid small type.** Small type (anything smaller than 10 points) is hard to read. You're much better off adding a few more pages than giving everyone eyestrain.

✔ **Use graphics to add interest.** Even if you can't afford an artist, plenty of inexpensive royalty-free clip art is available on many popular software packages, online, or in CD-ROM form.

Knowing what to include

Most policies and procedures manuals follow the same general format. What differs from one company to the next are the specifics.

You can find a sample table of contents for an employee handbook on the CD-ROM, along with an Employee Handbook and At-Will Employment Status Acknowledgement.

The following list gives you a look at a typical table of contents for a policies and procedures manual:

✔ Welcome statement by CEO

✔ EEO policy statement (including sexual and other forms of harassment)

✔ Company history and overview

✔ Employment at-will (if applicable)

✔ Company mission statement and values

✔ Essential company rules, such as work hours, business ethics, smoking, dress code, sick days, and so on

✔ Performance appraisal procedures

✔ Disciplinary procedures (you must have a lawyer carefully review this section)

✔ Health, safety, and security rules and procedures, including fire-exit maps

✔ Benefit, pension, and deferred-income programs

✔ Parking and transportation information, including maps

What about other languages?

In today's diverse, multilingual workplace, you may want to produce your manual in languages other than English. Such a practice is a good idea, especially if English is a second language to many of your workers. But be warned: You need a professional translator to do the work, not a staff member who took language courses in high school. It's a legal document.

Playing it safe

Whatever else your employee manual does, make sure that it doesn't do any of the following:

- ✔ Make promises you can't keep.

- ✔ Publish procedures you don't follow or can't enforce.

- ✔ Say anything that someone may construe as discriminatory.

- ✔ Use the phrase "termination for just cause" without specifying what you mean.

One last piece of advice: Always include a disclaimer that emphasizes that the manual is a general source of information and not for anyone to construe as a binding employment contract.

Forms on the CD

Onboarding Checklist

E-mail Policy

Drug-Free Workplace Policy

Employee Handbook Table of Contents

Employee Handbook and At-Will Employee Status Acknowledgment

Part III
Retention: Critical in Any Business Environment

The 5th Wave
By Rich Tennant

"The pay's not great, but where else can you get a retirement plan that will last for eternity?"

In this part . . .

After you hire the best people (see Part II), you need to *keep* all that great talent you've attracted. In Part III, I give you an overview of the tools that can help you hold on to top performers at every level of your organization.

Chapter 10

Ensuring an Effective Compensation Structure

In This Chapter

▶ Understanding compensation and benefits terms

▶ Creating a compensation system

▶ Knowing the legal implications of exempt versus nonexempt

▶ Using raises, bonuses, and incentives effectively

*T*he compensation system you establish for employees is one of the main engines that drive your business. If your company is like most companies, payroll is an expensive engine to maintain — probably even your No. 1 expense.

But payroll is more than simply an expense. How much you pay your employees and the factors you use to establish pay scales and award raises, bonuses, and incentives can profoundly affect the quality of your workforce. The way you compensate people plays a key role in your ability to attract and retain a productive, reliable workforce.

The following information is as legally accurate and comprehensive as I can present in this format. I prepared the material in collaboration with the esteemed law firm, O'Melveny & Myers LLP. However, you should still seek the sound advice of your own lawyer when making decisions of this kind. He can assist you in setting up policies and wage structures that can help keep you out of legal trouble.

Defining Your Role

Your goal is not to know everything that anyone can know about employee compensation. As you take on the task of managing your company's HR function, though, you do need to keep aware of changes taking place in this critical area. Although many traditional salary practices — automatic pay increases for time on the job, for example — are disappearing in favor of a wide range of other options, the basic challenges in developing a wage system remain.

So what is your role in building a compensation plan? Generally, if you're not the owner of the company, you don't to decide how much a particular individual should be paid. Your role, instead, is to alert senior management to the options available for building a compensation system. It's your responsibility to make sure that your compensation and benefits package is competitive enough to keep your top employees from being wooed away by companies that claim to offer better total compensation packages.

When you're establishing total compensation packages, you need to be both consistent and flexible. The two may sound contradictory, but they actually go hand in hand.

Consistency means that you have a logical plan and structure to everything you do in the area of compensation and benefits so that you don't inadvertently create employee discord by giving the impression that you're showing favoritism or acting capriciously. Flexibility means that you're doing your best — within reason — to adapt to the individual needs and desires of your employees.

The intended end result of balancing these two factors is a wage-and-salary structure that not only gives your employees equitable compensation, but also focuses on the market realities of your business.

Compensation and Benefits: Nothing Is Simple

The compensation and benefits aspect of the human resources function is very detail-oriented. And the bigger the company, the more complicated it can be to maintain the required paper trail. But benefits and compensation is also one of the more engaging areas of human resources. Companies have become much more creative in the ways they reward employees, from performance-based pay to stock options (see Chapter 11). Your business's overall compensation package plays a major role in your ability to recruit and retain employees. You don't need an advanced degree in economics to figure out the kind of financial hole you could put your company in if you're not paying attention to how you're managing this side of your business.

It's all about scale. For a one-person company, decisions regarding wages, health insurance, sick leave, retirement, and educational assistance aren't likely to bring a flood of red ink to your bottom line. You can give yourself a raise, take a few extra vacation days, add special areas to your medical coverage — do anything you please — without losing sleep over whether these extra expenditures will put you out of business.

But you enter an entirely new phase of operation when you hire your first full-time or part-time employee. Once you're responsible for someone else's well-being, you must become more structured in your basic approach to compensation and benefits — and, for that matter, to all HR issues.

And that's not particularly easy. Even a seemingly routine decision, such as what medical plan you want to offer, becomes a much more complex one once your employees start checking to see whether the plan covers their particular doctor, dentist, or chiropractor. The same principle holds true for all decisions regarding such benefits as overtime, holidays, vacations, and so on.

The Basic Language of Employee Compensation

Unless you specialize in employee compensation, terminology can get confusing. So, to start you out, the following list offers a quick rundown of key terms in the field, along with their definitions:

- **Compensation:** You use this term to define all the rewards that employees receive in exchange for their work, including base pay, bonuses, and incentives.

- **Base wage or salary:** The base wage or salary is simply the salary or wage — before deductions and other incentives — that employees receive for the work they do. (If you want to get really technical, you generally use *wages* to describe the pay arrangements of employees who work on an hourly basis and *salary* to describe the pay arrangements of employees who receive their compensation as a flat weekly, biweekly, or monthly amount, regardless of how many hours they work.)

- **Raises:** This term refers to increases in base salary or rate of pay, as opposed to one-time or periodic awards.

- **Bonuses and incentives:** It's tempting to treat these two terms as synonyms. To some degree, they are. What both have in common is an objective of making employees feel appreciated and valued.

But the terms also have key differences. A *bonus* is a reward for a job well done. Though usually financial, bonuses also can include rewarding time off, free membership in a local health club, or discounts on merchandise. In contrast, an *incentive* is a tool used to boost productivity. In other words, an incentive program sets a goal — "Contact ten new customers within a month" — and rewards employees who attain it. An easy way to remember the distinction: An incentive comes *before* work is done; a bonus comes *after*.

✔ **Benefits:** Benefits are also items that you offer to employees in addition to their base wage or salary. Examples include health insurance, stock options, and retirement plans. (Chapter 11 extensively covers benefits.)

✔ **Exempt workers:** You use this classification to define employees who perform certain types of duties and receive salaries (that is, those whom you pay on a flat, weekly, biweekly, or monthly basis, as opposed to an hourly basis) and, thus, are ineligible in most cases for overtime pay.

✔ **Nonexempt workers:** Nonexempt workers are those workers to whom you pay an hourly wage. Nonexempt employees are covered by the provisions of the Fair Labor Standards Act (FLSA) and comparable state laws, particularly with respect to minimum hourly wage, overtime pay, and other working conditions.

✔ **Commission:** This term refers to a percentage of the sales price of a service or product that salespeople receive in addition to (or in lieu of) salary. Commission arrangements are sometimes *straight commission* (with no salary), sometimes combined with a base salary, and sometimes part of an arrangement in which the salesperson receives a set amount (known as a *draw*) on a regular basis, regardless of how much commission is actually earned during that period, with adjustments made at set intervals, such as every three months.

The Foundation for an Effective Compensation System

When thinking about compensation, think *system*. Creating an effective compensation system requires thinking strategically — that is, with a constant eye toward the long-term needs and goals of your business. Your goal is a well thought-out set of practices that helps to ensure the following results:

✔ Employees receive a fair and equitable wage (from their perspective) for the work that they perform.

✔ Payroll costs are in line with the overall financial health of your company.

✔ The basic philosophy of compensation is clearly understood by your employees and has the strong support of managers and employees alike.

✔ The pay scale for the various jobs in the company reflects the relative importance of the job and the skills that performing those jobs require.

✔ Pay scales are competitive enough with those of other employers in your region so that you're not constantly seeing competitors hire your top employees away from you.

✔ Compensation policies are in line with state and federal laws involving minimum wages and job classifications.

✔ Compensation policies are keeping pace with the changing nature of today's labor market — particularly in recruiting and retaining your company's top performers.

Generally, state wage laws require employers to pay wages on time and at regular periods. The laws also regulate what employers may deduct from an employee's paycheck. Most states permit employers to automatically deduct only withholding taxes, social security, unemployment taxes, and state disability payments. All other deductions, such as medical-insurance premiums, life-insurance premiums, 401(k) contributions, or other employee paid benefits, require the advance written consent of the employee. You generally can't automatically deduct the costs to cover breakage, shortages in cash register receipts, or other job-related losses from an employee's paycheck.

Getting a compensation philosophy

If your company doesn't already have one, you need to formulate a compensation philosophy — a well thought-out, strategically driven set of criteria that becomes the basis for wage and salary decisions. Some questions you may want to ask yourself as you formulate this philosophy include

✔ Are you going to make your basic salaries simply competitive with the going rate for employers in your area or higher?

✔ Are you going to establish a structured pay scale for specific jobs in your company, or are you going to set salaries on an individual basis, based on the qualities and potential of the person filling the job?

✔ To what extent are the monetary rewards you offer your employees going to take the form of salary, performance bonuses, or benefits?

✔ Are salaries based on how well people perform or on other factors, such as how long they stay with you or what credentials they bring to the job?

✔ Are you going to award bonuses on the basis of individual performance, tie bonuses to company results, or use a combination of the two?

The payroll/sales ratio: What's an optimal balance?

Regardless of the compensation system you set up, you must make sure that your company can afford to carry the costs. No optimal ratio exists between payroll costs and revenues, but whatever you decide needs to be a structure that you can handle comfortably. Employees need to feel that their salaries are reasonably well insulated from the ups and downs of your business. Given a choice, most employees may be willing to take home a little less on a yearly basis (within reason) in exchange for the reassurance that they're going to receive their pay regularly throughout the year.

Most business consultants tell you that the key issue in determining an appropriate cost/revenue ratio is how much of a profit margin you realize on your products or services. Companies that operate on relatively high margins (50 percent or higher) can absorb higher payroll costs than can companies operating on smaller margins. According to a 2005 WorldatWork research project, payroll expenses (including benefits and taxes) run about 20 to 30 percent of total revenues in manufacturing industries and can reach as high as 80 percent in service industries. Finding out what your competitors are doing in this area pays off.

Keep in mind that no specific answers are right or wrong for every situation. What's important is that your compensation philosophy take into account your company's mission and goals. If your goal is to become the dominant company in your industry within five years, you probably must offer attractive wage-and-benefit packages to attract the people who can fuel your growth. And you may need to pay highly talented employees a little more than market value today so that you can reap the benefit of their contributions three or four years from now. If your goal is to improve productivity, you most likely want to tie compensation to performance and productivity. You start with your goals and work upward.

Setting pay levels in your organization

One of the fundamental tasks in any effort to create an equitable and effective wage and compensation system is to develop a consistent protocol for setting pay levels for each of the jobs in your organization. The more essential a job is to the fundamental mission of your company, the higher its pay range is likely to be.

The following procedure can help you determine some preliminary answers to this fundamental question:

1. **Make a list of all the jobs in your company, from the most senior to the least senior employee.**

2. **Group the jobs by major function — management, administrative, production, and so on.**

3. **Working on your own or with other managers, rank the jobs according to their relationship to your company's mission.**

   You wind up with two major categories — those jobs that contribute directly to the mission and those jobs that provide support for those mission-critical jobs. Following are some questions to ask yourself in making this particular distinction:

   - How closely does the job relate to our mission?

   - How indispensable is the job?

   - How difficult is the job — that is, does it require employees with special skills or training?

   - Does the position generate revenue or support revenue-producing functions?

   - Do political or other factors make this job important?

   Eventually, you produce a ranking or hierarchy of positions. Keep in mind that you're not rating individuals. You're rating the relative importance of each job with respect to your company's mission and strategic goals.

In setting the actual pay scale for specific jobs, you have several options, as the following sections describe.

Job evaluation and pay grading

How this approach works: You look at each job in your company and evaluate it on the basis of several factors, such as relative value to the bottom line, complexity, hazards, required credentials, and so on. A classic example of the traditional job-evaluation and pay-grade system is employed by the Department of Defense's Defense Logistics Information Service (DLIS). Most DLIS jobs fit into one of 15 numerical grade levels. This system keys the pay scale to the job level, and employees at those levels receive their pay accordingly. In the process, you create a measure of internal equity that contributes to each employee feeling that he or she is being treated fairly.

The rationale: In large companies, you must use a reasonably structured approach to deciding what pay range to apply to each job. Otherwise, you invite chaos. The more systematic you are as you develop that structure, the more effective the system is likely to be.

The downside: Creating and maintaining a structure of this nature takes a lot of time and effort. Compensation systems that you key primarily to the job (or grade) and not the person or the performance are currently out of fashion.

The going rate

How this approach works: You look at what other companies in your industry (and region) pay people for comparable jobs and set up your pay structure accordingly. You can obtain this data from government and industry Web sites and publications. Robert Half International (www.rhi.com) publishes a variety of salary guides focusing on professional disciplines like accounting and finance, law, technology, advertising and marketing, and the administrative field.

Rationale: The laws of supply and demand directly affect salary levels. Salaries in Stamford, Conn., and Richmond, Va., for example, are on average similar for the same job, although the cost of living in Stamford at the same time is 30 to 40 percent higher than in Richmond. Why? Because Stamford has a surplus of white-collar workers not found in Richmond, keeping salaries low. Assuming that you're able to rapidly and constantly discover what other companies pay, this system is fairly easy to set up and administer. Benchmarking salaries (and benefits) is an important way to ensure that you're paying people competitively.

The downside: Comparing even apples to apples can sometimes be difficult in today's job market. Many of new jobs that companies are creating today are actually combinations of jobs in the traditional sense of the word and, as such, can prove difficult to price, going only by how the job functions in other companies are paid, but it is a good starting point.

Management fit

How this approach works: The owner decides arbitrarily how much each employee is paid.

Rationale: The owner of a business has the right to pay people whatever he deems appropriate.

The downside: Inconsistent wage differentials often breed resentment and discontent. Lack of a reasonable degree of internal equity diminishes the spirit of teamwork and fairness.

Collective bargaining

How this approach works: In unionized companies, formal bargaining between management and labor representatives sets wage levels for specific groups of workers, based on market rate, and the employer's resources available to pay wages.

The rationale: Workers should have a strong say (and agree as a group) on how much the company pays them. This system, of course, is (arguably) the ultimate form of establishing internal equity.

The downside: Acrimony arises if management and labor fail to see eye to eye. In addition, someone else — the union — plays a key role in your business decisions. Also, in this system, employees who perform exceptionally well can feel less rewarded because their wages are then the same as less proficient colleagues in similar positions.

Accounting for individuals

You pay people, not positions. So, sooner or later, you must program into your salary decisions those factors that relate solely to the individual performing the job. The following list describes the key "people factors" that you may want to consider in defining your pay-scale structure.

- **Experience and education:** To a certain extent (and in certain occupations more than others), you see a fairly reliable correlation between the productivity of employees and their education levels and experiences. Be careful, however, not to take this principle too far. More experience and more education don't always translate into better work. People who are overqualified for positions, for example, often prove less productive than do their less experienced or not-so-well educated coworkers. The key here is to make sure that a logical connection exists between the employee's education and experience and the basic requirements of the job.

- **Job performance:** You should pay more to workers who produce more — in theory, at least. The challenge is putting this simple practice into practice. To do so effectively, you need to address the following questions:

  - What barometers are you using to measure job performance, and how do they tie in to your strategic objectives? If you're evaluating customer service specialists, for example, are you interested in quantity — the number of inquiries handled in a specific time frame — or are you more concerned about the satisfaction level reported in customer surveys? And if you're evaluating the performance of technical service personnel, are you going to key your pay levels to their technical proficiency or their ability to interact?

  - Who's responsible for measuring performance: Is it the employee's immediate supervisor, or do you use a team-based approach to performance evaluation? And what recourse are you giving employees who take issue with your evaluations? If they don't think the performance criteria are fair, can they take their case to someone other than their supervisor?

- Are the performance criteria you're using to reward performance discriminatory in any way? In other words, does any aspect of your company's job performance criteria favor one gender over another, one age group over another, or one ethnic group over another?

✔ **Seniority:** Length of service has long been a factor in the pay scales in most industries — unionized industries in particular. The rationale is that loyalty is valued and should be rewarded. The downside: No strong evidence suggests that seniority and productivity in any way directly correlate.

✔ **Potential:** Some companies justify higher pay for certain individuals because they consistently demonstrate the potential to become exceptional producers or managers. This consideration is generally why comparatively unskilled, inexperienced college graduates may receive extra compensation if you select them for management-trainee programs.

Thinking about wage plans

One major trend in wage systems of recent years is to base rewards on what employees can do — the skills, knowledge, and talents they bring to the company — and not the nature of the positions they fill. The following sections provide examples of how these approaches are taking shape.

Skill-based pay

Under a *skill-based pay system,* you set pay scales by skill level and not by job title. According to the American Compensation Association (ACA), the professional association of compensation managers, skill-based pay became quite popular in the 1980s, a time when companies were undergoing many changes and the focus of particular jobs was changing frequently. A 1990 ACA survey of 500 manufacturing firms and Fortune 500 service companies revealed that more than half were using some form of skill-based pay. Since then, it's become yet one of many compensation strategies employed by managers seeking to focus job responsibilities and compensation.

How the system usually works: You develop a list of skills that a broadly defined job requires — for example, those for the position of production-team member. You then develop criteria that underlie the mastery of each skill and peg pay increases to each step in the relevant skill ladder. The number and kinds of skills vary, of course, from company to company and from job to job. Generally, however, you can reasonably expect employees to pick up between five and ten new skills over a two- to five-year period — and to reward them accordingly.

Advantages:

✔ Lets you hire new employees at below-market rates with the promise that their pay is going to rise above the market rate as they master new skills.

✔ Provides strong incentive for employees to improve their job-related skills.

✔ Often results in higher levels of quality and production.

✔ Increases workforce flexibility and gives employees a good deal of power over the level of their base pay. (The quicker they master skills, the sooner they get increases.)

✔ Well suited to team-based organizations.

Disadvantages:

✔ Setting up the system takes time and care and may require the hiring of outside consultants.

✔ Implementing the program requires monitoring and vigilance. The process works only if everyone, from top management down, buys into it.

✔ After an employee tops out on the skills ladder, pay levels stagnate, which can produce morale problems if you don't make other arrangements.

✔ Rarely compatible with labor union contracts, most of which base wage "step-ups" on job title and seniority.

✔ If your company's required skills sets change rapidly, you must continuously reinvent the system.

Competency-based pay

Competency-based pay systems base compensation on an employee's traits or characteristics instead of on specific skills. Competency-based systems are traditionally limited to exempt employees, but in recent years, situations have also come up where it's relevant for nonexempt employees (such as when they're working on a team devoted to a specific project).

How the system usually works: A list of core competencies is developed for each job, and you base salary and subsequent raises on how well employees acquire those competencies. An advertising firm, for example, may look at what it perceives as the "ideal" account executive to determine what makes any account executive outstanding. These elements may include the ability to manage accounts or coordinate creative efforts. The agency then pays each account executive on the basis of how that account executive measures up in any particular competency.

Advantages:

- ✔ It creates incentives for sustained improved performance.
- ✔ It appeals to high performers who want you to pay them on the basis of what they contribute and not on seniority.

Disadvantages:

- ✔ It's very tricky to develop and administer. Everyone must generally accept the competencies you choose, or they're likely to perceive the system as subjective and unfair.
- ✔ It's incompatible with virtually all existing labor contracts, including those covering such professionals as teachers, journalists, and government employees.
- ✔ You must define competencies carefully (not an easy task) to avoid potential discrimination charges.

Broadbanding

With *broadbanding,* you reduce a lengthy series of narrowly defined base-pay categories to a few broad ranges.

How the system usually works: You boil down a cluster of related jobs into one pay *band.* Example: You currently have nine different job titles and pay groups for your administrative staff (office assistant, office manager, receptionist, executive assistant, administrative assistant, and senior administrative assistant) with base salaries ranging from $22,000 to $42,000 a year, depending on job title. Under broadbanding, you would eliminate all the job titles and salary ranges and combine everything into one band — administrative staff — with the same overall pay range as before, but with no hard-wired connection between specific salaries and job titles.

Keep in mind that the actual salaries you pay don't change: You may still have one person earning, say, $40,000 and another earning, say, $25,000. On the other hand, managers now have the option of basing pay on factors that are based on job performance or some other criteria, as opposed to the title of the job. Managers also have the option of moving employees around as the work requires, according to the employees' skills, without needing to worry about job titles.

Advantages:

- ✔ Gives managers flexibility in setting base salaries and work assignments.
- ✔ Eliminates bureaucratic barriers to transfers and employee development (job titles, and so on).
- ✔ Eliminates unnecessary distinctions between similar jobs.
- ✔ Lets managers reward superior performance more easily.

Disadvantages:

- ✔ May prove disconcerting to long-time employees who may see broadbanding as a threat to their status.
- ✔ Can result in inconsistent compensation decisions across departments.
- ✔ Unless guidelines are clearly established, management can be open to charges of favoritism or discrimination.
- ✔ In unionized industries, you can implement the system only through collective bargaining.

Variable pay system

Variable pay systems link a percentage of an employee's pay to defined performance and accomplishments.

How the system usually works: You establish a base pay rate and define group and individual objectives as a variable salary component. Some systems set base pay at about 80 percent of the possible compensation under the variable system. You can base proportions of the variable component on departmental or company objectives and on individual achievement.

Advantages:

- ✔ It imposes a direct relationship between pay and production.
- ✔ It guarantees employees a stable base income while providing incentives for superior performance.

Disadvantages:

- ✔ If employees can't meet performance targets, can lead to morale problems in an economic downturn.
- ✔ It can result in unequal pay among workers doing essentially the same jobs.
- ✔ It can prove exceptionally labor-intensive to administer.

Exempt and Nonexempt: Why the Distinction Matters

One of the main purposes of the Fair Labor Standards Act, enacted in 1938 and amended frequently since then, is to ensure that employers pay American workers a certain minimum hourly wage and compensate them appropriately (usually time-and-a-half) if they work more than 40 hours a week. Thus were born the two main employee distinctions in the workplace, exempt and nonexempt. The key difference between these two classifications is that *exempt* workers receive a flat weekly, monthly, or yearly salary, independent of the number of hours they work during any given week or month, while you pay *nonexempt* workers on an hourly basis (although some receive salaries). Nonexempt workers, however, are to receive overtime pay if the number of hours in their work week exceeds 40.

Who's exempt and why?

The exempt/nonexempt distinction is extremely subjective. Supervision of staff, management of a budget, or authority to do something outside of written guidelines, for example, can make a position exempt, while administrative work, filling out forms, or doing work that doesn't require judgments outside of specific guidelines can cause a position to be nonexempt.

If the labor authorities overturn your classification of a long-time employee as exempt, you become responsible for all the overtime pay that employee is due, going back two or three years of the individual's employment. This back pay can prove a substantial amount of money. How you choose to classify your workers can be a complicated affair depending on what industry you are in. Your best bet is to consult the labor authorities in your area or an attorney if you have any questions at all. Failing to properly compensate your workers can lead to serious repercussions.

An employee can't waive her right to overtime. So even a signed agreement with the employee stating that she isn't to receive overtime is meaningless. The employee can later claim that nonexempt status.

Bear in mind the following guidelines as you're classifying workers:

- **Don't rely on job descriptions and titles.** Remember that what people do and not what you call them is what counts the most in complying with FLSA regulations. If a certain job has been around for a while, its title may stay the same even though its duties change.

- **Analyze jobs to determine actual duties.** Focus on day-to-day activities and correlate them with the requirements of the law. Compare what the employee actually does with the formal job description. Lawsuits can arise as a result of conflict between the two.

- **Correct problems when you find them.** Don't wait for a lawsuit to drop in your lap or a government inspector — municipal, state, or federal — to walk in the door. The cost can be steep: A person who willfully violates FLSA regulations can be fined as much as $10,000 and imprisoned for as long as six months. And keep in mind that in many cases, state rules take precedence over laws established by the federal government.

✔ **Keep accurate records.** You need to keep timesheets for all nonexempt employees. If a dispute arises as to whether an employee worked overtime, the employee is probably going to win unless the company can produce an employee-completed time sheet.

The bottom line on overtime

Overtime seems an integral part of today's nonexempt jobs, and employees in many industries depend on the extra money they make in overtime wages to support their standard of living. No one disputes that overtime certainly makes sense in many situations. The question you need to ask yourself is whether overtime is the best option for your company in any given situation. The question doesn't lend itself to a from-the-hip answer, but the following list describes basic truths about overtime:

✔ Responding to increased demand by putting existing workers on overtime is less expensive than hiring new employees, which results in paying additional benefits and payroll taxes.

✔ Of course, cost savings from using overtime are true only for a short period of time. A steady diet of overtime to increase production can have negative long-term consequences. Numerous studies have demonstrated that excessive, long-term overtime can increase the rate of on-the-job accidents, erode employee morale, and cause family pressures.

✔ You're best off viewing overtime as a stop-gap strategy, reserving it for short-term situations, such as when people call in sick or take vacations or when the workload increases in the short term. If the need becomes constant, consider adding a new employee or filling the gap by using contingent workers (see Chapter 13).

Other legal considerations

The following list gives you a brief look at federal laws that affect how and how much you pay your workers (and don't forget to check your local and state regulations, too):

✔ **The Equal Pay Act of 1963:** This law prohibits unequal payments to men and women doing the same job, assuming that the jobs require equal skill, effort, and responsibility and that employees perform the jobs under similar conditions. Most states have similar statutes. The law permits a few exceptions, such as seniority, merit pay, or productivity, so check with a lawyer.

✔ **Civil Rights Acts of 1964:** Title VII of this law prohibits wage discrimination on the basis of race, sex, color, religion, or national origin. The U.S. Equal Employment Opportunity Commission (EEOC) enforces this law.

✔ **Age Discrimination in Employment Act of 1967:** As amended in 1978, this law bans wage discrimination based on age 40 or older, including pay increases, bonuses, and employee benefits. One of the most common violations is the denial of pay increases to people nearing retirement to avoid increasing retirement benefits that are based on an employee's salary. The EEOC enforces this law, too.

✔ **The Americans with Disabilities Act of 1990:** This law prohibits discrimination in compensation, including access to insurance, against qualified disabled workers.

✔ **Davis-Bacon Act of 1931, the Copeland Act of 1934, the Walsh-Healey Act of 1936, and the Anti-Kickback Act of 1948:** These four laws focus, in different ways, on the compensation policies of companies with federal contracts. Each law has it own wrinkle, but the basic purpose is to ensure that employers pay prevailing wages and overtime and prohibit excessive wage deductions and under-the-table payments by employees to obtain work.

✔ **The Wage Garnishment Law:** This law prohibits employers from firing workers whose wages, for whatever reason, are subject to garnishment by creditors or spouse for any one indebtedness and also limits garnishments in most cases to no more than 25 percent of an employee's take-home pay.

For more information on the first four laws, see Chapter 2.

What You Need to Know about Raises, Bonuses, and Incentives

Offering competitive compensation is key in attracting top talent to your organization, but once employees are on board, salary levels don't stay competitive for long. As staff develop new skills and increase their knowledge of your business, they become more and more valuable to you — and their value in the marketplace increases as well, meaning that they become attractive targets for other companies. To keep your best and brightest, you need to figure out fair (and affordable) ways to augment what you pay them. Most companies enhance their compensation through raises, bonuses, and incentives designed to retain their best workers and give them a reason to stay on.

Employers structure effective bonus and incentive programs around the following main principles:

✔ **Results-oriented:** Employees must accomplish something to receive a bonus.

✔ **Fair:** The rules for bonuses are clear, and you enforce them equitably.

✔ **Competitive:** The program rewards extra effort and superior performance.

Pay raises

Traditional pay systems often link raises to *tenure* (that is, time spent in that grade or position). Other systems frequently tie raises to performance. The most common types of raises include

✔ **Seniority step-ups:** These types of raises usually depend solely on an employee's length of service and are pretty much automatic. Such raises are a common feature of union contracts.

✔ **Merit raise:** These raises are increases for superior performance, usually as a formal performance evaluation system measures it, but sometimes driven by other considerations, such as attainment of an educational or training objective.

✔ **Productivity increases:** These raises generally involve increasing pay after employees exceed a certain norm — a production quota, for example. These systems usually apply to production or assembly workers or to clerical workers performing repetitive tasks.

Bonuses

Bonuses are one-shot payments that you always key to results: the company's, the employee's, or those of the employee's department. They come in a variety of flavors:

✔ **Annual and bi-annual bonuses:** These bonuses are one-shot payments to all eligible employees, based on the company's results, individual performance, or a combination thereof.

✔ **Spot bonuses:** Spot bonuses are awarded in direct response to a single instance of superior employee performance (an employee suggestion, for example). Employees receive the bonus on the spot — that is, at the time of, or immediately thereafter, the action that has earned the bonus.

✔ **Retention bonuses:** You make such payments to persuade key people to stay with your company. These bonuses are common in industries that employ hard-to-recruit specialists or to retain top managers or star performers.

✔ **Team bonuses:** These bonuses are awarded to group members for the collective success of their team.

Merit raises: What should you peg them to?

You should always key merit pay to a fair and consistent performance evaluation system (see Chapter 15). The key decision you often must make (or help others make) is whether you're going to peg performance standards to company performance or to departmental performance. Companywide merit pay systems are the rule traditionally, but managers in many firms have discretion to make individual salary increases that are outside the range if they feel someone's salary isn't competitive with market conditions or a strong performer is at risk of being recruited away. This increasingly popular method of allocating annual raises works something like this:

Mary Allen has 20 employees in her department. The company allocates her enough money to give each employee a 4 percent increase, based on the group's current salary dollar total. She may decide to give a 4 percent boost to the majority of the team because that is the general guidance from management. But she may decide to give superior performers more than 4 percent and underperformers less — or even

no raise at all. For example, 12 employees may receive 4 percent, 4 employees 6 percent, and 4 employees only 2 percent.

You need to set up merit-pay systems with the following principles in mind:

✔ You need to have a workable employee-appraisal system in place, and managers and supervisors must know how to implement it.

✔ Individual differences in performance must be large enough that you can measure them and significant enough to be worth extra pay.

✔ Merit pay increases must be large enough to be of value to the employee.

✔ Senior management must commit to an honest and equitable administration of the system.

✔ Employees must accept the principle of distinctions in pay based on performance. Merit-pay systems are especially contentious in highly unionized industries, where raises based on job title and seniority are more the norm.

Incentives

Incentives are like bonuses in that they don't increase base pay. The difference is that most incentive programs, unlike bonuses, are often long term in nature to cement employee loyalty or spur productivity. The following sections outline some common incentive programs.

Profit-sharing plans

Profit-sharing plans enable the company to set aside a percentage of its profits for distribution to employees. If profits go up, the employees get more money. You can focus these programs very sharply by allocating the profit sharing on a department or business-unit basis.

According to U.S. Chamber of Commerce's Employee Benefits Survey, since 1963, approximately one in five U.S. companies offer employees some form of profit sharing. Employees who stand to share in the company's profits have an extra incentive to work hard and be more aware of avoiding waste and inefficiency. After all, it's their business, too.

Profit-sharing plans fall into one of two categories: a *cash plan,* in which payments are distributed quarterly or annually, and a *deferred plan,* in which the company invests the profit-sharing payment in a fund and then pays out an employee's share if he retires or leaves the company. Deferred plans offer significant tax advantages to both the company and the employees. On the downside, deferred plans can have less effect on productivity: In some cases, the worker doesn't actually see the profit-sharing money, except as a figure on paper, until retirement.

Stock

Stock in the company is an incentive that publicly traded firms (or firms planning to go public) may choose to offer their employees. *Stock option* plans give employees at publicly held companies the right to purchase shares in the company at a time of their own choosing, but at a price that is set at the time the option is awarded. Employees are under no obligation to exercise that option, but should the stock go up, employees can buy the stock at the cheaper price and either hold on to it or sell it for the current value, thereby earning a profit.

Stock options have also given small, growing companies a way to attract top talent without having to pay high salaries. In the 1990s, these plans became commonplace in fast-growth industries such as technology.

If your company is thinking about offering stock options as part of your overall benefits package, there are certain aspects of the process everyone must be aware of. If you're a privately held company, for example, your employees need to recognize that a stock option plan isn't likely to mean anything to them unless your company goes public or is acquired. If you're publicly held, you need to make sure that you have an organized plan and some mechanisms in place that will not dilute the value of the stock to non-employee stockholders. Bear in mind, too, that these programs must comply with tax laws and also with the Securities and Exchange Commission (SEC) regulations.

Another major legal factor to take into account is that stock options must now be counted as a corporate expense, a change in law that has led many companies to offer fewer or no stock options to employees than they had in previous years. Get thorough legal and tax advice before you put together any sort of stock option plan.

Some other considerations you need to bear in mind about stock option plans:

- ✔ Most stock option plans include some form of *vesting,* meaning that options may not be exercised until an employee has been with the company for a specified period of time. Vesting is a retention strategy by the company.

- ✔ Most stock option plans set an expiration date, a point beyond which employees can no longer exercise options.

- ✔ Most plans require the approval of current shareholders.

- ✔ The plan you adopt may obligate you to provide periodic financial information and reports to option holders.

Many companies that eliminated stock options are instead offering *restricted stock* to their employees. Restricted stock is ownership in a company with rights to vote and receive dividends without the right to transfer or sell the shares until the shares are vested. Once the vesting conditions have been satisfied, the shares are employees' to hold, transfer or sell as they desire, subject to applicable securities laws and payment of withholding taxes and applicable commissions.

What's the difference between stock options and restricted stock? Basically, when a stock option vests, employees don't own any company stock until they exercise the option and purchase the stock. Once a restricted stock grant vests, however, employees automatically own the stock and can keep or sell it at their discretion. While they need to pay withholding taxes, they don't have to pay an exercise price as they would with stock options. As a recipient of restricted stock, they also are immediately eligible to receive any dividends declared by the company.

What's fair versus what works?

The easiest way to start a mutiny among your employees is to institute a raise or bonus process that people don't clearly understand and that neither managers nor employees buy into. The following list offers guidelines to help you avoid this all-too-common pitfall:

- ✔ **Set clear rules.** Whether you're dealing with an incentive system or a merit-raise program, everyone must clearly understand the rules concerning how you give out the rewards. The key information includes who's eligible for the program, what they must do to receive the reward, who decides on those who benefit, and how much the reward is.

✔ **Set specific targets or goals that you can quantify.** If you're going to establish incentives, make sure that you set a specific target: "125 percent of our annual sales quota," for example, or "more than 500 pieces per day." Specific numbers eliminate arguments and misunderstandings.

✔ **Make the goal worthwhile.** If the incentives aren't attractive, they're not incentives. So gear the reward to the group whose performance you're seeking to enhance. Think about setting up different rewards for varying levels of achievement: 4 percent increase, for example, for an "average" performer and, say, 8 percent for a top performer.

✔ **Don't ask for the impossible.** Such terms as "killer goals" may sound motivational, but if employees perceive incentive targets as being unattainable, you merely discourage them from striving for the rewards, and you also lose credibility with them.

✔ **Don't make promises you can't keep**. Never promise a bonus or incentive you're not sure that you can afford.

Communicate Your Policies

Many companies unfortunately spend a lot of time and effort designing a pay system and then leave it to the paycheck alone to communicate their pay philosophy and administration. Silence is not necessarily golden in promoting compensation policies. You need to thoroughly brief managers and supervisors in particular on your company's pay systems so that they can effectively explain, administer, and support your policies. Managers and supervisors need to possess the following information:

✔ Your company's pay philosophy.

✔ How to conduct a performance appraisal, if your company has such a system. (Many smaller companies may not have a formal system for performance appraisals.) I cover this topic extensively in Chapter 15.

✔ How to handle and refer employee pay complaints.

✔ Legal implications of all compensation policies.

You need to advise employees of the company's pay policies and how these policies affect them individually. You also need to communicate and fully explain any changes in these policies promptly. Employees need to possess the following information:

✔ The job's rating system, how it works, and how it affects them.

✔ How the performance-appraisal and incentive systems work.

✔ How they can raise their own income through performance and promotion.

✔ How to voice complaints or concerns.

You must keep your compensation system competitive and up-to-date. The key steps in doing so are as follows:

✔ Obtain and review competitive data at regular intervals.

✔ Review — and adjust if necessary — salary ranges at least annually.

✔ Review job descriptions regularly and make adjustments based on disparities between actual work performance and the formal description.

✔ Evaluate the performance-appraisal system. One common problem is that too many employees get superior ratings.

✔ Review salary systems in terms of your company's financial condition to determine whether the system is in line with the company's financial health and is tax-effective and efficient.

✔ Periodically measure and rate productivity and determine whether any links exist between productivity increases (or declines) and pay policies.

Chapter 11

Creating the Right Benefits Package

. . . .

. . . .

Managing the benefits side of the HR function today is a far cry from the way it was 50 or so years ago when the typical company benefits package was a one-size-fits-all healthcare and pension plan. You have a lot more to think about these days when you're administering benefits — more administrative details, more pressure to reconcile employee desires with the financial realities of your business, and more government regulation.

Much of this increased complexity is due to the changing face of the workplace. Today's diverse workforce has diverse needs, and this diversity extends to the benefits they want. Add to this a wide range of laws and healthcare and retirement plan options, and you quickly see how complicated it can be to create and implement effective benefits programs.

As challenging as all these factors seem at first glance, you have opportunity here as well. Once you get your arms around this area of human resources, you can do a great deal of good for your employees, your company, and yourself. And, best of all, if you know what you're doing in building and promoting a competitive benefits package, you can greatly strengthen your company's ability to attract and retain top talent.

What's a Benefit Anyway?

Strictly speaking, you can define a *benefit* as any form of compensation that isn't part of an employee's basic pay — and that isn't tied directly to either the requirements of their jobs or their performance in those jobs.

Specific employee benefits today take a multitude of forms — everything from the basics that you find in every benefits package (Social Security, workers' compensation, and unemployment insurance) to highly specialized offerings ranging from multiple-option healthcare coverage, tuition reimbursement, and childcare and eldercare assistance at one end of the spectrum to in-house concierge services, health club memberships, and on-site auto repair and detailing services at the far end of the spectrum. Exactly which benefits you offer and how much of your payroll expense goes to pay for benefits are decisions that your company's financial health and business philosophy must determine. Your job in taking on the HR function is to make sure that both your company and its employees are getting the best bang for their benefits buck.

Key Trends in Benefits Management

Much is going on today in the rapidly changing world of benefits administration. The following list provides you with a quick glimpse at four key trends:

- **Changing the definition of employee:** Demographic changes in the American workplace in the past 25 years have affected both the number and the nature of the offerings that you now find in the typical benefits package. Trends such as delayed retirement, second careers, and increased longevity mean that the age continuum of workers is greater than ever before. As a result, today marks the first time that four generations are working side by side in the workplace. This shift, as well as the growth of dual-income couples, domestic partners, and single-parent households, coupled with alternative work arrangements such as telecommuting, have drastically changed the profile of a typical employee and his expectations of a company benefits program.

    Most large companies are well aware of the incredible diversity shaping today's workplace and in response now offer flexible, or *cafeteria benefits,* which give employees a menu of choices instead of the traditional "one-size-fits all" approach. The plus side of this trend is that employees are clearly happier when they can tailor their benefits package to their specific needs. The downside is that the more choices you give your employees, the more complex your benefits plan becomes to administer.

- **Containing costs:** To offset the rising cost of employee benefits, more and more companies these days are asking employees to assume a larger portion of the overall benefits tab. For example, in the all-important realm of healthcare costs, the typical employee's contribution has risen considerably. Research from the National Coalition on Healthcare estimates that the average employee contribution to company-provided health insurance has increased more than 143 percent since the year 2000. To ease the sting of increased employee payments, progressive companies have introduced so-called *lifestyle benefits* — relatively inexpensive rewards or services, such as concierge services, that make life a little easier for employees but avoid substantial costs.

✔ **Home-based employees:** As the telecommuter population increases, a new need has surfaced — benefits geared specifically for people who divide their work time between the office and home. The biggest can of worms you face in this situation is how to structure a work-related injury- or illness-insurance program that accounts for the possibility that "on-the-job" injuries can now occur in an employee's home. The likely resolution? Hybrid policies that combine traditional workers' compensation policies with disability insurance.

✔ **Uncle Sam is watching:** In recent years, Congress and state legislative bodies have taken a more active role than ever in regulating many basic benefits policies, especially health insurance and 401(k) retirement and pension plans. In large part, increasing government involvement is a response to the well-publicized financial misconduct within some companies that triggered the failure of their pension plans. The most worrisome possibility on the horizon consists of potential lawsuits from employees who may claim that the company's healthcare provider failed to provide adequate medical care. Amid this environment, corporations need to be proactive in communicating the ins and outs of their benefits plans to employees.

The Basics of Benefits Coverage

Most employee benefits are voluntary: You're under no legal obligation to provide them. Three notable exceptions to this rule are *Social Security* and *Medicare, workers' compensation*, and *unemployment insurance*. The following sections take a brief look at each program.

See the CD-ROM for an Employee Statement of Benefits form.

Social Security and Medicare

Purpose: The Social Security system was originally designed to provide basic retirement income for all workers who have contributed to the plan and to provide healthcare benefits to Americans who are age 65 or older or become disabled. You and your employees may be eligible to begin receiving payments as early as age 62, but keep in mind that the benefit will be reduced permanently. On the other hand, if an individual delays in applying for this benefit past the age of eligibility, the benefit will increase. In 2003, the age of eligibility for full retirement began to increase gradually. People born between 1943 and 1954 must be 66 to quality for a complete retirement benefit. By the year 2025, the retirement age for full benefits will be 67.

Another key part of Social Security is *Medicare,* a federal health insurance program for people 65 and over. Beginning in 2006, the government passed laws reducing the cost of prescription drugs for those covered by Medicare.

How the system works: Payroll taxes finance Social Security and Medicare. Your employees typically surrender 7.65 percent of their gross take-home pay to fund both programs, and federal law obligates your company to match that amount. (Self-employed workers pay 15.3 percent.) The first 6.2 percent of the tax that goes to the Social Security fund is assessed only up to a specific income ceiling — \$94,200 in 2006. Any income over that limit isn't subject to Social Security tax. No ceiling exists, at present, on the 1.45 percent Medicare tax. Keep in mind, however, that these rules are subject to change.

Unemployment insurance

Purpose: *Unemployment insurance* provides basic income for workers who become unemployed through no fault of their own.

How the system works: The individual states run the unemployment insurance program, which was established as part of the 1935 Social Security Act, under loose federal guidelines. Except in a handful of states (Alaska, Pennsylvania, and New Jersey) that expect employees to pay a small percentage of the cost, employers pay for their workers' unemployment insurance. The cost to employers is generally based on the company's experience rating — how frequently its former employees receive payments through the program. The more people you lay off, the greater your potential assessment becomes.

Let employees know who's paying

Social Security, unemployment insurance, and workers' compensation are so common that your employees probably don't consider these programs as "benefits" and don't realize how much your company is paying on their behalf. You may want to list your company's contributions to Social Security, unemployment, and disability insurance annually right on the employee's pay stub, next to deductions from the employee's gross pay. If you contract out your payroll, your contractor may already have the software to do so.

Pitfalls and problems with workers' comp

The administrative nuts and bolts of Social Security and unemployment compensation are fairly straightforward. The payments and programs are well defined, and most employees understand both programs. Workers' compensation, however, is more complicated. The following list describes some issues that you need to watch out for in administering your company's workers' compensation program:

✔ **Matters of state:** If your company operates in more than one state, you must adjust your workers' compensation policies according to local rules. If you run into legal problems, you most likely must retain lawyers licensed to practice in the states in which the problems arise.

✔ **Expanding standards:** The definition of "work-related" illness has been expanding in recent years; some states are now permitting workers' compensation claims for psychological disorders, such as anxiety or depression, or chronic physical conditions, such as heart disease. As technology products such as laptop computers have become more prevalent, another source of concern is the rise in the number of repetitive-action medical conditions, such as carpal tunnel syndrome.

✔ **Fraudulent claims:** Fraudulent workers' compensation claims are one principal reason that costs for workers' compensation insurance in some states are rising. If you suspect fraud and have reasonable grounds for your suspicions, contact an attorney immediately.

✔ **Legal exposure:** Workers' compensation, contrary to what many people believe, doesn't automatically protect your company from lawsuits arising out of employer negligence. Exceptions vary from state to state. What's more, an excess number of workers' compensation claims by your employees may lead to your company being subject to prosecution and fines by state and federal agencies.

The experience-rating method of calculating employer unemployment costs is yet another reason for your company to avoid cycles of new hires in flush times and layoffs whenever demand sags, as well as a good reason to use contingent employees during times of reduced business or to handle normal workload peaks and valleys. It's also important for a company to regularly pay unemployment insurance taxes. This fact may seem obvious, but in recent years, a number of companies have behaved illegally.

Workers' compensation

Purpose: *Workers' compensation* provides protection for workers who suffer injuries or become ill on the job regardless of whether the employee or the employer was negligent. It pays medical bills, provides disability payments (income replacement) for permanent injuries, and pays out lump-sum death benefits.

How the system works: Workers' compensation is an insurance program. Depending on the state in which you work, your company contributes to a state fund, a private insurance fund, or a mixture of both. Some states permit private insurance, so if your company can demonstrate financial capability to state authorities, you may choose to be self-insured. Other states require you to contribute to one state-managed fund or permit a mixture of state and private insurance. Generally, however, contributory systems are *experience-rated:* the number of claims that employees file against your company determines your rates. Good workplace health and safety practices, therefore, pay off.

Some employers, especially those with large numbers of off-site workers or telecommuters, have integrated workers' compensation programs into health-insurance programs. Keep in mind, though, that certain laws — federal and state — can make such a combination difficult to manage. As with other areas surrounding employees who work away from a specific office, thoroughly explore this option with an attorney.

If you include the 50 states, the District of Columbia, Puerto Rico, and the Virgin Islands, at least 53 separate workers' compensation programs currently exist. You need to consult with your lawyer, insurance carrier, and state officials to determine your own liability. Workers' compensation, with very limited exceptions, is a no-fault system; no matter who's to blame for the illness or injury, it still covers the employee.

A Healthy Approach to Insurance

Health insurance is today's most expensive employee benefit. Without a doubt, it's also the most difficult benefit to administer, not just because of its cost but also because of the many options available and the challenges companies face balancing two seemingly contradictory objectives: keeping costs down while at the same time meeting employee needs.

A bird's eye view of the options

The number of individual healthcare plans available today is enough to fill a book — a book that, given the changing world of healthcare, would no doubt go out of date quite quickly. Following is a bit of information on the three most prevalent healthcare plan options. Bear in mind that these options (in fact, the entire structure of employer-provided healthcare) may change rapidly, given the pressure for companies to control healthcare costs:

- ✔ **Fee-for-service (indemnity plans):** *Fee-for-service plans* are insurance programs that reimburse members for defined benefits, regardless of which practitioner or hospital delivers the service. Under some fee-for-service arrangements, members pay the bills themselves and then submit their claims to the carrier for reimbursement. Under other plans, the physicians or hospitals assume the responsibility for filing and collecting on claims.

Fee-for-service plans have two fundamental parts — the Base Plan and Major Medical. The *Base Plan* covers certain "defined" services, usually in connection with hospitalization — an appendectomy, for example, but not routine mole removal. *Major Medical* — an option — covers such services as routine doctors' visits and certain tests.

✔ **Health Maintenance Organizations (HMOs):** *Health Maintenance Organizations* (more commonly known as HMOs) offer a wide range of medical services but limit your choices (both in medical practitioners and facilities) to those specialists or organizations that are part of the HMO network. Each person that the plan covers must choose a primary physician (sometimes known as the *gatekeeper*), who decides whether a member needs to seek specialty services within the network or services outside the network. As long as employees stay "within the network" (that is, they use only those facilities and medical practitioners who are part of the HMO network), the only additional cost to them if they undergo any procedure that the plan covers is a modest copayment. HMOs differ in their out-of-network policies. Some are highly restrictive. Others allow members to seek care outside the network but only with the approval of the gatekeeper; members who use approved services outside the network may also assume additional costs (up to a predefined deductible) for each out-of-network visit.

✔ **Preferred Provider Organizations (PPOs):** *Preferred Provider Organizations* (or PPOs) are similar to HMOs but with two key differences: Employees have a wider range of choices as to whom they can see if they experience a medical problem, and PPOs typically require no gatekeeper — members can go outside the network as long as they're willing to assume the costs, up to the agreed-on deductible. Also, the cost to employees for participating in a PPO is usually more than the cost to participate in a comparable HMO plan.

Weighing the options

In recent years, many companies have altered the options they most favor. The traditional fee-for-service, or indemnity, plans are still available, but most companies today make it most advantageous for employees to elect HMOs and PPOs, which are also known as managed-care programs. HMOs and PPOs provide the same benefits as the traditional fee-for-service plans but set limits on which practitioners and which facilities that employees on the plan can use to receive maximum benefits. Some managed-care programs provide no benefits at all if employees go outside the approved networks.

When deciding which type of plan to carry for your employees, you need to take into account the following factors:

✔ **Extent of coverage:** The procedures that health-insurance plans cover can vary widely, but most plans — both indemnity and managed-care plans — offer the same basic coverage. This coverage includes emergency trips to the hospital, illness-related visits to doctors, most routine tests, most surgical procedures (but not cosmetic surgery), and hospitalization. What varies widely, however, are any "extras" — the extent to which coverage includes, for example, chiropractic care or home nursing, or whether it accommodates long-term needs such as hospitalization for mental illness.

✔ **Quality of care:** The quality of medical services that members of managed-care programs receive has become an issue today for an obvious reason: Employees covered by these plans are obliged to use only those physicians or facilities designated by the plan's administrators. Therefore, you must make sure that any managed-care program you choose has high standards and a quality reputation. In addition, check to see whether the National Committee for Quality Assurance (NCQA) certifies that program at `http://hprc.ncqa.org/cvoResult.asp`.

✔ **Cost:** In shopping for your company's health insurance, keep in mind that you always get exactly what you pay for, regardless of the particular option you choose. Insurers generally base their pricing on three factors: the number of people that the plan covers; the demographics of your workforce (average age, number of children, and so on); and the amount of the deductible and copayment for the plan. The higher the deductible and the more money that members pay for each doctor's visit, the less expensive the premium.

✔ **Ease of administration:** A key factor in your choice of insurance carriers is the ease with which you can administer the program. The best plans, for example, offer an easy-to-use Web site and a 24-hour, 800 number that lets individuals swiftly modify benefit plans or levels. Some plans, on the other hand, curtail costs by shifting much of the administrative burden to you.

While you can save some money by using in-house resources to handle administration, servicing your benefits can require a major commitment of staff time and financial resources. If you decide to assume this responsibility, make sure that you have the administrative ability.

Rising costs: Staying ahead of the game

The good news about contemporary healthcare is that society takes its well-being very seriously. People of all ages are leading healthier and longer lives. But a major part of taking better care of themselves means more trips to doctors for examinations, more preventative procedures, and, when necessary,

Five ways to minimize healthcare costs

Even though it's true you pretty much get what you pay for in a healthcare plan, you can adopt a few strategies that will help you save money without compromising the quality of the medical care received by your employees. Here are five guidelines to keep in mind:

✔ **Affiliate with the largest group possible.** With regard to health-insurance premiums, safety lies in numbers. The larger the group of companies with which you affiliate, the more competitive the rates you're likely to pay. Shopping around pays off. Most local chambers of commerce, for example, offer group plans for member companies. So do most regional business associations and professional organizations.

✔ **Raise the deductible.** Increasing the deductible amount for which employees are responsible for covering on a typical indemnity plan can save you anywhere from 10 percent to 50 percent on premiums, depending on the size of the deductible. Bear in mind, however, that in some states the deductible in your insurance can't exceed $1,000.

✔ **Consider consumer-directed health plans (CDHPs).** CDHPs are a relatively new experiment in determining ways companies may be able to reduce healthcare costs. CDHPs usually consist of a high-deductible medical insurance plan coupled with *health savings accounts* (HSAs). HSAs were created by the Medicare bill signed by President Bush in 2003 and are designed to help individuals save for future qualified medical and retiree health expenses on a tax-free basis. To offer HSAs to employees, you first need to institute an HSA-eligible, high-deductible health plan.

✔ **Manage drug benefits.** Many companies have eliminated copay arrangements for prescription drugs, opting instead for plans that require coinsurance and/or deductibles on a cost-sharing basis. One cost-cutting aspect is to provide preferred coverage for generic drugs. Some plans offer reduced costs to participants who elect home delivery by mail for long-term prescription needs instead of purchasing these items each time at a local pharmacy.

✔ **Consider working with a benefits consultant.** Bringing in an outside benefits expert to analyze your company's healthcare needs and recommend the best approach to health insurance may cost you money in the short run. But the recommendations can more than offset the initial expense. Another option is to find a local insurance agent who specializes in medical insurance and ask that person to recommend the best program. Just make sure that the programs anyone recommends to you have an established track record. Bear in mind, too, that while some benefits consultants charge on an hourly basis, others act as insurance brokers and get a commission (anywhere from 3 percent to 10 percent). If you're a good negotiator, you may persuade the broker to make price concessions.

surgery. All these factors point to a pragmatic financial reality: Healthcare costs will continue rising.

You're right in the thick of this dialogue. In many ways, issues related to healthcare strike right to the core of a company's responsibility for its employees.

And there's no question that, depending on culture, history, and financial resources, different companies approach the matter of healthcare in different ways. Some see increased government involvement as an answer to rising costs. Others point to a benefit realignment in which employees bear most of the responsibility for healthcare costs and provider choices. You need to keep up with all these developments, but also understand what companies are currently doing to contain healthcare costs.

One key step is to encourage employees to stay healthy. Conducting regularly scheduled seminars, distributing literature, and offering a wealth of information on your company's intranet on topics such as stress, nutrition, sleep, and other health-related subjects can go a long way toward decreasing healthcare costs. Some large companies go further, building on-site facilities that offer exercise equipment and even spa services. But smaller firms can take many of these actions, including perhaps discounts on memberships at local health clubs.

This commitment to ensuring a healthy employee base fits in with much of what I cover in Chapter 12. HR can play an important role in creating and nurturing a culture where employees are urged to take good care of themselves. Be on the lookout, for example, for managers and employees who work themselves to the brink of exhaustion and end up getting sick. While dedication is valued, rarely is a short-term productivity gain worth the long-term expense.

Retirement Plans

In recent years, companies have made a major change in the way they structure and manage retirement planning. In the past, employees often spent their entire working lives with one company and received a set pension after they retired. If they changed jobs, they most likely lost all or a significant portion of the pension rights they'd earned at their old companies and had to start all over at the new firm. Employees had no say in how their pension money was invested and generally couldn't increase their contribution to boost retirement income.

But the business environment has changed radically. Rarely do you see cases of one employee working at a single company for an entire career. In response to this dynamic new business culture, retirement plans have become much more flexible and portable. And because many corporate pension plans have failed in recent years, employees are seeking ways to personally remain in control of this important benefit. Here's more on the many available options.

Defined-benefit pension plans

What these plans do: Generally limited to large, established companies, *defined-benefit pension plans* provide a fixed benefit after retirement, usually calculated by a formula that takes into account salary level and length of service. The employer can fully fund these plan *(noncontributory)* or require employee contributions *(contributory)*.

Advantages: Employees can count on a fixed, set amount of retirement income. The plan encourages employee loyalty and retention. Employees generally can make pretax contributions.

Disadvantages: These plans aren't generally portable: Employees can lose some or all benefits by changing jobs. Administrative costs can be high, and pension liabilities can significantly affect a company's balance sheet.

401 (k) plans: Pros and cons

What these plans do: The difference between a *401(k) plan* and a pension plan (see preceding section) is that each participant has his own tax-deferred account and doesn't need to remain with the company to collect the money. In addition, employees can contribute as much as 15 percent of their income into the 401(k) fund, deferring taxes until they withdraw the income. Another key difference between these two types of plans is that 401(k)s generally offer a variety of investment options, from conservative investments to moderately risky equity-oriented mutual funds. Also, employees often may borrow within certain limits against the investment account. Even if employed, withdrawal can start at age 59½.

Advantages: These plans are highly popular with employees; they also offer favorable tax treatment, lower administrative costs (usually), and are highly portable — employees can take most or all funds with them if changing jobs.

Disadvantages: These plans offer no guaranteed payouts. Investment risks fall on employees. Employees face heavy tax penalties (10 percent) for early withdrawals unless for limited reasons, such as disability.

See the CD-ROM for a 401(k) plan summary from the U.S. Department of Labor called "A Look at 401(k) Plan Fees for Employees."

Unfunded plans

In certain cases, the employer can simply set up a plan on an unfunded basis. For example, in return for an executive's reducing her salary 10 percent, the employer may promise an amount equal to this deferral (plus earnings) in the future. Or the employer may promise a pension in addition to that payable from the funded plan generally covering employees.

401(k) plans: Smart shopping tips

These days, many financial institutions — banks, mutual funds, insurance companies, and so on — are aggressively marketing 401(k) plans to employers of all sizes. These organizations usually also handle virtually all administrative details for employers. Finding a 401(k) vendor isn't hard, but finding the best one for your company can be a challenge. Following are some questions for you to ask of any potential 401(k) provider:

✔ Are the management fees reasonable? (Compare them with other plans and find out exactly what you're paying for.)

✔ Are the investment options all from the same family of funds, or can the employee choose individual funds from different companies?

✔ How easily and frequently can employees switch their investments — between an equity and a bond fund, for example? (If they can't change investments at least quarterly, your employees can't stay current with market trends.)

✔ How often do participants receive account statements?

✔ Does the plan offer a full-range of investments from the conservative to the moderately risky? The more choices employees get and the broader the range of those choices, the better the plan is for them.

✔ What's the reputation of the 401(k) plan vendor? How long has the vendor been offering and managing 401(k) plans? How have the investment options in the plan fared against similar options? (Stack the plan's equity funds alongside similar equity funds to see how they compare.)

✔ How good is the vendor's documentation for your employees — its brochures, investment-option explanations, and so on? Keep in mind that many employees require solid, easy-to-understand advice and guidance.

✔ Can the vendor support IRS and Employee Retirement Income Security Act (ERISA) reporting? (See the upcoming section "ERISA and other legal issues.")

✔ Does the provider offer self-service capabilities so that employees can access their accounts online to make changes?

Is an unfunded plan legal? Generally, the answer is yes if it covers only a "select group of management and highly compensated employees" (the terms of the Employee Retirement Income Security Act exception for unfunded plans). Is it desirable? It can be, when the employer doesn't want to benefit a broad group of its employees, unlike a funded plan.

An unfunded plan's benefits can discriminate in favor of highly compensated employees.

ERISA and other legal issues

Your company is under no legal obligation to provide a retirement plan for your employees. If you do offer a plan, however, you're subject to the regulations of ERISA — the Employee Retirement Income Security Act of 1974.

Since its passage, ERISA has created significant administrative requirements that small businesses feel the most. Some of ERISA's provisions have been modified by subsequent laws. In general, these combined retirement regulation laws mandate that any pension or profit-sharing plan you offer meets the following requirements:

✔ The plan can't exclude employees who are older than 21 or require an employee to complete more than one year of service.

✔ Beginning after three years, the plan must permit *graded vesting,* meaning that employees are permitted to own a certain percentage (20 percent is typical) of the employer matching contributions.

✔ After five years, it must permit *cliff vesting,* which is when the employer matching contributions become the complete property of the employee.

✔ You must fund it annually, with funding requirements calculated on the basis of future obligations.

✔ In the case of a pension plan, your company must be part of and pay for ERISA's government insurance fund to protect employees from the possibility of the pension plan dissolving.

✔ No more than 10 percent of the assets in your pension plan can be invested in your company stock.

✔ You must meet ERISA standards for the people who administer the program — for example, persons convicted of certain crimes or violations of ERISA can't administer the program.

✔ Employers must report pension activities to the government and inform employees of their pension rights and the status of their pension plan.

The Rest of the Benefits Smorgasbord

Besides health insurance and retirement plans, businesses frequently offer a number of other benefits. Here's a rundown of the most common benefits and what you should know about them.

Dental insurance

Dental insurance has become an increasingly popular employee benefit in recent years. According to the California Dental Association, more than 48 percent of all Americans — 113 million people — currently have dental insurance. That's nearly ten times as many as had it in 1970. Companies sometimes offer dental care as part of a health-insurance package and sometimes as a separate policy or an add-on. Costs and deductibles vary widely by region and by extent of coverage.

Generally, these plans cover all or part of the cost of routine checkups, fillings, and other regular dental procedures. They may cover orthodontics or extensive restorative dentistry (usually with stated limits). Most dental plans have deductibles and typically require the employee to pay at least 20 percent of the cost of each visit and/or procedure across all services.

Vision care

Most benefit plans usually restrict vision coverage to routine eye exams, and most plans impose a ceiling on how much is covered toward the purchase of eyeglasses. (Your employees can forget the Armani frames unless they pay out of pocket.) These plans, moreover, don't cover serious eye diseases and other conditions that, in most cases, the employee's regular health-insurance policy covers.

Family assistance

The much documented increase in the number of two-income families, single working mothers, domestic partner arrangements, and employees who care for both children and their aging parents has led to an accelerating demand for childcare and eldercare assistance from employers. And you can expect the need to intensify in the years ahead. The following list describes some ways in which companies are providing this benefit:

- **On-site care:** On-site child care is a great idea in theory — the convenience to the working parent is obvious. But only a handful of companies provide a day-care facility at the work location itself. The big problem is cost — liability insurance, in particular. Another obstacle is that state and county authorities extensively regulate on-site child-care centers, including the amount of play area required and the ratio of child-care workers to children.

- **Contracted day-care for children and elders:** This option is much more feasible for many employers but is still considered progressive. The company contracts with one or more outside providers to provide services for both the children and parents of employees. This approach to healthcare is becoming more prevalent, but it carries with it a good deal of responsibility. When your company selects a particular provider, you vouch for that provider's quality of care and services.

- ✔ **Vouchers:** *Vouchers* are simply subsidies that you pay to employees to cover all or part of the cost of outside child care. Voucher systems are the simplest form of child-care assistance to administer.

- ✔ **Dependent Care Reimbursement Accounts:** These accounts enable an employee to use pretax dollars to pay for dependent care. They're subject to both IRS and ERISA regulations. (See the previous section, "ERISA and other legal issues.")

Time off

Although many employees take the practice for granted, paying employees for days they don't work — whether for holidays, vacation, sick days, or personal days — is an important benefit that your employee handbook needs to spell out. Each company has its own philosophy, but the following list offers general observations about paid days off:

- ✔ Most companies provide employees with a fixed number of paid holidays a year, such as New Year's Day, Independence Day, Thanksgiving Day, Christmas Day, and so on.

- ✔ According to a 2005 study of international vacation policies conducted by the Economic Policy Institute, the typical American employee is awarded 8.9 days of vacation time after one year on the job. This figure rises throughout the employee's tenure: 11 days are granted after three years of service, 13.6 after five, and up to 19.2 after 25 years with a single company.

- ✔ Vacation accrual policies differ widely from one company to the next. Some companies enable their employees to bank vacation time, and others require employees to take all vacation during the year in which they earn it. The more popular option is to enable employees to accrue vacation time, but be careful! This policy can leave you with huge liabilities for untaken vacation time that you may need to pay in cash if the employee retires or leaves your company unless you put a cap on the maximum amount that can be accrued.

  The most important point here is that state authorities heavily regulate this matter. In some states, for example, the law requires companies to allow employees who don't use accrued vacation time in a single calendar year to "carry it over" to the next year up until a specified deadline. In other states, the policy is "use it or (eventually) lose it." Make sure that you consult legal counsel regarding your policy.

- ✔ Some companies combine sick time, personal time, and vacation time into a single paid time-off program.

Leaves of absence

A *leave of absence* is an arrangement whereby employees take an extended period of time off (usually without pay) but still maintain their employment status. In other words, they resume their normal duties when the leave is over. Employees either request or are granted leaves of absence for a variety of reasons: maternity, illness, education, travel, military obligations, and so on.

With certain key exceptions (military obligations and situations covered by the Family and Medical Leave Act, for example), the specific policies you adopt regarding leaves of absence aren't subject to federal and local law. It's up to you to determine how long employees can stay away from the job without jeopardizing their employment status. You decide what benefits will be maintained, and what job, if any, will be guaranteed them when the leave is over. Most companies reserve the right to decide these questions on a situation-by-situation basis.

The chief exception to the set-up-your-own-rules aspect of leaves of absence are those leaves that are covered by the Family and Medical Leave Act (FMLA). Under this act, which was passed in 1993, companies with 50 or more people within a 75-mile radius are in many instances obligated by law to grant employees up to 12 weeks unpaid leave per year for any of the following reasons:

- ✔ To care for newly born or newly adopted children (note that this right extends to both parents)
- ✔ To care for a child, parent, or spouse with a serious health condition
- ✔ To attend to a serious health condition that makes the worker unable to perform his or her job

Various states also have additional pregnancy leave requirements. Under FMLA regulations, you must maintain the employee's health coverage under any group health plan for the duration of the unpaid leave, and you must restore the employee to the same or equivalent job when she returns. The law also requires you to post notices advising workers of their rights under the law. Note that some states (California, for example) provide greater benefits to employees.

See the CD-ROM for a Sample FMLA Posting, an Employer Response to Employee Request for Family or Medical Leave, and a Certification of Health Care Provider to be filled out by the healthcare provider upon an employee's request to implement FMLA rights. You can find all forms on the U.S. Department of Labor's Web site (www.dol.gov).

Family-friendly policies: A checklist

What follows is a list of progressive benefit categories that are generally classified as family-friendly:

✔ Adoption assistance

✔ After-school and holiday care

✔ Child-care centers and family day care (on- or off-site)

✔ Domestic partner coverage

✔ Eldercare

✔ Employee assistance programs

✔ Flexible benefit plans (includes dependent-care assistance plans)

✔ Flexible scheduling options (compressed work week, part-time, job-sharing)

✔ Health and wellness plans

✔ Housing/relocation assistance

✔ Lactation programs

✔ Leave (parental, personal, family; in certain industries, can also include *sabbaticals,* which are extended leaves usually for concentrated study in a field)

✔ Long-term care

✔ Paid time off (sick leave, paid leave banks, leave donation programs)

✔ Resource and referral services

✔ Sick-child care

✔ Telecommuting

Sick days

Failure to formulate and communicate to all employees a formal sick-day policy can be dangerous to the health of your company. If you have a loosely defined policy that sets no limits on paid sick days, for example, you may run into legal problems should you ever decide to discipline or fire an employee who's clearly abusing the policy. A court may rule that, because you have no policy, the employee is simply following the firm's customary practice.

Formal sick-leave policies generally limit how many sick days the company is willing to pay for (anywhere from 6 to 12 days a year). In addition, companies usually impose a limit on the number of sick days that employees can take in succession (after which employees may be entitled to nonpaid leave of absences). Most companies have short-term disability plans that kick in either immediately following an accident or on the eighth calendar day after the onset of an illness. Short-term disability ends after a predefined interval (typically either three or six months after it has started), at which point long-term disability begins.

Guidelines for domestic partners

Extending benefits to domestic partners (either opposite-sex or same-sex nonmarried partners) has become a rapidly accepted practice at thousands of companies across the United States. This new benefit speaks powerfully to the ways corporations have become aware of the changing lifestyle arrangements of many of their employees.

The Human Rights Campaign Foundation's release of the "The State of the Workplace 2005-2006" report shows that, for the first time, a majority of Fortune 500 companies, 253 (51 percent), offer domestic partner health insurance benefits. Although large employers are more likely to offer these benefits than small and midsize businesses, 31 percent of respondents in Mellon's 2005 "Nontraditional Family Benefit Coverage Survey," which studied 550 U.S. companies with an average of more than 5,000 employees, offer domestic partner benefit coverage — a significant increase from the 19 percent who offered the coverage when responding to a Mellon survey in 2001. Among all organizations, Mellon said, the most frequently offered domestic partner benefits are medical, dental, and prescription drug coverage.

Though no official, nationally recognized set of requirements determine eligibility for this benefit, here are a few to keep in mind should you decide to offer it:

- ✔ Both partners occupy common residence, as proven by lease or title deed, for at least six consecutive months.

- ✔ Both partners are at least 18 years of age and not related by blood.

- ✔ Joint bank account, joint credit cards, or other evidence of shared financial responsibility exists.

- ✔ They're registered as partners in a state or locality that permits registration of domestic partner relationships.

Sometimes companies offer a reward for employees who don't use their allotment of sick-days — for example, a cash payment for a percentage (usually half) of an employee's unused sick leave at year-end or if he leaves the company. Many companies have CTO (choice time off) or PTO (personal time off) plans that combine vacation and sick days.

Setting Up an Employee Assistance Program

Employee Assistance Programs (EAPs) originated in the early 1970s as a mechanism for helping employees deal with certain types of personal problems (alcohol abuse, for example) that had on-the-job implications. In a way, EAPs were "ahead of the curve" in addressing employee well-being in a variety of areas that previously hadn't been covered by benefit programs. The following list will likely look familiar to you, as a great many of the issues historically addressed by EAPs have also become the province of HR. Today, EAPs are usually presented as a benefit rather than included in work environment programs.

Here's a sampling of areas in which EAP providers can assist employees:

- ✔ Stress management and conflict resolution
- ✔ Social, psychological, and family counseling
- ✔ Referral to legal services
- ✔ Preretirement planning
- ✔ Termination and career transition services (sometimes called *outplacement*)
- ✔ Alcohol and substance abuse
- ✔ Mental-health evaluation and referral
- ✔ Gambling addiction and other compulsive behaviors
- ✔ Marriage counseling
- ✔ Financial issues and credit counseling

Many large companies operate their own in-house EAPs, staffed with psychologists, social workers, counselors, and support staff. Smaller companies that have EAPs generally rely on outside sources, such as EAP providers. These providers range from fully staffed organizations to small groups of individuals who have arrangements with outside firms.

If your company has fewer than 3,000 employees, you probably can't justify the cost of an in-house professional counselor. Your best option is to find an outside source. You can obtain a list of EAP providers in your region by getting in touch with the Employee Assistance Professionals Association (EAPA), at its Web site, www.eapassn.org, or by calling its office in Arlington, Virginia at 703-387-1000.

Other suggestions: Check with your local business associations, chambers of commerce, and other businesses in your area for referrals. When the time comes to make a choice, here's what to do:

- ✔ **Check references.** As you would with any outside provider, carefully check references and make sure that the staff members of EAPs you're considering have the required training, certifications, and licenses. Companies normally do this during the Request for Proposal (RFP) process, comparing factors such as average call center wait times and the level of medical and psychological education of staff before they sign up for a particular service. You should ask providers to demonstrate the quality of their care though surveys or case studies.

✔ **Clarify fees.** EAP costs can vary widely, but in most situations, a basic per-employee fee can range anywhere from $12 to $20 a year, depending on the number of employees in your company. This fee is frequently adjusted on a yearly basis depending on how extensively your company actually uses the services. Ask about additional charges, such as referrals to therapists. The EAP's base fee should cover everything, including materials and administration.

✔ **Check with your health insurer.** Your health insurance policy may not offer mental-health benefits or substance-abuse rehabilitation. You may want to upgrade your benefits to provide these services or find an alternate means of providing them.

If you offer an EAP, remember that confidentiality is essential for legal and practical reasons. Employees must have confidence that they can talk privately to a counselor without repercussions (information reported back to a supervisor, for example). The Americans with Disabilities Act (ADA) prohibits using information on employees' health problems in a way that would negatively impact their jobs. The Health Insurance Portability and Accountability Act (HIPAA) also protects health-related data from inappropriate intrusion. Your EAP contracts should provide for this confidentiality.

Five Ways to Make Your Life Easier

As this chapter emphasizes, benefits administration can get very complex. The good news is that five simple principles, if followed, can make the job of administering benefits in your company a whole lot easier.

✔ **Remember that one size doesn't fit all.** With businesses more diversified than ever, employees bring a wider range of values, desires, and expectations to their jobs. As a result, you need to constantly evaluate which mix of benefits works best for your company and its broad spectrum of employees.

Members of various age groups, for example, often have different preferences about benefits policies and workplace accommodations. Many younger workers are more likely to expect balance between their personal and professional lives than their older counterparts who began their careers in highly structured business environments. Therefore, younger professionals frequently value options such as flexible schedules and telecommuting. But avoid stereotyping or jumping to conclusions. These accommodations can also appeal to some older employees who want to "cycle" between periods of work and leisure as they approach retirement.

The point is that your benefits offerings need to be broad and flexible enough to appeal to a variety of diverse groups, but it's not your job to make assumptions about which will appeal to whom. The single most important thing that you can do to win employee support for your program is to involve them as much as possible in all aspects of the plan, particularly as you're deciding which options to offer. If your company is small enough, you can keep your employees in the loop informally — simply by meeting with them regularly to discuss your benefits package and whether it's meeting their needs. If you have ten or more employees, however, a survey is a better option. Suggestion: Rather than ask employees to list benefit options that are important to them, provide them with a list of options to rate on a scale of 1 to 5.

✔ **Get to know your programs cold.** You and the people who work with you in benefits administration need to have a thorough knowledge of your benefits package and about the benefits field in general. Otherwise, you can't explain your offerings to employees, help employees sort out problems, or make the best benefits choices for your company. At the very least, you need to be able to write a brief description (in simple, clear language) in an employee handbook of all the programs that your company offers. And regardless of your level of experience in HR, you should make it a point to stay current. Be on the lookout for seminars and short courses that are offered in your region and make sure that you route important benefits articles that appear in HR journals or business publications to all those accountable for or interested in benefits administration.

✔ **Make benefits education a priority in your onboarding program.** Making sure that your employees have a thorough understanding of their benefits options should be one of the main priorities of your orientation/onboarding program. Take the time to develop an information package that spells out what you offer but that doesn't overload employees with overly detailed information. Make sure that the person who handles the benefits side of the orientation/onboarding program can answer the most frequently asked employee questions. (For more on onboarding, see Chapter 9.)

✔ **Monitor your program for problems and results.** Don't make the mistake of waiting for resentment and dissatisfaction to build before you do something about aspects of your benefits package that aren't working. Whether you do so informally through conversations or through some other means, such as a survey, make sure that you're attuned to employee attitudes, particularly about health insurance.

✔ **Provide feedback and problem-resolution procedures.** If you haven't already done so, establish formal mechanisms to receive employee comments and complaints and set up a system to resolve problems. Many problems aren't really problems at all but misunderstandings that stem from miscommunication. Try to develop some means of tracking problems through various stages of resolution. (One method is to use a form that lists the complaint and includes spaces for the various steps you need to take to resolve it.) The benefits complaints that employees voice most commonly today involve denial of health-insurance claims. Use employee feedback as a resource to periodically revise your communications about benefits.

Forms on the CD

Employee Statement of Benefits

A Look at 401(k) Plan Fees for Employees

Sample FMLA Posting

Employer Response to Employee Request for Family or Medical Leave

Certification of Health Care Provider

Chapter 12

Creating an Employee-Friendly Work Environment

A wise man once said that the mark of an outstanding mind is the ability to hold two seemingly opposing ideas at the same time. Consider two aspects of contemporary business: On the one hand, in order to thrive, your organization must be diligent, competitive, and keenly focused on bottom-line results. But at the same time, most of the companies that earn respect and profits know that nothing is more critical to attaining their goals than a workforce that feels not just engaged, but valued. Companies that are appropriately attuned to creating a supportive, nurturing work environment stand the best chance for long-term growth. What appear to be opposite ideas — unwavering attention to business results, coupled with an employee-friendly environment — go together like bees and honey. Your skill in linking the two can go a long way toward building a first-rate organization.

A People-Oriented Workplace: What Matters Most

What do you have to do as a company to become known in today's highly competitive market as employee-friendly? That's the basic question asked by the Great Place To Work Institute, a research and management firm that each year identifies the "100 Best Companies To Work For," a study published in

Fortune Magazine. The cofounder of the Institute is Robert Levering, who along with Milton Moskowitz coauthored the classic book, *The 100 Best Companies to Work For in America* (Plume).

The Institute believes that the cornerstone of a great place to work is trust built on open, engaged relationships between management and employees. Only from that foundation can employees feel the profound sense of engagement that marks a great company. The following sections provide more information on how that spirit of trust plays out.

Employee well-being as a core value

Without exception, companies known for their "people-friendly" HR policies have adopted the notion that employees are a cherished asset — and need to be treated accordingly. The steps that organizations actually take to integrate this value into their day-to-day business practices vary from one company to the next. And the existence of this value doesn't mean that human concerns always take precedence over fundamental principles. It simply means that the welfare of employees is routinely taken into consideration when companies are making bottom-line decisions.

At minimum, a business must follow operational and physical standards if it expects employees to be productive, loyal, and satisfied. The Occupational Safety and Health Administration (OSHA) establishes protective workplace standards and enforces those standards. OSHA's cornerstones are simple: education and enforcement. OSHA is exceptionally important in monitoring the safety and health of employees in manufacturing industries, where factories, assembly lines, and heavy-duty equipment create a wide range of stressful factors. But OSHA is also a useful resource for any kind of business. Its Web site (www.osha.gov) offers insights into the complexities of such vital topics as workplace ergonomics, health management, and other issues. Though it's often the case that your operations managers will be familiar with OSHA guidelines, it's important for you to be aware of what OSHA offers — and requires — too.

A reasonable commitment to job security

Though even the most employee-friendly businesses in today's marketplace can't guarantee lifetime employment, companies that place a high value on the personal well-being of their people tend to view massive layoffs as a last resort, not a reflex response to a business downturn. When your management is weighing the possibility of layoffs, make sure that they're taking into consideration the bottom-line implications. What will be the effects on customers and remaining staff? Of course, layoffs may end up being inevitable, but the takeaway message from you to senior managers should be as follows: Staffing is a long-term process, so make sure that a short-term crisis doesn't derail your bigger objective of building a successful company.

People-friendly facilities

Virtually all businesses today are obligated by state and federal law to provide a safe working environment. Employee-friendly companies, though, go above and beyond, creating facilities and introducing policies that far exceed legal requirements. In a section on its Web site called "What's it like to work in Mountain View?" Google speaks with pride of the "elements that define a Google workspace" at its corporate headquarters. These perks include a workout room with weights, rowing machines, massage rooms, video games, pool table, ping pong table, foosball, beach volleyball, and on-site bike service. A 2005 article in *Workforce Management* magazine praises Abbott Laboratories' headquarters and its $10 million state-of-the-art childcare center that more than 400 preschool children attend daily. According to *The Wall Street Journal*, a major reason why Analytical Graphics, a Pennsylvania-based software company, topped the "Best Small and Medium Companies to Work For" list in 2005 was its on-site laundry, car maintenance, and haircut services.

Other more modest but progressive investments have included private lactation areas for breast-feeding mothers; on-site automatic teller machines; fitness centers; and employee cafeterias with healthy menus, ultra-low prices, and after-hours take-out service. Every step your company takes to make life easier for its employees, no matter how large or small, sends a big message to employees: You care.

Sensitivity to work-life balance issues

A company's ability to attract and retain employees with the expertise it requires relates increasingly to the "human" side of the day-to-day working experience — the general atmosphere that prevails in the workplace. This includes, in particular, the extent to which company practices help people balance the pressures they face at work with the pressures they have to deal with at home.

Benefits packages in employee-friendly companies often feature policies to help staff better balance work and personal priorities (see Chapter 11). These policies may include anything from allowances for childcare and eldercare to a sensitivity to simpler, occasional needs. Workers in employee-friendly companies can count on the support of their employers whenever a medical emergency occurs, for example, or, on a happier note, some special event takes place at their child's school. Permission to attend to these matters is granted almost implicitly.

A high degree of employee autonomy

The one thing you almost never find these days in companies known for their employee-friendly policies is the traditional "command-and-control" management style, with its highly structured hierarchy and military-like "chain of command." Employee empowerment in employee-friendly companies is more than simply a catch phrase; it's one of the key values that drives day-to-day company operations (see Chapter 16). The rationale behind true employee empowerment is that most people work harder and do a better job when they're accountable for their own decisions and actions, as opposed to simply "following orders."

Open communication

A hierarchical management approach was effective in a time when individuals were but one part of a corporate machine. Today's business environment is far more fluid and fast-paced. With information flowing much more rapidly and employees frequently forming project teams that draw on a range of disciplines and personnel, smart leaders know that they must be more forthcoming in how they communicate.

As much as they must be willing to speak, leaders also must be willing to listen. They need to be receptive to feedback from employees at all levels, and, from operational matters to company financial results, the emphasis is on a two-way flow. With that in mind, no matter if your firm has five, 50, or 500 employees, look for ways to hear their thoughts on a regular basis. Gathering employee input can take the form of focus groups, a planned series of manager-employee conversations, quantitative surveys that measure attitudes, or other means. The more that managers and employees are aware of one another's priorities and concerns, the better equipped everyone in the company will be to create productive solutions.

Open communication is particularly key in today's fast-paced companies, where the entire workforce must marshal its efforts around the organization's strategic goals. Managers have a vital role in explaining to employees how their individual goals support organizational objectives, and a two-way dialog helps staff understand how overall business priorities should affect their work. Bear in mind that company strategies can change, sometimes rapidly, and you and your firm's line managers need to communicate any shifts throughout the organization to allow employees to adjust their individual goals. Employee morale and, in turn, retention increases when staff feel they play important roles in carrying out corporate objectives (see Chapter 9).

A sense of belonging

To be truly productive, people need to feel "good" about being a part of an organization. I can virtually guarantee that morale will be low for anyone in your company who feels he's an outsider. Sharing knowledge is one way to make people feel more a part of things and "in the know." But today's diverse workforce means that creating a sense of belonging must go even deeper. A commitment to diversity requires that you create a workplace environment that is supportive of a wide range of perspectives and approaches (see Chapter 3). Part of that commitment is an effort to ensure that everyone feels accepted and valued by their colleagues, subordinates, and supervisors. The more people feel comfortable with being who they are at work, the higher their morale, the greater their contributions, and the more their creativity is unleashed.

Some larger companies attempt to achieve this comfort level by encouraging the creation of *affinity groups.* The term *affinity* refers, in this context, to a connection or relationship, especially as marked by a community of interest. Affinity groups (sometimes referred to as employee networking groups) in the workplace are voluntary, employee-driven associations organized around commonalities including everything from job responsibilities and experience levels to gender, race, ethnicity, sexual orientation, or any other factor where a cluster of employees occupies the same or similar ground. The goal of an affinity group in the work environment is to create an open forum for exchanging ideas and encouraging a supportive, friendly dialogue.

Employer support for affinity groups usually includes use of company facilities and equipment for meetings, though it can also sometimes include funding for group projects. Such support not only advances a firm's diversity goals, but can also serve to retain employees whose loyalty is enhanced by knowing the company recognizes their value.

Keep in mind, though, that if people in your organization create affinity groups, their membership must still be open to anyone within the company. Some people argue that this requirement defeats the purpose of these associations, but allowing anyone to join guards against divisiveness, a common criticism leveled at affinity groups, and also promotes mutual understanding among all employees, whatever their backgrounds. For example, it can be helpful for a midlevel executive to participate in an affinity group of administrative assistants so that he can find out how to better understand them and, in the process, become a better manager.

By the numbers: What's behind the push to help employees achieve work-life balance

Here's a look at some of the statistics driving the need for programs that support employees' efforts to balance work and personal priorities:

✔ Percentage of couples where both members are in the workforce: 78 percent (2002), up from 66 percent in 1977

✔ Percentage of American children living in single-parent households in 2004, according to "Kids Count" study conducted by The Annie E. Casey Foundation: 31

✔ Percentage of large U.S. employers (1,000 or more employees) that provide on- or near-site childcare, according to Families and Work Institute: 17

✔ Percentage of women with children under 18 who currently work, according to the U.S. Department of Labor (2004): 70.7

✔ Percentage of Americans under the age of 60 who expect to be responsible for the care of a relative within ten years, according to a 2004 study conducted by the National Partnership for Women and Families: more than 60 percent

---

Smaller companies lacking the resources or critical employee mass to create affinity groups should still strive to promote the basic objectives of these associations. In other words, HR professionals can emphasize with managers and employees in meetings and workshops that a better understanding of all individuals in the company leads to stronger working relationships and helps remove barriers to cooperation and team spirit that people may encounter if they feel isolated.

Goodbye, 9 to 5: Alternate Work Arrangements

One of the most popular management concepts of recent years has been the scheduling concept known as *alternate work arrangements*. Broadly speaking, an alternate work arrangement is any scheduling pattern that deviates from the traditional Monday-through-Friday, 9-to-5 workweek.

Alternate work arrangements are an approach employees care about very much. According to a survey commissioned by Robert Half International, the benefit that employees say they value the most is — guess what? — flexible scheduling.

Flexibility is the basic idea behind alternate work arrangements. You give employees some measure of control over their work schedules, thereby making it easier for them to manage nonjob-related responsibilities. The business rationale behind the concept is that by making it easier for employees to deal with pressures on the home front, they'll be more productive when they're on the job — and less likely to jump ship if one of your competitors offers them a little more money.

Options for alternate work arrangements

Alternate work arrangements are generally grouped into the following general categories:

- **Flextime:** *Flextime* refers to any arrangement that gives employees options on structuring their work day or work week. In the most extreme (and rarest) form, employees decide for themselves not only when they work, but also for how long. More typically, though, employees working under flextime arrangements are expected to be on the job during certain core hours of the workday. They're given the opportunity to choose (within certain parameters) their own starting and quitting times — as long as they work the required number of hours each day.

   Here's an example: Say that you have a six-person customer service department, and the phones are answered from 9 a.m. to 7 p.m. And assume that the peak period — when the most calls come in — is between noon and 3 p.m. You can institute a flextime arrangement that obliges all six customer service representatives to be in their offices from noon to 3 p.m. but also gives employees the latitude to work together to set up their own eight-hour days so that the department is never left unstaffed.

- **Compressed work week:** Under this arrangement, employees work the normal number of hours but complete those hours in fewer than five days. The most common variation of the compressed work week is the so-called 4/10, in which employees work four 10-hour days instead of five 8-hour days.

- **Job-sharing:** As the term implies, *job-sharing* means that two part-time employees share the same full-time job. Salary and benefits may be prorated on the basis of what proportion of the job each worker shares. Apart from the obvious consideration (both people need to be qualified for the job), a successful job-sharing arrangement assumes that the employees sharing the job can work together harmoniously to make the arrangement work.

✔ **Telecommuting:** *Telecommuting* refers to any work arrangement in which employees — on a regular, predetermined basis — spend all or a portion of their work week working from home or from another noncompany site. I give you more details in "Telecommuting: The Adult Version of Homework," later in this chapter.

✔ **Permanent part-time arrangements:** The hours in these arrangements usually vary from 20 to 29 hours per week, with employees sometimes given the right to decide which days they work and how long they work on those days. The key attraction of this arrangement is that the employees may be entitled to company benefits, albeit on a prorated basis.

Making alternate arrangements work

In theory, alternate work arrangements offer a win-win situation. Many studies have shown that flexible scheduling policies improve morale and job satisfaction, reduce absenteeism, cut down on turnover, and minimize burnout — and with no measurable decline in productivity.

That's the good news. The not-so-good news is that these arrangements don't work for every company at every level, and thus the practices may have to be carefully implemented with some legally sound ground rules. In addition, instituting a policy of alternate work arrangements involves a good deal more than simply giving your employees a broader selection of scheduling options. The process needs to be carefully thought out. It must be implemented with consistency, patience, and discipline because you can easily ruin a good thing. The following sections offer some guidelines if you're thinking of setting up a flexible scheduling policy in your company:

Be willing to rethink processes

Implementing a successful flexible work arrangement policy requires far more work than merely changing when jobs get done. More often than not, alternate work arrangement policies need to be accompanied by changes in how the work actually gets done and, in particular, how people are supervised.

So when considering new work arrangements, think about this question first: How will the work itself be affected by the new scheduling? All subsequent decisions should be based on the answer to that question.

Establish guidelines

Flexible work arrangement policies don't have to be set in stone. At the very least, though, you need a set of guidelines that serve as the basis of the program. Some specifics:

✔ Make sure that the flexible work arrangement policies your company develops are logically keyed to the nature and the demands of your business.

✔ Be consistent. Decisions regarding who should be offered the option of flexible scheduling should be based on the nature of the job as opposed to the needs of the individual. You can certainly be lenient and take into account the special needs of individual employees, but you can sabotage a formalized flexible work arrangement policy by making too many individual exceptions to it.

✔ Make sure that managers and supervisors have some say in policy development. (Bear in mind that supervisors are always affected by the scheduling patterns of their direct reports.)

Consider phased retirement options

One option that's become quite popular in recent years is the notion of a *phased retirement,* or allowing tenured employees to gradually ease their way out of the organization by reducing the number of hours they spend on the job. This plan has many positives. Phased retirement gives your company the ability to retain the valuable institutional knowledge of longstanding employees that would otherwise walk out the door with them. It also provides a better means of transitioning job responsibilities.

In many cases, phased retirement simply means lowering an employee's workload and training his replacement. But another approach is for the employee to technically retire and then continue to work for your firm on a contract or consulting basis. Given the numbers of the baby boom generation expected to leave the workforce in coming years, a phased retirement option can be extremely productive for both employer and employee.

Pay attention to legal implications

With certain groups of employees (hourly employees or unionized workers, in particular), flexible arrangements can easily run counter to existing agreements. Check with your legal counsel or state labor department to see whether flexible scheduling violates state or local laws, and, in particular, how certain arrangements — compressed work weeks, for example — may affect overtime obligations.

Get managerial buy-in

Regardless of how thrilled your employees may be with a flexible work arrangement, the policy itself will face rough sledding if it doesn't have the enthusiastic support and involvement of both senior management and line supervisors.

FedEx Kinko's, a company that prides itself on round-the-clock service, invariably must have its stores managed by people who know how to cope with a variety of scheduling arrangements. Accordingly, aspiring local managers are put through a nine-month training program. What's great about this program is that it includes courses taught by the company's chief executive officer, chief technology officer, and chief financial officer. The involvement of these senior C-level managers drives home the message that the company cares a great deal about how it conducts its business.

Telecommuting: The Adult Version of Homework

Telecommuting is one of the fastest-growing alternate work arrangements in corporate America. A 2005 OfficeTeam study conducted for the "Office of the Future" project estimates that by 2015, more than 100 million Americans will telecommute to work. Several factors are fueling this trend:

- ✔ Increased demand from employees for this option
- ✔ Pressure on companies in certain parts of the country to alleviate commuter traffic and air pollution
- ✔ The growing availability of technology-based solutions — broadband and Wi-Fi access from remote locations, mobile phones, picture phones, video conferencing, and, of course, access to information provided by the Internet — has created the phenomenon generally known as the *virtual office*

Strictly speaking, telecommuters are employees of a company who regularly work out of their homes or other locations all or part of the work week. The key word in the previous definition is *regularly*. The structured aspect of the arrangement is what differentiates telecommuters as a group from those employees who routinely take work home from the office.

Telecommuting arrangements vary. In some cases, employees never come into the office except for special events. More typically, though, a company's telecommuters spend part of the week — one or two days, usually — working out of their homes and the rest of the week in the office.

Identifying prime candidates for telecommuting

Candidates for a successful telecommuting arrangement can include, but should not be limited to, those who:

- ✔ Perform a function that doesn't require extensive interaction with other employees or the use of equipment found only on company premises.
- ✔ Have a compelling personal reason (a long commute, for example, or family responsibilities) for working part of the time from home.
- ✔ Have the temperament and the discipline to work alone.
- ✔ Can be absent from the office without creating an inconvenience for others in the company.

These factors are just a few to consider when selecting telecommuting candidates. Beyond these managerial issues, you should also take into account a number of sticky legal and operational aspects

But does telecommuting work?

Unquestionably, telecommuting provides many opportunities and rewards. It's a highly productive way for certain employees to get their work done. It's also a good way to draw on the skills of talented, high-performing employees who may otherwise be unable to work for your company under a standard scheduling arrangement. This advantage makes it a compelling recruiting strategy.

But you should also take into account certain other factors before permitting someone to telecommute. For example, consider the temperament and discipline of the telecommuter. Can the individual continually work effectively in relative isolation? How does his work fit into a broader team environment — not just now, but as you look ahead to future growth? What is the impact of the telecommuting arrangement on others? If the telecommuter is a manager, for example, supervising people even part of the time by telephone and e-mail is not always productive.

Worker safety and health

An accepted principle of employment law is that employers are responsible for the safety and health of their employees regardless of where the employees are working. As I mention in "Employee well-being as a core value" in this chapter, OSHA provides guidelines and training for setting and enforcing safety and health standards in all industries. But safety and health guidelines are tricky to create and monitor when employees work from home-based offices. Even OSHA, for example, generally will not conduct inspections of employees' home offices. You can take two key steps to protect both your company and the telecommuter:

- ✔ Check with your legal counsel or insurance carrier to see what additional coverage, if any, you may need.

- ✔ Verify that your liability coverage covers third parties who are injured at the telecommuter's home, such as a repair person, another employer, a client, and so on.

Home office expenses

The basic question is simple: Who pays for what? The answer isn't simple and can depend on any number of factors, including the safety and health of the employee. The general guideline is that if the expense involves a piece of equipment that an employee must use to perform his job and that you would routinely be responsible for if the employee were working on company premises, your company should consider paying for it.

This guideline doesn't mean that you're obliged to replicate in the telecommuter's home office everything that he would have access to if he were working in company space (the corporate gym, for example). But most companies view basic resources — at least one dedicated phone line, a computer with proper Internet connections, a scanner, photocopier, and fax machine —as business expenses. Common sense needs to prevail.

Viability of service contracts

Some office equipment vendors provide service only at the employer's office locations. If your company intends to furnish a telecommuter's home office with equipment that would normally be covered by a service contract, double-check with the service provider to make sure that your policy covers residential visits.

Security

The mere fact that telecommuters are working on company business in their homes — well outside the sphere of normal company security procedures —

creates a hornet's nest of potential security problems, none of which has an easy solution. Technology-driven security measures, such as access codes and passwords, can reduce but never eliminate the chance that confidential company information will end up in the wrong hands, particularly in an era when the Internet is an integral part of many people's job. At the very least, you should have a written agreement with all telecommuters that spells out the company's confidentiality policies and sets down specific guidelines.

Tax implications

Telecommuting arrangements may have tax implications for employees who are working out of their homes, particularly because home office deductions have come under increasing IRS scrutiny in recent years. Make sure that any employees who have set up home offices understand what they are legally entitled to deduct. What they can't deduct, to be sure, are expenses for which they're being reimbursed.

Local zoning issues

Many communities have zoning restrictions against conducting certain business activities in residential neighborhoods. While these rules generally are loosely enforced, the restrictions can create legal problems. Somebody — either the employee or a company representative — should take the initiative to investigate the situation before a problem arises.

Setting up an agreement

Consider preparing a formal agreement with any employee who is going to be telecommuting. The agreement, at the very least, should spell out the following:

- ✔ The specific scheduling terms — that is, how much time is to be spent at home or at the office.
- ✔ The specific equipment the company is willing to provide, and how the equipment is to be installed and maintained.
- ✔ Reporting requirements: How often should the telecommuter send e-mail updates? Should he be part of a weekly departmental conference call? What kind of voice mail setup will the employee have (on both the business home office line and cell phone)?
- ✔ How proprietary information is to be controlled and handled.

Avoiding Burnout

The Japanese have a word for it: *karoshi*. The term means, literally, "death from overwork." *Karoshi* may not be a major cause of death in the United States, but almost everywhere you look in today's lean and mean environment — even in companies known for employee-friendly policies — you sometimes hear complaints and concerns raised about employee burnout. Often it relates to the psychological, social, and physical problems that result when workers literally "wear down" from stress and become unable to cope with workday demands.

Most psychologists explain burnout as the convergence of two forces:

✔ High job demand

✔ Low job control

In a typical burnout situation, employees not only feel tremendous pressure to extend themselves, but they also perceive that they lack the ability or the resources to meet the demands. Whether this latter perception is justified doesn't really matter. As long as employees believe they're both overworked and under-resourced, the potential for employee burnout exists.

Employee burnout can manifest itself any number of ways. Among the most obvious signs are the following:

✔ Noticeable increase in staff absenteeism or tardiness

✔ Any obvious change (for the worse) in the general mood of the workplace

✔ Uncharacteristic emotional outbursts from employees who are normally calm

✔ Increased customer complaints about the quality of goods and services

Burnout doesn't happen overnight; it's a gradual process. And if there's any good news here, it's this: If you can become sensitive to the warning signs of burnout, you can frequently avert a crisis.

Your managers and supervisors are your first line of defense against burnout and the workplace problems it causes. Make sure that they're trained to recognize burnout symptoms before the situation gets out of hand.

Be sensitive to extended periods of excessive workload

The prime cause of employee burnout is overwork, or, to be more precise, sustained periods of overwork. Most successful businesses, of course, run into periods of peak workloads from time to time, and expecting good employees to rise to the occasion isn't unreasonable. But even if you're giving your regular employees extra income to meet the increased demand, at some point even the most dedicated employees will reach their physical, emotional, and mental limits. When they reach this point, you have two options:

- Hire additional full-time employees.
- Hire supplemental workers to ease the burden.

Give employees more day-to-day job autonomy

Productive, happy employees generally feel that they're making unique contributions that provide a sense of personal pride. Peter Drucker, a prominent management scholar for more than 50 years, repeatedly emphasized the importance of personal ownership. If you've haven't already done so, take a look at the responsibilities your employees have, make sure that they have the necessary resources, and then be certain to provide them with plenty of independence.

You've no doubt heard of or even experienced firsthand the dreaded micromanager. And perhaps you've found moments when you yourself have taken on some of those characteristics and suffered the consequences. I'm not saying that you must abandon demanding accountability (such as weekly update meetings or written reports), but think how you much you like it when your own supervisors display ample trust in your ability to get your work done. Nothing is more important to wedding productivity and an employee-friendly culture than encouraging self-reliance and, as The Great Place to Work Institute emphasizes, the accompanying spirit of trust.

Provide help

No matter how good your work environment, some employees will develop personal problems that have nothing to do with your company but that they nonetheless bring to work. The most damaging effects include behavior and attitudes that hinder the ability to do their jobs. The HR professional has a responsibility to offer resources to assist employees in addressing these issues.

In the HR world, programs that help workers cope with personal difficulties are known as *Employee Assistance Programs* (EAPs). EAPs include such activities as confidential counseling or seminars for employees seeking to better handle job pressures. Employees need to know that help is available and that their careers will not suffer if they seek it. For more about EAPs, see Chapter 11.

Employee Surveys: Keeping Tabs on Company Morale

In many cases, particularly if your company has fewer than 50 employees, you don't have a hard time getting a good read on the general atmosphere in the workplace. You're able to personally make your way around offices and work areas enough to observe how employees interact with one another, how they feel about the way they're treated by senior management, and whether morale is rising or falling. But if your company is larger, periodically conduct a more rigorous employee survey. Here are some tips:

- ✔ Watch your timing. Don't conduct surveys during holidays when many employees may be taking days off. And avoid exceptionally heavy work-load periods.

- ✔ Think carefully about your objectives before crafting your survey questions. What do you want to find out? What do you intend to do with the information?

- ✔ Share survey objectives with employees, but do so in language that's relevant to them. In other words, instead of using HR terms such as "We want to assess employee attitudes," tell them that "We want to hear your thoughts since we merged with Company X."

- ✔ Before you unveil your survey to the entire company, test it out on a small group of employees to see whether your questions are appropriate and what you can refine.

> ✔ A key step: Assure employees that their comments are confidential.
>
> ✔ Communicate to employees the results of the survey on a timely basis and take action, as appropriate, when employees make recommendations. Let employees know how their input has affected company policy.

To get an idea of some of the questions you may want to ask on such a survey, see the Employee Satisfaction Survey on the CD-ROM.

Exit interviews

When you're trying to "take the temperature" of the organization, some of the most candid employees are often those who are leaving your company. To gain valuable ideas about improving your working conditions and making the workplace more inviting, consider conducting exit interviews with employees who have resigned or are otherwise voluntarily leaving your company. (People you've had to fire, while potentially the most candid of all, are not good subjects for two reasons: They're unlikely to cooperate and, if they do, their input will probably be overly negative rather than constructive.)

For a Exit Interview Questionnaire, see the CD-ROM.

Forms on the CD

Employee Satisfaction Survey

Exit Interview Questionnaire

Chapter 13

Getting Permanent Benefit from Interim Staffing

• •

In This Chapter

▶ Recognizing the increasing role of interim employees in today's workforce

▶ Identifying staffing assistance

▶ Maximizing the use of project professionals

▶ Avoiding legal troubles

• •

Many years ago, the notion of assigning work to anyone other than full-time employees was viewed primarily as a stop-gap measure. In those days, change came more slowly, it was easier to anticipate business cycles, and, when necessary, companies could supplement their ongoing work efforts by adding a few extra personnel. Though the pace of business certainly had its volatile side, staffing needs were frequently predictable.

Today's business environment is drastically different. Advances in technology and communications, coupled with increased competition from all corners of the globe, have raised customer expectations about speed and quality. The new pace of business has triggered the need for companies to be more agile and responsive to changing circumstances than ever before. As the speed of business activity accelerates, as companies create new opportunities and strive to meet new challenges, and as long-term planning efforts become trickier by the minute, HR's approach to staffing has also had to change to keep up. Managers have become increasingly aware of the need to explore smart approaches and carefully assess their mix of employees.

Tapping the Growing Ranks of Project Workers

Adopting a strategic staffing plan allows you and other company managers to assemble a combination of talent you can expand or reduce as necessary to help meet both current and long-term business goals (see Chapter 3). A central element of this approach is making judicious use of interim employees. No matter what term you use — project professionals, supplemental workers, contractors, contingent staff, interim employees, freelancers, part-timers, or consultants — these individuals have become a significant part of today's workforce.

According to the American Staffing Association (ASA), contingent jobs accounted for one out of every 384 non-agricultural jobs in 1970. In 1997, that ratio was one out of every 50 jobs. By 2005, the number of contingent workers in the American workforce on any given day exceeded 2.9 million people, an increase of 8.7 percent over 2004. ASA data reveals that U.S. annual sales for contingent and contract staffing totaled $69.5 billion in 2005.

Sound reasons exist for this growth. More and more professionals today are drawn to project work because of the flexibility and opportunities these positions provide. It enables them to pursue personal and professional goals and, at the same time, explore a variety of industries. Project assignments allow job seekers to "try out" work in different firms and office cultures, and in fact, many times a project engagement may become a full-time job.

But project work is not pursued only by job seekers. Increasingly, professionals who desire a flexible work schedule along with the diversity of working in different offices and work environments are attracted to this arrangement as a long-term work style. This group includes working parents, who want more time to devote to their children, as well as people nearing retirement age, who still want to be active but perhaps not on a full-time basis. For these and many others, project work fits the bill.

The use of project workers is not news, of course. What's new is not only the enormous growth in their numbers, but also the level of experience and expertise that you and the line managers you work with can bring into your company on an interim basis. A company can now engage a highly skilled professional in virtually any specialty: finance, sales, marketing, operations, information technology, law, medicine, human resources — even an interim CEO. And in contrast to the past, the specialist who joins your firm is likely to be part of the contingent workforce by choice rather than necessity.

In short, you can find talent galore in today's contingent workforce. The challenge is to discover the best way to capture that talent for your own company.

Weighing the Pros and Cons

Contingent workers are part of a larger staffing mosaic, and you and the line managers you work with need to approach the use of these workers strategically — with a clearly defined sense of current business requirements and long-term objectives.

The pros of interim staffing are as follows:

- ✔ Lets departments adjust staffing levels to the ebb and flow of business cycles, thus helping keep overhead costs under control.

- ✔ Eases the work burden on employees who may already be spread too thinly because of business demands.

- ✔ Eliminates the need (on your part) to recruit outside workers who can make an immediate contribution. (The staffing firm locates people for you.)

- ✔ Offers departments a way to handle special projects — or special problems — that lie beyond the expertise of current staff members.

- ✔ Gives the company an opportunity to hire — on a short-term basis — high-level specialists it can't afford to bring on-board for the long term.

- ✔ Creates job stability for a core group of full-time workers in highly cyclical businesses that would otherwise need to subject their workforce to nerve-wracking cycles of constant hiring and layoffs as the needs of the business fluctuate.

- ✔ Provides what amounts to a no-obligation trial period for newly hired employees: A person is hired for a limited time — until the manager is satisfied that the individual can handle the job on a full-time or permanent part-time basis.

If, as your needs evolve, you decide to consider converting an interim employee to full-time status, you have the advantage of already knowing some of the individual's capabilities and personal attributes. Even so, since you will now be taking this person into your firm as a full-time employee, it is your responsibility to supplement any evaluation made by your staffing firm with reference checks made by you. This is no different from your role when you use the assistance of recruiters to secure full-time employees who do not first work for you on a contingent basis (see Chapter 8).

The cons of contingent staffing, on the other hand, are as follows:

- Can be more expensive in the short term than traditional hiring practices. (Remember, your company is paying a premium to the staffing firm for finding and conducting preliminarily skills evaluations of prospective hires.)

- Best suited to project-oriented positions that are skills-based and don't require an extensive knowledge of your particular company or its customers.

- Produces morale problems if you don't pay attention to how line managers integrate project workers into their day-to-day operations and if they (with your help) don't communicate to existing staff the rationale behind the contingent hiring strategy.

- Requires a certain amount of preparation at the departmental level to make sure that you're getting the most out of contingent workers.

Knowing When to Begin

Strategic staffing requires that you don't wait until the need actually arises to respond to peak demand or to fill in for employees who are vacationing or on extended leave (by which time you're already in an emergency). Instead, work with your company's managers to help them forecast their needs well in advance. Help them budget for those needs. And take the time to identify the staffing firm you're going to call to fill the needs.

The more proactive and systematic you and line managers are in approaching your staffing needs, the bigger the payoff.

Here are some threshold questions as you consider the use of contingent workers:

- **What specific tasks do you need someone to perform and over what time period?** The key points here are "project" and "short term" in nature versus activities that last for years. The shorter the time period, the more inclined you should be to seek contingent help.

- **What skills or expertise are necessary to perform those tasks?** Generally speaking, contingency hiring enables you to tap into a knowledge base that's far broader than you find in your current staff.

✔ **Can people who are already on the company's payroll perform those tasks — without affecting other aspects of their job performance and without creating excessive overtime costs?** It's not easy to balance basic responsibilities with additional tasks. To answer this question, departmental managers will likely look to you and your HR colleagues, as you're probably more familiar with the skills and workloads of people in all parts of the company.

✔ **Can the department and company afford the extra cost involved to bring in highly skilled supplemental staff?** Think overall value, not just cost.

Interim staffing makes the most sense if the tasks or duties of the position meet the following criteria:

✔ A department needs someone to perform within a limited time frame or for a specific project, rather than an ongoing basis.

✔ Only one specific skill set or area of knowledge is generally required, as opposed to needing a variety of skills or a broad area of knowledge.

✔ Tasks don't require an extensive knowledge of your company or your customers.

Finding the Right Staffing Source

You can hire interim workers on your own without going through a staffing firm. You can also run a marathon in a pair of sandals. But here's the question: Why put you and the already-busy line managers you're working with through the extra work? If help is required, managers are probably in a time bind already, so why add to everyone's miseries by all of you having to get involved with such labor-intensive details as recruiting, interviewing, hiring, payroll, and so on?

The case for using a staffing firm to help execute a contingency staffing strategy is fairly airtight. Firms that specialize in providing interim employees already have a pool of experienced people they can assign to your company. They understand the complex legalities (including tax-related issues) of contingency staffing. They handle all the paperwork.

True, the cost is a little more than the average pay rate for people in that particular specialty, but remember that the staffing firm handles all the preliminary skills evaluations and government-mandated benefits and also assumes responsibilities as the employer of record.

In the course of their preliminary evaluation process, staffing firms often check selected references for their candidates from past employers to gather skill proficiency information and job performance history, but employers should perform their own reference checks as well. This is because a preliminary check may or may not reveal all the information you want to consider in making your final decision as to whether to bring an individual into your company. (See Chapter 8 for more on reference and background checks.)

The number of firms specializing in contingency placements has mushroomed over the past few years. That's good news in one respect: Your company has more options today than ever before, and staffing firms are expanding their services in efforts to remain competitive. But with so many options available, making the right choice can be a problem.

Reputation is important. The best job candidates — and these are the people you want access to — work for the best staffing firms. Specialization is a key factor in attracting skilled talent, so look for businesses that specialize in the types of positions you're looking to fill.

One way to ensure satisfaction with the staffing firm you select is to get a personal recommendation from other business people who use the service — assuming, of course, that the staffing firms they use have expertise in your industry and the positions you're seeking. You can also check with professional and trade associations, many of which maintain an active file on staffing services that specialize in their particular areas. The Internet, of course, is also a great tool for evaluating a firm's approach and capabilities.

Checking things out

The one thing you always want to do as you're deciding on the staffing firm to partner with is to visit its local office. Pay attention, in particular, to the general environment and atmosphere. Is the firm professionally and smoothly run? Ask yourself the following question: If you were a specialist with a skill in high demand, is this firm the sort you'd want representing you?

To help you on your way, the following checklist offers several questions you may want to ask whenever you're checking out staffing firms:

- ✔ Does the firm specialize in the areas where you need help?
- ✔ How long has the firm been in business?
- ✔ Does the company have locations in other cities where you have operations?
- ✔ How does the service recruit and retain a highly skilled workforce?

✔ How does it evaluate and select the workers?

✔ How broad and deep is its candidate base?

✔ How does the service match needs with skills?

✔ Does the service guarantee its contingent workers, and does it provide replacements?

✔ Is your contact available after hours?

One last thing: Make sure that you nail down all the costs ahead of time — and clarify this information with the departmental supervisor who's going to be managing the worker(s). A reputable firm is always willing to communicate its fee structure in writing.

Asking the staffing manager to visit your business

The more familiar a staffing firm is with your business — how it operates, who your employees are, the needs of various departments — the greater is its ability to provide you with workers who can excel in your environment.

Have the staffing firm's representatives come to your office and give them a tour of your facilities. Introduce them to the managers and supervisors who are going to be working with the contingent workers or consultants.

And, most important of all, make sure that you've worked with line managers to provide the staffing firm with a detailed, written description of the job, including the required skills, hours, and anticipated length of the assignment. Another good idea is to tell the firm whether your company is thinking of turning the assignment into a full-time position. Remember that some contingent workers have more interest in landing a full-time job than others do, and you want to make sure that you bring in people whose personal goals are consistent with the nature of the assignment.

Getting the Most Out of Project Professionals

The following incident actually happened. An experienced editor arrived one Monday morning at an office for a two-week assignment with a consulting firm that had a rush special project. The manager who had hired him was nowhere to be found, and none of the ten or so people in the office that day had the vaguest idea of why the editor had shown up that morning, where he was to go, or what he was to do.

After an uncomfortable hour, the manager arrived and said, "Well, I guess we better find somewhere for you to sit." The manager then led the editor to an unoccupied desk in a corner that was being used as the office coffee bar. After the coffee pot, the cups, and the rest of the items were cleared off, the manager pulled over an empty chair, gestured to the editor to sit down, and disappeared without another word. Two hours later, an office clerk appeared with an unopened carton that contained a computer. The computer was quickly unpacked, and the editor was told to wait until "Mel, the computer guy, hooks you up."

Mel showed up two days later.

The scary part of this story is that it's reflective of a common error in using staffing firms. Far too often today, contingent workers find themselves in offices that aren't adequately prepared for their arrival. The unhappy result is a waste of everyone's time — and money.

The following list describes simple steps that go a long way toward sparing the project employee who comes to your company from the same fate that befell the editor described in the preceding paragraphs.

- ✔ **Get the workplace ready.** Ready means a number of things: You've coordinated with the manager who the project employee will report to and arranged an adequate workspace, and the materials and supplies the worker needs are already there upon her arrival. The equipment must be free of glitches: computers have the latest versions of software used by your company, the Internet connection is safe and fast, any necessary logon IDs and passwords are provided, and so on.

    Adjusting to a new workplace is one of the constant challenges that interim workers face. Don't give them additional hoops to jump through.

- ✔ **Make safety a priority.** Be sure to provide appropriate safety and health training, particularly for workers in manufacturing or other non-office settings.

- ✔ **Brief your staff.** Pay attention to how you integrate project workers into your day-to-day operations. You're inviting trouble if you don't communicate beforehand to your staff the rationale behind your strategy. Failing to do so can cause trouble on two fronts: First, it leads to needless confusion or even tension among your full-time employees who may wonder why the individual has been engaged, what his role is to be, and what may be amiss that caused the need for a project worker in the first place. This speculation in turn can lead to morale and productivity problems. Second, it creates unnecessary pressure for the project professional who must work with or near a group of people who are puzzled by his mere presence.

Here's a better approach that you can use with interim employees you bring in or suggest to managers who engage them. Rather than merely announcing that a project professional is arriving, involve core employees weeks earlier in the staffing process to help you clarify the scope of the department or project team's workload. In many instances, staff members can offer input about specific tasks that require attention or skills that are lacking among the workgroup. Or they may provide creative solutions, such as reassigning certain activities among themselves and subsequently allocating the most appropriate set of activities to the supplemental worker. This way, as a team, under the supervision of a manager, the entire workgroup can be clear about what the individual is going to be doing (and, equally important, not going to be doing), how long the assignment is going to last, and how the situation is going to affect each of them (if at all). Stress the positive: Make sure that full-time employees are aware of how they stand to benefit and how the presence of an interim professional is going to lighten their own workloads.

✔ **Set up a plan.** You need to have a clear idea — before the project worker arrives — about the scope of the project, when it should be completed, and, as appropriate, matters related to quality. Just make sure that your expectations and those of other managers are realistic, particularly regarding the difficulty of the task. Also factor in the reality that even seasoned project workers need time to acclimate themselves to a new working environment. Again, other staff members can provide valuable input in clarifying the scope of work and the amount of time it takes to get specific tasks done.

✔ **Create a friendly atmosphere.** The more "at home" a company can make interim employees feel, the more productive they're likely to be. It's not necessary to go to extreme lengths — no need for a big welcome sign or a desk covered with roses. At the very least, however, make sure that that the receptionist has been alerted (if you have one) ahead of time. Either you or someone in the department to which the worker has been assigned should conduct a mini-orientation: a quick tour of the immediate work area, location of restrooms, fire exits, lunchroom, vending machines, and any tools that will be needed for the job. Take time to explain lunch-hour policies, security procedures, office protocols, parking and so on.

✔ **Be explicit about the tasks.** One of the concerns that contingent workers who have unsatisfying work experiences voice most often is that they're not given sufficient direction at the start of the assignment. General rule: The lengthier and more complex the assignment is, the more time you or a line manager needs to spend on orientation and an explanation of the nature of the assignment. Putting down the instructions in writing is a particularly useful technique.

✔ **Provide adequate supervision.** Regardless of how busy your company is, try to keep reasonably close tabs on the project employees you bring in — especially in the early stages of the assignment. Check in with line managers and make sure that they're communicating well with interim professionals. Bear in mind that some people consider admitting that they don't know how to do something a sign of incompetence — and thus waste an enormous amount of time trying to figure out for themselves a problem that you or another staff member can solve in seconds. The manager and others within the department should encourage the employee to ask questions if anything is not understood.

✔ **Intervene early.** As important as it for managers to provide clear direction to interim staff, sometimes the work is simply not getting done properly. As the person handling HR for your firm, you are a value-added resource for every department and each full-time employee. Let managers know that if they're not pleased with the quality of a contingent employee's work that they should contact you immediately and, if necessary, you'll lead the way in working with the staffing firm to make a change.

✔ **Don't settle.** A reputable staffing firm will not argue with you if the person who's been sent to your firm isn't doing a good job. The firm simply sends a replacement. And it handles communication directly with the individual (who's their employee, after all) regarding termination of the assignment. For everyone's sake, however, try to be as specific as you can when expressing displeasure. If you do a good job of telling the firm where the individual fell short, you're more likely to get a suitable replacement.

Provide evaluations at the end

Prepare evaluations at the end of each project professional's assignment. Doing so helps you and each department get maximum benefit from project workers, and it also helps the staffing firm do a better job of meeting your company's needs. (Note: Many staffing firms offer evaluation forms after an assignment to solicit this type of feedback.) As you go through this exercise, you and line managers who have used contingent staff should ask yourselves whether the interim employee:

✔ Met your expectations

✔ Finished the job on time and professionally

✔ Required little, some, or too much guidance

✔ Fit well into the workplace

What most interim employees need to know

One of the best things you and the line managers you work with can do to ensure that project workers are as productive as possible is to anticipate their information needs. Here's a list of the questions the typical interim employee is likely to have the first day he shows up for work:

☞ What's the job?

☞ What are your policies and procedures?

☞ What does your company do? What's its culture like?

☞ Who's the boss?

☞ Whom do I go to if I run into a problem?

To save time, consider preparing a one-sheet flyer that covers the preceding issues and provides space for the interim employee to take notes.

Additionally, ask yourselves:

☞ What could the interim employee have done differently? Done better?

☞ Would you hire this person as a full-time employee? If no, why not?

Where appropriate, take advantage of the opportunity to get feedback from a contingent worker or consultant about your company or department and its procedures and approaches. Interim employees can usually offer unbiased opinions that are invaluable. And there's a good chance they'll be more forthcoming with an HR practitioner than they might be with the managers they've been working with each day. If problems arose with the project, the employee's comments may help you prevent similar situations in the future.

Avoiding Legal Hassles

Apart from whatever strategic benefits contingent staffing produces, the growing influx of interim workers, independent contractors, and part-timers introduces some thorny legal issues as well. One key question: To what extent are companies who hire contingent workers directly (instead of relying on staffing firms) obliged to provide these workers with the same benefits and protections that full-time employees receive?

Equal coverage

The EEOC believes that discrimination is discrimination — and whether or not the victim of discrimination is working for you on a full-time, part-time, or contingent basis doesn't matter. The bottom line is that project workers have the same fundamental rights with respect to EEOC legislation as do regular, full-time employees — and this fact holds true for all forms of discrimination, including sexual harassment.

Workplace injuries

Even if a staffing service pays someone working for your company on a contingent basis, your firm is still responsible for that individual's health, safety, and security while on the job at your company. Check with your staffing firm to determine whether your workers' compensation package adequately protects you. And remember: You can always face a lawsuit from anyone who's injured while working on your premises.

Chapter 14

Training and Development

• •

• •

*I*n a perfect world, every employee you hire would already possess the combination of knowledge, skills, and background required to perform every facet of the job flawlessly. However, employees can always discover something that can help improve their performance. This simple, universally acknowledged principle underlies the HR function generally known as employee training and development.

Broadly speaking, employee training and development refers to a wide range of educational and learning-based tools. Activities aren't inherently built into job functions but generally produce some positive change in the way employees handle their work. These activities can range from a live seminar, to a CD that employees listen to while commuting, to an online or DVD instructional session they participate in at home or at their desks. I discuss these and more options in this chapter. In taking on the HR role for your company, it's your responsibility to not only determine the best training approaches but also to organize and run these programs in a cost-effective way that's in line with your organization's overall culture.

Organizational Development Never Stops

Training and development refer to everything you do in your organization to upgrade the skills and improve the overall job performance of your employees, both in the short term and long term. In the "command-and-control" era, companies tended to take the notion of organizational development for granted. With job responsibilities and roles clearly defined, it was much easier to know which skills mattered most year after year.

But over the last 20 years, companies are approaching training in a different way. No longer is sending an employee off to a developmental session a perk or bonus. It's a competitive necessity. To keep pace, skills development must be a constant priority. More and more companies view training and development not just as a way to keep up, but to get ahead.

No matter what the nature of your business is, you won't find it easy to stay on top without a commitment to helping your people stay ahead of emerging trends and changing needs. Increasing the knowledge of your workforce not only enhances your ability as a company to compete but also makes for more satisfied employees. Even in lean times, cutting back on training to reduce expenses can be "shooting yourself in the foot," both in terms of company success and employee retention.

The Changing Face of Training and Development

The biggest change in training is the degree to which it has become intertwined with other HR functions (hiring, promotions, and so on) and the company's long-term business goals. Because training is so valued by companies and employees alike, it's also become a big business in its own right, with a wide range of products, services, seminars, and materials available for businesses of all sizes.

In recent years, a major shift has occurred in how companies approach training. It used to be the case, for example, that training departments operated as independent entities with their own budget and their own objectives. Typically, the training department each year developed a curriculum of courses and seminars that employees enrolled in, either on their own or in conjunction with their managers. Rarely was any real thought given to whether this mix of courses was logically keyed to a company's business goals. Nor was much attention paid to what happened to employees after they participated in the training course.

To be sure, some companies today may still use this model of training administration. But if you're responsible for training in a growth-oriented firm today, you're working more closely than ever with senior managers, supervisors, and employees themselves. You're making sure that a logical connection exists between the programs being offered and the skill sets necessary to keep your firm competitive. Here are key factors that are fueling this shift:

✔ **The "learning" route to competitive advantage:** Profitable organizations recognize that in today's highly competitive and changeable business environment, it's not so much what employees currently know that shapes a company's future; it's what they must *eventually* know that's most important. That's why one major objective of training is to increase each employee's intellectual capacity for acquiring the knowledge and skills needed to thrive amid the increasing demands and pressures of a global marketplace.

✔ **The need to attract and keep talented employees:** The degree to which your company is genuinely committed to developing the skills of your employees is a critical factor in attracting and keeping high performing employees. The only true job security people have today is largely a function of the skills and knowledge they can bring to an employer. Workers understand this fact of business life, which is why companies that provide their employees with opportunities to learn and grow have an edge when recruiting.

✔ **The competition for skilled labor:** Many companies discovered the hard way that they can no longer solve performance and productivity problems by simply getting rid of employees who aren't measuring up and quickly replacing them with employees who are better equipped to meet performance standards. Forgetting for the moment the expense and disruption created by excess turnover, what compounds the problem today is the reality that skilled workers are at a premium. Simply put, the "shape up or ship out" approach to managing is no longer feasible in most industries, even for entry-level positions. In response to the realities of the workplace, companies are investing more time and money in training, mentoring, and developing other employee activities.

✔ **The disappearance of hierarchies and the emergence of team play:** As more and more companies have moved away from the command-and-control approach to supervision, tens of thousands of old school managers found themselves in workplace environments that require stronger interpersonal skills, a talent many of them were never called upon to develop. The ability to communicate effectively and build a spirit of teamwork, for example, is far more important in today's workplace than it was when most communication between supervisors and their employees took the form of instructions that had to be followed or behaviors that needed to be corrected.

Creating the Right Environment for Training

It takes more than a curriculum of well-designed, well-delivered courses and workshops to make a training program successful. What's needed most of all is a corporate culture that values continuous learning and development. There's no single formula for creating such an environment. Clearly, though, it's hardly a coincidence that companies frequently singled out for their commitment to training and development are headed by chief executives who are themselves strong advocates of employee education.

Here's a brief look at some of the best practices found in companies that are known for their outstanding training and development programs. You may want to use them as a checklist against what is currently going on in your company.

- ✔ **A mission statement** that incorporates continuous learning as a core value. Beyond this mere statement, there should also be a steady flow of communication from senior management that reinforces this commitment.

- ✔ **A systematic approach** to identifying the skills and knowledge needs of managers and employees that is explicitly connected to business objectives and goals.

- ✔ **An administrative support system** that makes it easy for employees to gather information about education and training offerings, to relate those offerings to their needs, and to arrange the time in their work schedules to take advantage of the offerings.

Assessing Your Training Needs: Where It All Starts

In today's business environment, you can't afford to let training be an afterthought. The cornerstone of an effective training program is a focused and disciplined approach to the process. In Chapter 3, I discuss the concept of a needs assessment and how it works when it comes to staffing. In the case of training, a good needs assessment helps you determine which skills or knowledge your employees require to enable your company not just to respond to competitive challenges, but also to create new opportunities for the future. This big picture goal is precisely in sync with the major trend I discuss throughout this book: the elevation of HR administrators to HR strategists.

How that works in training is that you want to ensure (to the extent possible) that you're staying ahead of demands for training rather than merely reacting to events. The following sections offer pointers on how to make that proactive approach happen.

Assessing your training needs

A growing number of consulting companies and individuals specialize in helping clients identify their training needs. If your company is large enough and you don't have the time or resources to engage in this process yourself, it may well be in your best interest to hire one of these outside sources. If you do decide to manage this process yourself, consider exploring the following options.

Keep in mind that some options work better at larger companies, while others are more effective in smaller companies.

Time, money, mentors: Principles of first-rate training

Fortune 100 companies like General Electric spend in excess of $1 billion a year on training. Though your firm does not likely have that kind of budget, the most important factor is that you show your employees you support their ongoing professional development. Training your employees does, of course, require spending money, but what matters most is the level of your commitment. Here are just a few ways to "walk the walk."

✔ A progressive tuition reimbursement policy

✔ A scheduling policy that doesn't oblige employees to attend training sessions during nonworking hours

✔ Excellent communication channels between HR professionals involved in training and line managers

✔ Performance appraisal systems that take into account what managers have done to enhance the individual development of the employees they manage

✔ A mentoring program that gives employees the chance to learn from and interact with others in the company who might not necessarily be that employee's immediate supervisor. (See also "Mentoring as a training tool" in this chapter. I also discuss mentoring in Chapter 9 as part of the onboarding process.)

✔ If possible, comfortable, well-equipped on-site facilities (a library or training room, for example) where employees have access to books, periodicals, research studies, CDs, DVDs, and self-administered courses. This level of commitment communicates to employees the importance management places on their growth as individuals. And, of course, to the extent possible, this information should also be available through the company's intranet.

Employee focus groups

Generally implemented at larger firms, *employee focus groups* often represent the ideal first step to a needs-assessment process. You pull together a group of employees from various departments or levels of your organization. If time permits, you spend a day or two (possibly off-site) discussing as a group what your company needs to do to achieve its strategic goals and what skills are required to meet this challenge. In the event this time commitment isn't plausible, even a 2 to 3-hour session in a conference room at your company's offices can be illuminating.

No matter how much time you're able to take, two keys make sure that this process is productive:

- ✔ **The make-up of the group:** The group should include representatives from a wide cross section of departments and experience levels.

- ✔ **The ability of the facilitator:** It can be either you or someone else, but the facilitator needs to promote open discussion and keep the focus group from disintegrating into a "gripe session."

Surveys and questionnaires

Surveys and questionnaires are standard tools in the needs-assessment process. Depending on the size of your company, surveys may represent the most cost-effective approach to needs assessment. In a typical needs-assessment questionnaire, employees are given a list of statements or questions that focus on a specific skill. They're invited to indicate whether they think improvements in that area will enhance their ability to perform their jobs or advance in the company.

If you intend to survey employees in this way, also gathering feedback from supervisors is a good idea. Each group may offer a unique perspective. Yet another way of enhancing the utility of questionnaires is to get some survey feedback from customers.

Employees may well have an accurate sense of what they themselves need to improve in order to perform more effectively, but these areas may not necessarily connect directly to the strategic objectives of the company. The goal is to view the information you gather from employees as simply one tool in a process.

Observation

Simply observing how employees are performing on the job and taking note of the problems they're experiencing can often give you insight into their training needs. Here again, you should be careful about the conclusions you draw. It's tempting when observing employees who are struggling with some aspect of their jobs to attribute the difficulty to a single cause — some problem that you can solved by scheduling a training program or by sending them to a seminar. This assumption is dangerous. If you were to notice, for example, that your customer service reps aren't being as courteous to customers as you would like, you may assume that what they need is training in phone skills. Phone training may indeed be called for, but other factors may be involved as well, such as inappropriate pressures from supervisors that are contributing to the negative behavior.

One way to avoid the common pitfall of jumping to conclusions is to speak directly with the employees you've observed and give them the opportunity to explain why their performance may be falling short.

Tying training needs to strategic goals

Whatever approach (or approaches) you take to evaluate your training requirements, the needs-assessment process should be strategically driven. After you've gathered the data — regardless of how you've gathered it — you need to process it within the framework of the following questions:

- ✔ What are the strategic goals of this business — both long term and short term?

- ✔ What competencies do employees need to achieve these goals?

- ✔ What are the current strengths and weaknesses of the workforce relative to those competencies?

- ✔ What improvements can training be expected to offer that differ from day-to-day supervision?

- ✔ What kind of a commitment — in money, time, and effort — is your company willing and able to make in order to provide necessary training?

Deciding whether to train or not to train

Getting a clearer sense of what skill and knowledge deficits you have in your company is one thing, but figuring out where you go from there is something else entirely. The basic question you need to ask in this regard (and it's a question you have to ask yourself over and over) is whether a training program (whichever form it may take) represents the best and most cost-effective approach to reducing the gap between job demands and current employee capabilities. How do you determine whether or not to train a group of employees, and how do you determine how much time and money to invest? There are no simple answers, but certain factors can help guide you:

✔ **State of the labor market:** Training decisions are often dictated by the nature of the labor market in your region. The tighter the labor market, the more pressure on you to develop employees rather than replace them.

✔ **Current workload in the company:** Training sessions can be difficult to schedule and run successfully in companies where employees are already under excessive pressure to meet the day-to-day demands of their jobs. Before you go to the trouble of setting up training sessions, make sure that the targeted employees can take part in those sessions without creating serious problems for their coworkers or supervisors. Someone, preferably in senior management, needs to communicate whether the training sessions will take priority over the day-to-day needs of the business.

✔ **Internal resources and budget:** Training invariably requires an investment of time and resources. True, you can take steps to keep these expenses under control, but at some point, the lack of a budget may produce training activities that will only worsen rather than remedy the performance problems you're trying to correct. Keep in mind that there's a direct correlation between the results you achieve with training and employee attitudes about your company's intent. Programs that employees view as simply a bandage or flavor-of-the-month are almost certain to be counterproductive.

Evaluating Training Options

If you think that conducting an effective needs-assessment process (see "Assessing Your Training Needs: Where it All Starts" in this chapter) is the biggest challenge you face in setting up an effective training program, think again. Needs assessment is simply the first step to effective training and development: You then have to figure out the most intelligent and cost-effective way to meet those needs. This aspect of training administration — figuring out what programs to offer employees — used to be fairly cut and dried. Until recently, most corporate training was delivered the old-fashioned way: through instructor-led, classroom training.

Not so today. Classroom training options still abound, but numerous other training delivery options are available as well. What follows is a brief look at the range of approaches that are possible today, along with the pros and cons.

In-house classroom training

With *in-house classroom training,* the traditional and most familiar form of training, a group of employees gathers in a classroom and is led through the program by an instructor. These sessions occur on-site or off-site and can be facilitated by trainers who are either employees themselves or outside specialists.

Pros: The main advantage to classroom training (apart from its familiarity) is that it provides ample opportunities for group interaction and gives instructors a chance to motivate the group and address the individual needs of students.

Cons: In-house classroom training requires considerable administrative support (coordinating schedules, reserving training space, and so on). Also, in most cases, for larger companies with far-flung offices, this form of training can entail major expense (travel and lodging, for example), which is not directly connected to the learning experience.

Public seminars

You can encourage employees to attend topic-specific workshops that are organized and run by training companies. These public seminars are usually held at a public site, such as a hotel or conference center. Companies that stage these seminars typically market them through direct mail or advertising.

Pros: Public seminars require little or no administrative support. The per person cost is reasonable (usually less than $150 for a one-day course).

Cons: Most public seminar offerings are, by necessity, generic: Topics covered don't necessarily have direct relevance to your particular company. Another problem: inconsistent quality from one seminar to the next.

Executive education seminars

Seminars and workshops offered by universities and business schools are targeted, in most cases, to middle and upper-level managers. Typically they cover a wide range of both theoretical ideas and practical pointers for putting these principles into practice.

Pros: Instructors are usually faculty members with a high level of expertise. These kinds of seminars are a good opportunity for attendees to network and share ideas.

Cons: Courses at the more prestigious schools can take the executive away from the office for more days than desired. They're also expensive, in some cases as much as $5,000 (including room and board) for a five-day course. Choose these courses wisely: Make sure that events cover management concepts and techniques that are relevant or applicable to your firm's business focus and culture.

E-learning: Its growing influence

E-learning, or the use of computer and online technology to house and deliver training content, has gained rapid acceptance throughout corporate America. The concept of learning from sources based far away is, of course, hardly new. Correspondence courses were popular long before computers, CDs, or the Internet entered the workplace. But the great payoff of e-learning is its flexibility and speed, delivering the real-time immediacy of classroom instruction without the need to actually be present in a classroom.

Pros: E-learning has a number of important benefits:

- Vastly increases the scope and reach of a corporate training effort
- Eliminates, or greatly reduces, ancillary, nonlearning expenses of training, such as travel and lodging costs for participants
- Enables students to work at their own pace and convenience so they avoid production downtime
- Enables participants to not only experience training in real time but to also store and subsequently retrieve information transmitted through the course
- Enables students to set up individualized objectives and to establish milestones to mark different levels of achievement
- Liberates you or your training staff from classroom presentations, enabling more one-on-one consultations

Cons: The downside of e-learning is that lack of human interaction and direct instructor involvement can hamper the learning process among people who are not self-motivated. Then again, if an employee is not driven to succeed, then she may not be right for your company.

For more on e-learning, see the next section.

Making E-Learning Work

The growing influence of e-learning as a business practice is being fueled by a number of technologies, primarily computers and the Internet. Here's a look at the ways e-learning is delivered by large, midsize, and many small companies:

- **Internet:** As is the case with virtually everything in the business world, training has benefited greatly from the Internet. By far the primary technology responsible for the growth of e-learning, the Internet is a remarkable online training mall, offering a rich and rapidly growing variety of online workshops, courses, blogs, discussion groups, and literature. Its impact increased tremendously when high-speed access became widely available.

  You can access training courses, experts, and materials that cover an immense range of topics and sources. Many courses are sponsored and run by colleges and universities, as well as a large number of other organizations.

  Besides courses employees can take at their own pace, some Internet training takes place in real time, where the instructor directs a course via e-mails, chats, webcasts, or webinars. Other courses are taught over a period of days, weeks, or months, with students turning in assignments, occasionally communicating in a group format, or intermittently checking in with the instructor. In some situations, these courses are conducted without any face-to-face contact. In others, the instructor employs a Web camera, which can be quite useful when, for example, an instructor wants to provide a role-play scenario on a topic such as offering constructive criticism to a subordinate.

- **Intranets:** Thousands of companies have created internal computer networks known as *intranets* that use the Internet as their backbone. An intranet's biggest asset is security. Businesses find intranets very useful in confidentially sharing information and resources with employees, including training. Once it's set up, an intranet-based training program vastly simplifies the task of administration and keeping track of results. The big drawback: It can take considerable time and expertise to set up a training curriculum of this kind.

  You can contact vendors specializing in e-learning that can help customize their courses to your company's specific needs and integrate it into your intranet.

- **Video teleconferencing:** Though in many ways the Internet has absorbed video teleconferencing as a training device, video teleconferencing can still be useful when you want to gather all your employees in one place to receive a particular course of training. Much of your decision depends, of course, on the size of your company and employee body. For midsize to large companies, an orientation event, a critical part of the onboarding process, may be an ideal time for video teleconferencing so that an entire group can hear one message and discuss it at the same time (see Chapter 9).

If video conference technology is rarely used, it's probably not worth the expense. And while hiring outside specialists to handle teleconferencing may make sense for major, one-time events, it's hardly as efficient as the Internet for ongoing training purposes.

✔ **CDs and DVDs:** Some courses and seminars come packaged in kits and sold as CD-ROMs or DVDs. (Some recorded training still comes in VCR or audiotape format, but new technology is rapidly replacing them.) CDs and DVDs are easily administered to a group without the need for an instructor who's an expert in the topic. Many companies combine off-the-shelf programs with company-based activities that address local problems and issues. Employees who drive long distances as part of their jobs can access training via audio CDs in their cars or trucks, but the importance of road safety makes this option more of a voluntary solution than one you should require.

✔ **Podcasts:** Portable MP3 players, PDAs, and mobile phones can allow employees to conveniently access digitally recorded course segments while traveling or in places where even a laptop computer would be impractical. Though an unlikely substitute for an entire training program, these devices are an undeniably convenient way to supplement instruction. Portable devices can be an easy way for an employee who missed a live session, lecture, or module to keep up.

With all these offerings, you need to shop intelligently. Anytime you're considering a training course or program, find out more about the credentials of both the organization and, if appropriate, the instructor. Ask for references, and if you're not given any, look elsewhere.

Don't forget you've got to monitor and manage e-learning if it's to be successful. If you simply upload a slew of training courses and tell employees to "have at it," then you shouldn't expect it to do much good. The good news is that e-learning is easy to monitor. In fact, one of the benefits of e-learning is that you can track its usage to make sure that employees are engaged in the learning and are actively participating and completing the required workshops and courses. Encourage — and maybe even offer incentives — to employees who complete training. Set aside specific times for training so that employees feel comfortable temporarily stopping their day-to-day tasks to complete an online course.

A word of caution: Lead, but don't bleed

E-learning has unquestionably enhanced the training process. But as is the case with any new resource, you have to know what you're doing and why you're doing it. With that in mind, avoid the *bleeding edge syndrome,* wherein you feel the need to experiment with every new form of technology. No matter whether it's a new technique useful for wireless computers, or content that you can transmit swiftly via mobile phones, or a Web site that incorporates downstreaming video, don't lose sight of the basics. Easy as it is to get swept away by all these bells and whistles, any single delivery method is secondary to the primary goal: Creating efficient and effective ways to improve employee skills and knowledge in a manner consistent with the company's strategy and goals.

In short, e-learning is a productive training technique, but also one that requires careful attention. You need to determine which mix of approaches best matches your real needs. To evaluate effectively, you need to create a team consisting of yourself, technology experts and line managers to collectively create the best possible set of solutions. For example, the time and expenditures required to set up an effective system of intranet-based training makes sense only when you have a large population of potential students — and only when your long-term strategy is to make your intranet your primary training delivery system.

Mentoring as a Training Tool

Some skills, such as interpersonal abilities, are not easily taught in the classroom or through online courses. In fact, some skills aren't taught well in groups at all. Enter employee mentors. Just as appointing a more experienced employee to serve as a mentor for a new employee can help her acclimate to your work environment (see Chapter 9), well-chosen mentors can likewise assist staff at any stage of their careers with longer term developmental learning.

In a mentoring role, an employee who excels in a given area — customer service, for example — can help fellow employees discover how to more smoothly interact with customers and colleagues or develop additional skills that require more long-term and individualized attention than a classroom or online course can offer. Regarding interpersonal, or people skills, employees who are paired with an appropriate manager can pick up such abilities as persuasiveness and diplomacy.

Mentors can also serve as valuable training facilitators for high-potential employees you may want to groom to eventually take over key roles in your company. Mentoring programs are among the most effective ways to transfer tacit knowledge from seasoned leaders to aspiring ones. As firms brace for significant turnover among their most experienced employees due to the retirement of many baby boomers, such arrangements may become increasingly important as a means of passing on valuable know-how to less experienced workers and preparing them take on positions of greater responsibility.

Deciding on a Training Program

Again, evaluating the effectiveness of each training program independent of the variables at play is virtually impossible. The point is that now, more than ever, learning is a highly individual process, and because of that you must remain leery of taking the "one-size-fits-all" approach. In general, here are some of the factors that most often influence the effectiveness of a program, regardless of which form it takes:

Receptivity level of students

You should consider the extent to which participants are open and receptive to the concepts that are covered in the training.

How to control it: Do your best to communicate to all potential participants the specific learning objectives of the course and how they will benefit. Make sure that supervisors who've recommended that certain employees attend the program communicate to employees why that decision was made.

Applicability of subject matter

The success of any program will hinge largely on whether participants believe that what they're being taught has direct relevance to the day-to-day challenges they face in their jobs.

How to control it: Take all reasonable steps to ensure that the workshop focuses on issues that are the most important to employees taking the program. If you're using an outside training provider, make sure that the instructor is aware of those issues. Arrange to have examples and exercises customized, making ideas easy to relate to.

Eight common pitfalls of ineffective training

Your ability to put together a training program that achieves its desired results is often determined by the common mistakes you avoid. Here's a brief look at the most common pitfalls of training administration — and the consequences of those pitfalls.

Pitfall: Failing to incorporate business goals into the overall training effort.

Consequence: Because training efforts aren't aligned with business goals from the start, the results rarely have any impact on company operations, and the training initiative doesn't get any further support from senior management.

Pitfall: Not taking enough time to go through a systematic needs assessment process.

Consequence: The offerings have little or no impact on the performance issues that have the most bearing on employee performance and business results.

Pitfall: Inefficient process for identifying training participants.

Consequence: Courses attract employees who, for any number of reasons, shouldn't be in the course to begin with, and whose presence can be disruptive to employees who badly need the training. An example is employees who fail to meet the prerequisites for an advanced software course and spend the majority of the course getting up to speed on the basics.

Pitfall: Lack of a disciplined process for evaluating training programs brought in from the outside.

Consequence: Training initiative, in general, loses credibility among key constituents.

Pitfall: Failure to solicit feedback from supervisors during the needs-assessment process.

Consequence: Supervisors never really buy into the training initiative and fail to reinforce what participants learn.

Pitfall: Conducting the training in substandard facilities.

Consequence: Discomfort and inconvenience sends the wrong message to employees and inhibits their ability to absorb the training.

Pitfall: Trying to accomplish too much in a limited time frame.

Consequence: Employees who go through training feel more frustrated at the end of the course than they did when they first entered the class.

Pitfall: Lack of *experiential learning* (for example, simulations, hands-on exercises, and role playing).

Consequence: Employees like the ability to actually practice what they're learning during training sessions. Experiential learning ensures that they retain more of what they learn, and its popularity makes it a retention tool as well.

The overall learning experience

Consider how interesting or entertaining the training session is, content notwithstanding.

How to control it: Bear in mind that adults aren't as accustomed as children to the passive nature of traditional classroom learning. Training sessions should be as interactive and participant-oriented as possible. The best courses use a variety of learning tools: lecture, discussion, and exercises.

Quality of instructor

A big factor in determining the effectiveness of a program is the ability of the trainers or instructors (whether they're giving live presentations or are on videotape) to capture and sustain the interest of participants.

How to control it: Try to get as clear a picture ahead of time of how effective the instructor is as a presenter. Ask for a videotape or attend an actual session. Instructors' level of knowledge should be equal to or greater than that of the audience. Don't have someone who's never coached a team, for example, teach a class in management techniques.

Reinforcement of class concepts

Devise techniques to reinforce the skills learned in the seminar and apply them to the job or task at hand.

How to control it: Ask seminar participants to create followup plans during or at the end of a session. Alternatively, trainers can create a followup plan and send it to participants' managers with a request to integrate certain aspects of training into the job, if feasible.

Making sure that you get feedback

E-mail has made it much easier to measure the effectiveness of training in a timely manner. You can quickly send surveys to large groups of employees. If you want, you can distribute them and ask for responses within a few days or even hours of the session's conclusion, though in many instances you may want your employees to reflect for a short time prior to providing feedback. You can also record survey responses online, with results organized into databases and available to HR team members and line managers.

But Is It Working? Measuring Results

As the person in your company responsible for the training effort, you can safely assume that you're going to be called upon at some point to answer a simple question: Is the money and time being invested in the program paying any real dividends?

If you're not sure of how you go about answering this question, join the club. HR professionals have long wrestled with the problem of quantifying the results of a process that doesn't readily lend itself to quantifiable measures. It's generally acknowledged, for example, that one of the primary benefits of employee training is that it enhances morale. But how do you measure the bottom-line benefits of morale? Not easily, to be sure. Yet another problem with measuring the results of training is that the skills and knowledge that people bring to a task represent only one factor in job performance. In many situations, factors that are independent of an employee's knowledge and skills will either impede or enhance job performance.

These issues apart, following are four generally accepted practices for measuring the results of training:

- ✔ **Initial employee reaction:** The most common way to gather feedback from participants immediately following a training session is to distribute a questionnaire to each one at the end of the session. The answers give you a general idea of whether your employees thought the training was worthwhile and how impressed (or unimpressed) they were with the instructor and instructional materials. This feedback is useful but limited. Post-training surveys measure initial reactions, but offer little insight into how effective the training was in the long run.

- ✔ **Effectiveness of learning:** Your ability to gain an accurate measure of how much people have actually learned in a training session depends in large part on the subject matter of the course. You can measure the learning that takes place during programs that focus on well-defined technical skills (using new software programs, for example) by administering tests before and after the training and comparing the results. Remember, though, that the subject matter of many training programs (leadership skills, for example) doesn't lend itself to specific metrics. One way around this limitation is to observe the accomplishments or behavior of employees in the weeks and months after soft skills training. Did those who had leadership training, for example, report lower attrition rates for their staff? Do more trainees win promotions than the average employee base? What about staff who participated in team-building exercises? Are they becoming better collaborators?

✔ **Impact on job performance:** Determining whether training has had a positive impact on actual job performance depends on the nature of the training and the specific tasks. The problem? Performance in most jobs is influenced by variables that may have little bearing on what was taught in a workshop. It is not at all unusual for participants to bring back to their jobs new skills, but they may run into resistance from supervisors when they try to put their newly acquired skills to practical use. That's why it's important to educate company managers about the advantages training sessions bring to their employees. Conducting executive briefings or a quick "Benefits of Training for Your Staff" course can help managers appreciate what their employees are learning and become more supportive in helping them grow beyond the training period.

✔ **Cost/benefit analysis:** Measuring the bottom-line benefits of training is, by far, the most imposing challenge you face in your efforts to build a business rationale for training. The reason is simple: Training simply doesn't easily lend itself to familiar cost/benefit analysis. The costs are easy enough to quantify. The problem lies with attaching a dollar value to the many indirect benefits that training brings, which may include reduced absenteeism and turnover, reduced employee grievances, a less stressful workplace (with fewer medical problems), and the need for less supervision. If you're pressed by senior management to come up with a return-on-investment rationale for training, work with line managers to develop some reasonable financial barometers for these indirect benefits.

TIP

Key questions to ask in a post-training questionnaire

Employees' answers to the following survey questions can help you gauge the effectiveness of your training sessions.

✔ Did the course meet your expectations, based on the course description?

✔ Were the topics covered in the course directly relevant to your job?

✔ Was the instructor sensitive to the needs of the group?

✔ Were the instructional materials easy to follow and logical?

✔ Would you recommend this program to other employees?

✔ Were the facilities adequate?

Part IV
Keeping Things Together: Monitoring Ongoing Performance

The 5th Wave   By Rich Tennant

A pie factory is no place to let motivation slip, Brad.

In this part . . .

You may have moved mountains to hire the best staff in the world, and you may be offering them the most comprehensive and cost-effective benefits package known to man, but that's only half your job. You have to keep the machines well oiled, turbocharge them occasionally, and fix them when they break down. That's what this part of the book is all about. From assessing the way your team is handling their jobs and inspiring them to achieve even more, to handling the not-so-un aspects of HR, I show you what it takes to keep things together.

Chapter 15

Assessing Employee Performance

• •

In This Chapter

▶ Creating a performance appraisal process

▶ Introducing the program

▶ Handling difficulties

▶ Following up

• •

*F*ew management practices are more basic or prevalent than performance appraisals — the mechanism through which managers or supervisors evaluate the job performance of their employees. Yet, as common as the practice may be, many companies, both large and small, experience difficulty in structuring and managing the process.

To be sure, the problem doesn't lie in the concept itself. Everybody agrees that effective managers have to monitor the performance of direct reports, note which areas of job performance need to be improved, and then communicate assessments to them in a positive and constructive way. How else is it possible to determine how people get promoted, if they deserve salary increases, and how much they should be making?

The problem seems to be not with the concept, but with the format and mechanics. In many companies today, managers as well as employees aren't convinced of the value of appraisal systems. To many supervisors, they simply represent additional work, and some employees remain skeptical and apprehensive regarding the process. In addition, traditional approaches to performance appraisals aren't necessarily well suited to today's flatter management structures, which de-emphasize direct supervision, promote employee autonomy, and often involve collaboration with many different employees from a wide range of disciplines. In fact, many younger companies were created with the goal of intentionally *not* resembling older command-and-control corporations and, as a result, are reluctant to create formal employee performance evaluation procedures. Yet another problem with performance appraisals in today's workplace is that the difficulty in finding highly skilled employees, coupled with the fear of litigation, has made some managers gun-shy about being too critical of their staff members.

These problems notwithstanding, performance appraisals are a vital management function, and it's up to you to help your company implement a structured and systematic program that takes into account the realities of today's workplace — and the nuances of your firm's unique culture. As I point out in Chapter 10, merit raises should always be pegged to your performance evaluation system.

The information in this chapter is legally sensitive. As they have with this entire book, the firm of O'Melveny & Myers LLP generously helped with this chapter, and we strongly recommend that you consult with an attorney before adopting an official appraisal system. The policies you set in place can make or break your company in a potential lawsuit. So do yourself a favor: Hire a lawyer before you *must* have one.

Reaping the Benefits of Performance Appraisals

Creating and implementing a structured performance appraisal process is by no means a modest challenge. For one thing, performance appraisals invariably create additional work for supervisors. The process also puts pressure on employees by forcing everyone to establish specific goals and identify the behaviors necessary to achieve those goals, which some may view in the short term as simply "busy work." What's more, the very nature of appraisal systems puts both employees and supervisors into situations that most people find uncomfortable. Being, in effect, "graded" makes many employees feel as though they're back in school, for example. And most managers, even those who've been involved with an evaluation process for many years, find it difficult to be both candid and constructive when they're conducting an appraisal session that involves negative feedback.

Why, then, should you put in the time and effort needed to create and implement this process? The answer, simply put, is that the long-term benefits of an effectively structured and administered performance appraisal process far outweigh the time and effort the process requires. Here's what a well-designed, well-implemented performance appraisal system can do for your company:

✔ Creates criteria for determining how well employees are truly performing — and, to that end, makes it clear how their job descriptions and responsibilities fit in with company and departmental priorities

✔ Provides an objective — and legally defensible — basis for key human resources decisions, including merit pay increases, promotions, and job responsibilities

✔ Verifies that reward mechanisms are logically tied to outstanding performance (see Chapter 10)

✔ Motivates employees to improve their job performance

✔ Enhances the impact of the coaching that is already taking place between employees and their managers

✔ Establishes a reasonably uniform set of performance standards that are in sync with company values

✔ Confirms that employees possess the skills or attributes needed to successfully fulfill a particular job

✔ Irons out difficulties in the supervisor-employee relationship

✔ Gives underperforming employees the guidance that can lead to better performance

✔ Keeps employees focused on business goals and objectives

✔ Helps employees clarify career goals

✔ Validates hiring strategies and practices

✔ Reinforces company values

✔ Assesses training and staff development needs

✔ Motivates employees to upgrade their skills and job knowledge so that they can make a more meaningful contribution to your company's success

Deciding on a Performance Appraisal System

The first step you need to take after you've decided either to introduce a performance appraisal system in your company or to change your current one is determining which kind of system is best for your company. All performance appraisal systems are driven by the same objective: to establish a systematic way of evaluating performance, providing constructive feedback, and enabling employees to continually improve their performance.

The basic ingredients in all systems are pretty much the same: setting performance criteria, developing tracking and documenting procedures, determining which areas should be measured quantitatively, and deciding how the information is to be communicated to employees. Where the different methods vary is in the following areas:

✔ The degree to which employees are involved in establishing performance evaluation criteria

✔ How employee performance is tracked and documented

✔ How performance is rated and how it's aligned with corporate priorities, objectives, and goals

✔ The specific types of appraisal tools used — in some cases, for example, certain approaches are more appropriate for evaluating managers and professionals than other employees

✔ The amount of time and effort required to implement the process

✔ How the results of the appraisal are integrated into other management or HR functions

✔ How the actual appraisal session is conducted

The following section offers a brief description of performance appraisal methods most commonly used today.

Goal-setting, or management by objectives (MBO)

First created by influential business thinker Peter Drucker in 1954, *management by objectives* (MBO) is still an extremely popular appraisal system because of its focus on results and the activities and skills that truly define an employee's job. Even more recent forms of appraisal that require reciprocal feedback, such as the increasingly popular multi-rater assessment I describe later in this section, are in large part based on the principles of MBO.

In a typical MBO scenario, an employee and manager sit down together at the start of an appraisal period and formulate a set of statements that represent specific job goals, targets, or *deliverables*.

What makes MBO so powerful is its direct link to organizational objectives and priorities. In the case of MBO, goals, targets, and deliverables should be as specific and measurable as possible. For example, instead of "improve customer service" (too vague), try something like "reduce the number of customer complaints by 5 percent." And instead of "increase number of sales calls" (too vague), go with "increase the number of sales calls by 5 percent without changing current criteria for prospects."

This list of targets becomes the basis for an action plan that spells out what steps need to be taken to achieve each goal. At a later date — six months or a year later — the employee and the manager sit down again and measure employee performance on the basis of how many of those goals were met.

Advantages:

✔ Is familiar: MBO has been used for decades and provides a sharp focus for evaluating employee performance

✔ Draws the employee into the appraisal process

✔ Can be easily integrated into companywide performance-improvement initiatives

✔ Gives employee a blueprint for successful performance

✔ Emphasizes action and results

Downsides:

✔ Takes time and involves considerable paperwork

✔ Works effectively only if supervisors are trained in the process

✔ Can lack sufficient specificity of goals

✔ Doesn't work well for employees who have little discretion over how their jobs are performed

Essay appraisals

Though less popular than it was a few years ago, the *essay approach* still has merit. It can be quite useful for a supervisor to periodically compose statements that describe an employee's performance during the appraisal period. The statements are usually written on standard forms, and they can be as general or as specific as you want. A supervisor may describe an employee's performance in terms of "his or her ability to relate to other work-team members." These written statements can either be forwarded to the HR department or can be used as one element in an appraisal session. Any written evaluation also needs to include more measurable evaluation tools, such as rating scales applied to specific objectives, tasks, and goals.

Advantages:

- ✔ Is easy to administer
- ✔ Lends itself to most supervisory and professional functions
- ✔ Forces supervisors to give serious thought to worker performance

Downsides:

- ✔ Can vary in its effectiveness according to the writing skills of the evaluator
- ✔ Can vary in length and content, making appraisals from different supervisors difficult to compare
- ✔ Promote highly subjective perceptions

ON THE CD

See the CD-ROM for a sample Essay Appraisal Form.

Critical incidents reporting

The *critical incidents method* of performance appraisal is built around a list of specific behaviors, generally known as *critical behaviors,* that are deemed necessary to perform a particular job competently. Managers, the HR department, or outside consultants can draw up the list. Performance evaluators use a critical incident report to record actual incidents of behavior that illustrate when employees either carried out or didn't carry out these behaviors. You can use these logs to document a wide variety of job behaviors, such as interpersonal skills, initiative, and leadership ability.

Advantages:

- ✔ Records employee performance as it happens
- ✔ Always links employee behavior to job performance
- ✔ Provides documented record of behaviors over time
- ✔ Identifies the most important dimensions of a job
- ✔ Offers more insight into job descriptions and core competencies

Downsides:

- ✔ Requires disciplined and regular attention
- ✔ Can often compromise objectivity of recorded incidents because of the evaluator's emotional state when the incident is recorded
- ✔ Depends on a clear definition of critical behaviors

Job rating checklist

The *job rating checklist* method of performance appraisal is the simplest method to use and lends itself to a variety of approaches. To implement this approach, you supply each evaluator with a prepared list of statements or questions that relate to specific aspects of job performance. The questions typically require the evaluator to write a simple "yes" or "no" answer or to record a number (or some other notation) that indicates which statement applies to a particular employee's performance. More often than not, the responsibility for developing the list lies with the HR department.

A more sophisticated variation to this method is to establish a *weighted rating system* in which a number is used to reflect the relative importance of each criterion being evaluated. The weighted variation presents a clearer picture of how employee strengths and weaknesses measure up against the priorities of the job.

Advantages:

✔ Minimizes the amount of paperwork for the evaluator

✔ Can customize lists in any number of ways

✔ Can purchase lists commercially

Downsides:

✔ Unsuited to jobs with evolving or frequently changing requirements

✔ Offers only a sketchy outline of job performance

✔ Doesn't encourage evaluators to focus on "improvement" strategies

See the CD-ROM for a sample Job Rating Checklist Appraisal Form.

Behaviorally anchored rating scale (BARS)

Behaviorally anchored rating scale (BARS) systems are designed to emphasize the behavior, traits, and skills needed to successfully perform a job. A typical BARS form has two columns. The left column has a rating scale, usually in stages from Very Poor to Excellent. The right column contains behavioral anchors that are the reflections of those ratings.

If the scale were being used, for example, to evaluate a telephone order taker, the statement in one column may read "1-Very Poor," and the statement in the right column may read, "Occasionally rude or abrupt to customer" or "Makes frequent mistakes on order form."

Advantages:

✔ Reduces the potential for biased responses

✔ Focuses on specific, observable behaviors

✔ Provides specific and standardized comments on job performance

Downsides:

✔ Can be time consuming and complicated to develop

✔ Depends on accuracy and appropriateness of "anchor statements"

✔ Must be updated as job requirements change

✔ Impractical for jobs with frequently changing requirements

Forced choice

Forced-choice methods generally come in two forms: paired statements and forced ranking. In the *paired statements method,* evaluators are presented with two statements and must check the one that best describes the employee; it's either one or the other. In the *forced ranking method,* a number of options are listed, allowing the evaluator to select a description that may fall somewhere in between the two extremes.

The following example illustrates how each version may be used to cover the same aspect of job performance for a field service representative.

Paired statements:

____ Provides sufficient detail when filling out trip reports

____ Doesn't provide sufficient detail when filling out trip reports

Forced ranking:

____ Provides sufficient detail when filling out trip reports

____ Exceptional

____ Above average

____ Average

_____ Needs improvement

_____ Unsatisfactory

Advantages:

✔ Minimizes bias

✔ Is somewhat more objective than other ranking methods

Downsides:

✔ Requires skill and professional training to develop

✔ Must be redesigned when job requirements change

✔ Doesn't lend itself to behaviors that are difficult to quantify

Ranking methods

Ranking methods compare employees in a group to one another. All involve an evaluator who asks managers to rank employees from the "best" to the "worst" with respect to specific job performance criteria. The three most common variations of this method are as follows:

✔ **Straight ranking:** Employees are simply listed in order of ranking.

✔ **Forced comparison:** Every employee is paired with every other employee in the group, and in each case, the manager identifies the better of the two employees in any pairing. The employees are ranked by the number of times they're identified as the best.

✔ **Forced distribution:** The employees are ranked along a standard statistical distribution, the so-called *Bell Curve*.

Advantages:

✔ Can be helpful in presenting an overall picture of employee strengths and weaknesses throughout the company

✔ Requires little training

Downsides:

✔ Is the most subjective of appraisal methods

✔ Provides little information on training and development needs

✔ Focuses on individuals rather than job outcomes or behaviors

> ✔ Forces raters to evaluate employees in terms of other employees
>
> ✔ One of the ranking methods, forced distribution, is suitable only for large groups to be statistically valid, typically thousands of employees.

Multi-rater assessments

Multi-rater assessments are also called *360-degree assessment.* The employee's supervisors, coworkers, subordinates, and, in some cases, customers are asked to complete detailed questionnaires on the employee. The employee completes the same questionnaire. The results are tabulated, and the employee then compares her assessment with the other results.

Advantages:

> ✔ Draws assessments from a wide variety of sources
>
> ✔ Gives maximum feedback to employee

Downsides:

> ✔ Need to have the questionnaires professionally developed
>
> ✔ Relies on people outside the employee's immediate work circle, which may cause resentment

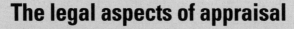

The legal aspects of appraisal

Depending upon how you develop and conduct it, an appraisal system can do one of two things with respect to your company's legal exposure:

> ✔ Unnecessarily expose your company to the danger of discrimination lawsuits
>
> ✔ Provide your company with a strong defense if you're taken to court by an employee or former employee over an unfavorable personnel action.

The best defense against wrongful dismissal is a carefully documented record of unfavorable performance evaluations, coupled with an employee's inability or refusal to carry out suggestions to correct poor work or on-the-job behavior.

At the same time, you need to be sure that no aspect of your appraisal system violates state or federal antidiscrimination legislation.

Launching an Appraisal Program in Your Company

When you set up a new performance appraisal system, you need to gather input from both senior management and employees and also make sure that the program is workable and well communicated throughout the organization. The results can be disastrous when well-meaning HR professionals attempt to impose an approach on the organization without fully considering how it will be perceived. (See the sidebar "Overcoming obstacles," later in this chapter.) The success or failure of an appraisal system hinges on factors that are based more on company issues than on the system itself. The following sections list successful guidelines culled from studies of companies with successful performance appraisal systems.

Enlist the support of senior management

Because appraisals can be a difficult sell with both employees and managers in some organizations (especially in companies that have never formalized the process), you must make sure early in your development process that senior management is willing to give the initiative strong support.

One major way you can generate support for your ideas is to explain to top management how the particular approach you're recommending is tailored to the company's business and culture. For example, a retail environment has a heavy emphasis on teamwork and collegiality. In this instance, where on-floor sales personnel, clerks, and cashiers are all highly dependent on one another, a multi-rater assessment (see "Multi-rater assessments" in this chapter) can be quite useful. On the other hand, take the case of a professional services firm. While collaboration is also important in that environment, it may be less valued than intellectual problem-solving skills, in which case an essay written by a supervisor may prove more insightful.

Give employees a say in establishing performance criteria

Bring in employees who are going to be evaluated as early as possible into the developmental process. At the very least, invite employees to offer input on what specific skills, attributes, behaviors, and goals should be the basis of the performance criteria.

Choose performance measures with care

The cornerstone of a successful performance appraisal process is the criteria used as the basis of evaluation. Here are some of the key factors you should bear in mind when formulating criteria, along with the questions you should ask yourself with respect to each factor:

- ✔ **Job-relatedness:** Are the criteria connected to strategic business goals? How are these big-picture goals linked to successful work performance?

- ✔ **Feasibility:** Do employees have the resources, the training, or the autonomy required to meet the goals?

- ✔ **Measurability:** Can the behaviors that underlie each performance be observed, measured, and documented?

Develop a fair and practical tracking mechanism

In small companies, when supervisors and employees are working closely together, keeping track of day-to-day behavior is not much of a problem. In larger companies, though, tracking can become a key issue. Essentially, you need a reliable and fair mechanism (on-the-job observation, for example) to ensure that the results of the appraisal are an accurate reflection of day-to-day employee performance. Here are some questions to ask yourself when confronting this issue:

- ✔ What specific procedures will be used to track and monitor behavior?

- ✔ During what specific periods is behavior going to be tracked and observed?

- ✔ What training, if any, do managers need to carry out these procedures without placing undue pressure on themselves?

- ✔ To what extent will employees be made aware that their behavior is being observed and measured?

- ✔ What recording mechanism is going to be used to document performance?

- ✔ Where is the documentation going to be kept and what assurances of confidentiality, if any, will be given to employees about the tracking procedure?

Devise a workable evaluation method

There is no one "right" way to determine which specific evaluation method (See "Deciding on a Performance Appraisal System" in this chapter) will work best in your company. Here are factors to take into account:

- ✔ **The level of employees being appraised:** Some methods, such as MBO or essay appraisals, are more suitable for managers and professionals than for other workers. An essay can evaluate such nuanced, qualitative skills as problem-solving, decision-making, and the ability to supervise other people. Are these skills important for a warehouse worker? Certainly, but they're likely less vital than more quantitative factors that you can evaluate through such techniques as a job checklist. One key variable that helps shape your range of evaluation techniques: the degree of autonomy an employee enjoys.

- ✔ **The degree of training needed to implement the program:** Some systems, such as MBO and critical incidents, require more training than others to implement effectively. Make sure that you take into consideration the current workload of your supervisors before you introduce a program that requires extensive training.

- ✔ **The availability of development resources:** The more complex the appraisal system, the more time and effort you'll need to develop it. So if you decide to launch a system that involves extensive research into how jobs are performed and what constitutes outstanding performance, make sure that you have the appropriate time and resources available. Remember, too, that as job requirements change, the evaluation forms must also change, which can mean additional work down the road. In short, don't bite off more than you can chew.

Keep it simple

Resist the temptation to create the perfect system. Keep in mind that no matter how hard you try to quantify the measuring of any performance criterion, you can never remove the human element. It's not a science. Don't shoot yourself in the foot by creating a system that is so complicated that no one will take the time or effort to learn it.

Develop a communication game plan

Most appraisal processes live or die on the basis of how clearly and how openly you communicate the aims and the mechanics of the system to employees. At the very least, everyone involved in the process should be aware of the following information before you actually launch the program:

- ✔ The overall goals of the initiative
- ✔ How employees themselves will benefit from the program
- ✔ How performance criteria will be developed
- ✔ The length of the appraisal periods
- ✔ The degree to which appraisal results will be linked to bonuses, merit pay increases, and other HR-related activities
- ✔ What recourse employees have in the event they disagree with the results
- ✔ What training, if any, will be made available to managers expected to implement the program

You can communicate this information in any number of ways. The important thing is to have a communication strategy. Make sure that everyone has a clear understanding of how the program will work and their roles in ensuring the program's success.

Getting the Most Out of the Performance Appraisal Meeting

At one point or another in the process of creating a performance appraisal process, you have to address the "people" component — what happens when managers and employees sit down together to set goals or to discuss work performance during the appraisal period.

More specifically, the one thing you can't afford to do is to assume that this aspect of the process will simply "take care of itself." The simple truth is that very few managers have ever been trained to conduct an effective performance appraisal session. So while your managers may be responsible for what happens during the session, you and your HR colleagues are responsible for making sure that they're prepared for the challenge.

Overcoming obstacles

Regardless of how much time you take to gather feedback and incorporate it into a new performance appraisal system, you may still face objections. Some employees approach appraisals with skepticism and even trepidation. Some supervisors may not appreciate the reasons for the additional work. And the senior management of some younger companies, eager not to mimic what they perceive as the harshly judgmental cultures of older corporations, resist the idea of conducting performance appraisals at all. It's your job to demonstrate to your team that, in order for companies to grow, its managers need to evaluate what's working, what isn't, and what can be improved.

So when it comes to the potential obstacles encountered by performance appraisal systems, here's what you can expect — and what to do about it:

Employee resistance: Employees often feel threatened by appraisal systems, and some employees actively dislike being appraised. How to respond: Communicate as clearly and as openly as possible the purpose and mechanics of the new appraisal system and that it was built with their input. Make sure that employees understand what role the appraisal will play in influencing the things they care about: raises, promotions, and so on. Spell out the role they're expected to play in the process.

Supervisor resistance: Appraisal systems require extra work by supervisors and managers, as well as create additional paperwork and administrative overhead. How to respond: Keep forms and paperwork to a minimum, but provide forms for continuing tasks such as critical incidents reporting. Train evaluators and audit their performance to see whether follow-up training is needed.

Preparing for the meeting

Managers should be thoroughly briefed on what they need to do prior to holding a performance appraisal session. The key point to emphasize when you're talking to managers about the meeting is being ready: that is, not waiting until the last minute before thinking about how the meeting is going to be handled. Managers should have a clear idea before the meeting begins of what specific behaviors are going to be the focal point of the session. Other points to stress include the following:

- ✔ Give employees sufficient time to prepare for the session
- ✔ Allot sufficient time to conduct a productive session
- ✔ Have all documentation ready prior to the meeting
- ✔ Choose a suitable place (private, quiet, relaxing, with no interruptions) for the meeting

Conducting the session

If more than a handful of managers will be involved in your performance appraisal process, think about setting up training sessions for them on how to conduct an effective appraisal session. Whether you conduct this training yourself or bring in an outside company, here are the points that should be stressed:

- ✔ The appraisal meeting should always be a two-way conversation, not a one-way lecture.

- ✔ Positives should always be emphasized before negatives are discussed.

- ✔ The emphasis should be always on what needs to be done to improve and not what was done wrong.

- ✔ Employees should be encouraged to comment on any observation managers share with them.

- ✔ Managers should know how to explain to employees the difference between effort (how hard employees are working) and quality results (whether the results of those efforts are contributing significantly to business objectives).

Giving constructive feedback

If your company is like most, the toughest thing for your managers to do during the appraisal meeting will be to talk about performance areas in which the employee is lacking. Here again, it's in your best interest to work in advance with your managers so that they're sufficiently prepared to handle this undeniably tricky aspect of the process. Here are the points to emphasize:

- ✔ **Focus on why candor is important:** Managers who, when the need arises, fail to focus on the negative aspects of employee performance are not only doing the employee a disservice, but can also be harming your company as well. The employee can't very well improve if the manager doesn't communicate the need. Additionally, should it become necessary to fire an employee, a manager's failure to mention the employee's weakness in a performance appraisal can jeopardize the company's ability to defend the firing decision.

- ✔ **Stress the importance of documentation.** Managers should always be prepared to back up critical comments with specific, job-related examples. The documentation for these examples should be gathered prior to the meeting.

✔ **Highlight the importance of careful wording.** Managers should be made aware (if they're not already aware) that how a criticism is worded is every bit as important as what behavior is being described. Remind managers to focus on the behavior itself and not on the personality quality that may have led to the behavior. For example, instead of saying, "You've been irresponsible," be sure to describe the specific event that reflects the irresponsibility, as in "For the past few weeks, you've missed these deadlines."

✔ **Encourage employee feedback.** Once managers have issued any piece of criticism, employees should be given the opportunity to comment. Managers should be advised that, given a chance, employees will often admit to their shortcomings and may even ask for help.

✔ **End on a positive note.** No matter how negative the feedback may be, performance appraisal meetings should end on a positive note and with a plan for improvement.

Preparing for a negative reaction

In a well-managed company, most employees are probably performing adequately or better, but some people don't take criticism well, no matter how minimal or appropriately delivered. In any performance appraisal meeting, an employee whose work is being criticized has the potential to become agitated, confrontational, verbally abusive, and, in very rare instances, violent. Managers should be alerted to this possibility and given a strategy for response. Here's some advice to share with them:

✔ **Within reason, let the employee blow off steam.** Don't respond, comment on, or challenge the employee while he is agitated or angry. In certain situations, a calm, nonthreatening demeanor can defuse a situation.

✔ **Don't fake agreement.** The worst thing you can say in this sort of situation is "I can see why you're upset." It can very well set the employee off again.

✔ **When the storm passes, continue the meeting.** A lack of response usually ends most outbursts, and the employee quickly realizes he has made a serious mistake. Accept the apology and move on.

✔ **If she has any hint that the employee may become violent, the manager should leave the room immediately and seek help,** either from an in-house security guard, calling 911 for the police, or, if necessary, other nearby employees.

Choosing areas for further development

What's most important following the delivery of any constructive criticism is a mutual effort between employees and managers to begin the process of making changes that will help staff perform at a higher level. As part of the appraisal meeting, supervisors should recommend areas for improvement and, together with their employees, build a set of workable performance-development activities.

To prepare, supervisors should take time prior to the meeting to create a concise, one-page list of potential developmental activities for the employee. The list can include

- Recommended readings, both current and ongoing, devoted to the topics where development is suggested
- Possible classroom or online courses
- People within the company who may offer useful input. ("John became a supervisor last year, so you can talk with him about the challenges of managing people.")

Employee development isn't just for underperformers, of course. Even the very best employees have room to improve and further develop themselves. For any professional, appraisal time is the ideal opportunity to tie a look backward with a look forward.

Performance-development activities are a means to help employees better achieve their job objectives set at the start of the appraisal period. (See "Goal-setting, or management by objectives (MBO)" in this chapter.) As a result, the employee and manager should revisit these objectives during this phase of the appraisal meeting to ensure that they're still on target. Many companies require an annual goal-setting meeting, and the appraisal meeting may be a good time to tackle that task. You certainly don't want to establish developmental activities around goals that will soon be changing.

Appraisal Followup Is Ongoing

Some managers may feel that the performance appraisal meeting is the conclusion of the appraisal process. The truth is, the days following this session are extremely important. You need to explain that it's also key to provide adequate followup, including regular monitoring of employee progress toward performance-development goals. Without sustained followup — both formal and informal —any input an employee receives is unlikely to be long-lasting.

The employee and supervisor should have both short- and long-term methods to review progress on the improvement areas discussed and schedule specific dates to do so. Many companies advise managers to conduct interim meetings after six months, but the interval can be shorter or longer depending on the situation. Between these sessions, supervisors should be encouraged to remain easily accessible so that employees can share thoughts, concerns, or suggestions on any of the topics covered during the appraisal. Managers should understand the benefits of providing input to staff throughout the year: If feedback is ongoing, nothing in the performance appraisal should come as a surprise to employees.

One thing I recommend at the end of any appraisal process is to evaluate your own performance. Were you able to thoroughly explain the evaluation approach to line managers? Did employees feel the session was conducted appropriately, with their supervisors providing enough time for discussion? Did you recommend specific actions to take following the appraisal — courses, reading, or contacts within the organization who may offer a different perspective? Again, the evolution of your job from "personnel administrator" to "business strategist" requires extensive attention to these very human, delicate matters. It's not easy, but I guarantee it can be quite rewarding — for the company, for employees and also for your own personal growth.

Evaluating your appraisal system

Here's a list of questions to ask yourself about your company's current program. If you can answer "yes" to all the questions, you can probably relax. A "no" answer may indicate an aspect of your program that needs to be reexamined.

✔ Are all performance criteria job-related?

✔ Is the focus on results, as opposed to personal traits?

✔ Do your employees understand how the process works and how appraisals tie into other aspects of their jobs?

✔ Have managers been adequately trained to implement the system?

✔ Is the program thoroughly understood by employees?

✔ Have all relevant employee behaviors been documented?

✔ Have promises of confidentiality been kept?

✔ Are all subsequent HR decisions consistent with employee evaluations?

✔ Are follow-up plans built into appraisals?

✔ Have you reviewed all elements of your program with legal counsel?

Forms on the CD

Essay Appraisal Form

Job Rating Checklist Appraisal Form

Chapter 16

Encouraging Extraordinary Performance

*P*redicting the future of the American workplace is no easy task. A quarter-century ago, who anticipated the way information technology would simultaneously create so many new opportunities— and, at the same time, so much increased complexity? But for all the talk of technology determining economic success, it's still sitting in the back seat. What's driving success? What most business leaders agree on is that the winning ingredient for success in today's business environment is a company's employees.

Employees who possess both familiar and new skills — and the fortitude to apply them with tenacity and intelligence — will determine the future of the economy. With competition coming from all corners of the globe and the pace of business accelerating rapidly, companies are pressured to keep costs down while delivering first-rate products and services. The key to making this value happen is to have a workforce that's highly motivated, engaged, and dedicated to success.

If you're particularly interested in this topic, check out my book *Motivating Employees For Dummies* (Wiley).

People: Your Most Important Competitive Strength

Logical as this observation may seem, the idea that your employees are a valuable asset whose creative potential needs to be constantly nurtured was not always part of traditional organizational thinking, especially in old-line, mass-production industries. Throughout much of the 20th century, the prevailing view was that employees were primarily the "instruments" in a system that succeeded or failed on the basis of strategic decisions formulated by senior management.

Bound heavily by rules and procedures, this thinking was strongly inspired by the military and worked well for a heavily centralized workplace that was expanding so rapidly it needed a rigid, structured bureaucracy. Good employees, according to this mode of thinking, were people who did their jobs and followed the rules. And good managers, by definition, were people who made sure that employees did their jobs and followed the rules.

But beginning in the '80s, this "command-and-control" management style began to prove cumbersome. Faced with both increased competition and a wider range of domestic and international needs, companies began to spread out, expanding not just geographically but also organizationally by adding new business units and, in some cases, broadening their focus through mergers and acquisitions. Along with these changes in corporate infrastructures came advancements in information technology. Everything from desktop computers to local area networks to the Internet made it possible for more people to have more information in their hands faster than ever before. Expectations at all levels of business — customers, resellers, employees, senior management, and investors — were revolutionized. All these changes have made the methodical, hierarchical decision-making process of old extremely unwieldy.

The HR professional is probably the one person in your organization who is ideally positioned to help the broadest range of employees understand and maximize the opportunities created by this new management model. Because you work with all levels and departments, you're the person best qualified to spearhead management practices that foster extraordinary employee performance. Creating a workplace environment that taps full employee potential is a monumental challenge, but, if you're successful, you can significantly impact productivity and profitability.

Many of the companies that have grown up in Northern California's Silicon Valley over the last 30 years — Apple Computer, Intel, Cisco Systems and, more recently, Google — have been among the leaders in trying new approaches to employee motivation. Some of these ideas — like on-site sushi bars and ping-pong tables — may have been well-intentioned, but perhaps were a little lacking in substance. But other motivational techniques — such as bringing in special speakers on topics like creativity, offering a variety of foods at an affordable company cafeteria, or letting employees evaluate their managers — have proven effective. Employee empowerment is more than a catchy phrase.

Making the Case for Employee Empowerment

Here's a quick definition that hopefully crystallizes the essence of *employee empowerment:* It's an all-purpose term (probably too all-purpose) whose cornerstone notion is that employees ought to have as much control and autonomy as is reasonably possible in the performance of their day-to-day tasks. In an empowered environment, in other words, the authority to make decisions doesn't originate at the top and work its way down on a diminishing scale, as was the case decades ago. Power and decision-making responsibility is spread more equitably throughout the organization. Individual judgment replaces "rules" and "procedures" as the decision-making mechanism in day-to-day situations. The need for supervision and micromanaging declines. Employees become increasingly accountable for their own actions.

In theory, employee empowerment is a terrific concept. Organizational studies conducted over the past 25 years have repeatedly shown that, all things being equal, employees who enjoy significant autonomy in their jobs are more productive, resourceful, and responsive to customer needs than those who don't. It's clear, too, that most measures of job satisfaction — low turnover, high morale, strong team spirit — are considerably higher in companies that encourage employee initiative and participation than they are in companies that operate under the traditional "command-and-control" structure. Employee empowerment is particularly important in an economy where employees at all levels of an organization are constantly facing new problems and must come up with new ways to solve them.

In your career, you've no doubt been exposed to and experimented with your share of employee empowerment techniques, all designed to boost creativity, productivity and, most of all, encourage employee "ownership," "initiative" and "responsibility." But I suspect — and I've heard this concern from dozens of HR professionals — that you've also been somewhat frustrated at how the term has become such a buzzword, causing the eyes of many employees to glaze over whenever they hear it. In fact, I'm told that many HR professionals hesitate to use the term "empowerment" at all for fear of alienating employees.

So what went wrong on the way to employee empowerment? The problem was that, in far too many cases, companies failed to provide the support or make the fundamental structural changes that employees needed in order to exercise the "power" they've been granted. When that support or change doesn't happen — when, for example, a supervisor repeatedly shoots down his team's ideas or constantly shows up late for meetings that his subordinates have called —employees feel significantly less motivated. And motivation is really what's at the heart of empowerment: motivation, and the willingness of everyone in the company to foster an environment where all the hallmarks of empowerment — initiative, accountability, ownership — are highly valued.

Keep in mind, though, that effective motivation is heavily a trial-and-error process, one that requires constant experimentation and vigilant study — not just of your company dynamics, but also that of others. No "silver bullet" solution exists that magically makes your organization perfect. It's simply impossible. Even such enduring, successful companies as Ford Motor Company, IBM, and HP (whose "HP Way" of bygone years is a prominent ancestor of the spirit of empowerment) have been through their share of the ups and downs that accompany change. Still, what makes these companies admirable is their capacity for weathering these shifts and their efforts to stay close to their core principles. Here's a look at the principles of an environment in which employees are motivated — and where employee empowerment is no mere buzzword but a way of life.

Recognizing that it's a process, not a flavor of the month

The biggest difference between companies successful in their empowerment initiatives and those that aren't lies in the mindset that underlies the initiative itself. In companies genuinely committed to a more open and participatory management style, senior management recognizes that the changes needed to make employee empowerment a reality do not occur overnight. The process takes time. It needs to be carefully thought through. And it needs to be monitored and supported, even when the early results are confusion and uncertainty.

Creating a safe-to-fail environment

More than any other nation in the world, America's economy has been built on the spirit of enterprise and risk-taking. As the economy has become more global and competitive, the ability to generate new ideas has become even more important — not just big ideas for new products and services, but those little, keenly creative concepts that streamline processes, cut costs, and create new opportunities.

Successful companies encourage employees at all levels to develop and experiment with new ideas. Brainstorming sessions, exposure to techniques that jump-start creativity, and even the occasional off-site session should all be regular parts of each department's ongoing series of activities. Think of it as your mission to instill this mindset throughout the organization. Unless your company is willing to take smart risks, your company won't thrive.

I'm not saying that you should encourage managers to support every single idea they receive. A smart risk is well thought-out. Employees have looked at other options and genuinely believe that risk is worth the gain.

But perhaps the most important aspect of risk-taking — the factor with the most profound long-term implications — is the way a manager treats a new idea once it's implemented. An old adage says that while success has many parents, failure is an orphan. Effective managers don't abandon employees who suggest ideas that don't pan out. Nor do they take full credit if the idea proves successful. Instead, they reflect collectively, talking candidly and supportively with their team. What worked? What needs to be improved? What factors impacted the idea's implementation? And, most importantly, how can this problem or project be better tackled in the future?

Finally, here's another simple technique that's vastly underused: When good managers make a mistake, they openly admit it. It's remarkable how motivational it can be for employees to hear their boss concede that she, too, was wrong about something.

Providing training and support

Empowerment initiatives invariably create the need for new skills at all levels of the organization. Front-line workers who are being called upon to make on-the-spot decisions frequently need training in problem solving, decision-making, and time management. You shouldn't assume that those skills are already in place. You'll probably need to provide special training for managers and supervisors, particularly those who have operated throughout most of their careers in a more traditional environment.

Supervisors must recognize — and accept the fact — that the primary role of a supervisor in a participatory environment is not to enforce rules or micro-manage, but to coach, train, and support. The specific training required for this new role often includes conflict resolution, facilitation, and two-way communication. For both front-line workers and supervisors, the training needs to be ongoing.

Sharing information: Communication as a strategy

Thanks to computer technology and the concurrent globalization and diversification of business, organizations are now able to exchange information much more quickly than in the past.

What's most notable in successful companies is that communication starts at the very top of the organization. Senior executives encourage an open and constant approach to communication, where information moves freely up and down the organization. Information sharing takes many forms, from frequent e-mail and Web site updates to planned departmental meetings to impromptu discussions and, as appropriate, printed literature, DVDs and special events that involve the entire company. And good communication addresses the widest possible set of corporate topics. Short-term objectives, long-term strategies, data on new products and services, research on competitors, updates on employee benefits, financial results — all are fair game.

At the same time that information is flowing freely from the top of your organization downward, you want to ensure that there's also a steady upward flow. In other words, it's essential that senior management is not simply talking to the rest of the organization but is listening openly as well.

The best way to maintain a steady flow of information is to impress upon managers the importance of creating an overall atmosphere that encourages employees to become involved and to openly communicate their concerns. Managers shouldn't just wait for employees to come to them. They must make an effort to proactively check in with employees. HP years ago dubbed this technique "management by walking around." It may seem simple, but visiting employees at their desks (rather than only hosting them in your office, which is often bigger and somewhat foreboding) can be exceptionally effective in raising morale, triggering new ideas, and increasing productivity. This philosophy ties in with the notion of encouraging risk-taking and being supportive when employees ask tough questions or raise doubts about a particular direction that's being taken. To be effective, managers must become great listeners. But the only way they can do that is to get in a position where they're willing to hear someone speak. As the best companies demonstrate, communication is a two-way street.

Rewarding initiative

Employees in empowered environments are more motivated by the desire to be creative, resourceful, and responsive to customer needs than they are by the fear of making mistakes. The most progressive companies allow staff to do whatever they consider necessary to please the customer, with no "rule book" to determine what is or isn't permitted.

An all-too-common pitfall in companies where empowerment initiatives have failed is that the empowerment was conditional. The first time that employees made a mistake, their power to make key decisions was curtailed. There's a fine line, of course, between giving employees enough latitude to encourage initiative and entrusting them with powers that, if misused, may jeopardize your business. The mistake that most companies make today, however, is to pull the plug too soon. If you want to elicit the best from your employees, be patient. Progressive companies create values and set broad parameters, trusting employees to make sound decisions.

Putting Team Power to Work

One complicated consequence of the break-up of the "command-and-control" approach to management is that the concept of teamwork has taken on a life of its own. (See the section "Making the Case for Employee Empowerment," earlier in this chapter, for more on this concept.) Of course, working in teams is the best way to accomplish organizational objectives, but the dialogue surrounding this topic has become overwhelming. Just consider all the terms that have entered business vocabulary over the last few decades — quality circles, self-directed work teams, performance-based work teams, empowered work teams, and team-building. The list goes on and on.

Defining how team members can best work together can be so complicated and confusing that a great many books and articles have drawn on analogies from an increasingly wide range of disciplines. I'm sure you've seen some that borrow from the world of sports — whether the fluidity of basketball, the structure of football or the baton-passing speed of a relay race. Others are influenced by the arts — the free-form of jazz, the harmony of an orchestra. Fables, fiction, poetry, philosophy — they're all part of it, too. You may feel at times that to understand teamwork, you need an extra four hours a day merely to absorb the literature.

One reason for all this dialogue is that teams exist in a much different context than they once did. Time was when a team pretty much meant the same group of people in a department, working on a fairly narrowly defined set of tasks. More recently — and with increasing frequency — teams are formed across an exceptionally wide range of skills and corporate demands. Some exist for the short term, while others are around for the long term. Some draw in executives from various departments to address an ongoing initiative, while others are established strictly to address and solve an immediate problem. Some are based in a single office and meet face-to-face on a daily basis; other teams occupy offices all over the globe and may never meet in person. All this diversity in structure and focus has created the need for a common language of understanding.

Teamwork is not an abstract or "trendy" concept. By now, organizational experts who've studied high-performance work teams in all industries and sectors of the economy report that when the concept of team play is successfully implemented, it produces dramatic results in productivity, employee morale, and customer satisfaction.

The better you understand the challenges of making teamwork a reality, the more you'll be able to keep things in perspective. Moreover, if you're called upon to spearhead a work team initiative in your company, you'll move ahead with a realistic understanding of the issues.

The following sections describe the fundamental factors that characterize effective teams.

Task appropriateness

Not every function or challenge in a company lends itself to a team approach. So the first question that needs to be asked is whether the work that needs to be done will benefit from a team approach. To determine task appropriateness:

✔ Keep an open mind as you analyze which functions lend themselves to a team effort and which functions are better handled by individuals.

✔ Bring employees themselves into the process that determines which tasks should be handled by teams.

Shared vision

Teams that succeed are unified by a clear sense of mission. Members of the team understand why the team was formed, what its goals are, and what steps are needed to achieve its goals. To create a shared vision:

✔ Take time to formulate a clear statement of purpose.

✔ Ensure that the team mission is understood and embraced by all team members.

✔ Make sure that the mission is consistent with the overall mission and strategic vision of the company.

Strategic focus

The specific tasks that teams perform need to be driven by the strategic goals of the organization. To develop these goals:

- ✔ Set priorities. Make sure that team members are focused at all times on the issues that are directly keyed to strategic considerations.
- ✔ Ensure that goals are realistic and are accompanied by specific action plans that have their own measures of success.
- ✔ Make sure that teams can measure their progress.

Role clarity

The individuals who make up high-performance teams must understand — and accept — the role that they themselves play within the team and must also be aware of the responsibilities of their team members. If the team chooses a leader, the group should agree on and clearly define her role and responsibilities. To clarify roles:

- ✔ Spell out — in writing — the roles and responsibilities of each member.
- ✔ Hold regular meetings to ensure that team members are living up to their responsibilities.
- ✔ Establish protocols for intervening when people aren't living up to their responsibilities.
- ✔ Encourage team members to ask for help when they're having trouble handling their individual responsibilities and then make sure that assistance is provided.

Individual motivation

Team members should be given the opportunity to develop new skills at the same time that they're contributing to the success of the team's mission. To help develop those skills:

- ✔ When assigning specific tasks, make it a point to pair team members who have expertise in a particular area with other team members who can benefit from that expertise.

- ✔ Set aside time for group learning, giving individual team members the opportunity to share their knowledge and experience.

- ✔ Create reward mechanisms for team members who share information.

Conflict resolution

Good teams anticipate disagreement and diversity and have developed workable means for resolving differences. To effectively resolve conflict when it occurs:

- ✔ Establish ground rules for resolving differences and conflicts.

- ✔ Encourage team members to voice concerns about the performance of others early on in the process.

- ✔ Emphasize the importance of individual accountability.

Appropriate reward mechanisms

Creating reward mechanisms that support team initiatives has emerged as one of the prime challenges facing companies that want to move to a more team-oriented work system. The main reason: Appraisal and merit systems have traditionally been based on individual performance and individual rewards. Some systems also factor in company performance, and some consider all three: the company, individuals, and teams. To reward teams appropriately:

- ✔ Make sure that all reward mechanisms give proper weight to both individual accomplishment and group success.

- ✔ Challenge team members to develop their own system of rewards (within company parameters, of course).

- ✔ Keep in mind that rewards can be nonmonetary as well as monetary.

No organizational barriers

Your "star" performers help drive your company's success and are good role models for other employees as well. Don't make the mistake, though, of letting your attention to these individuals overshadow your support of your team as a whole. A key way to avoid the "star" syndrome is to eliminate barriers within your organization — infrastructure, policies, procedures — that focus too heavily on individuals rather than teams. Here are a couple of pointers for overcoming those barriers:

- ✔ Communicate openly with senior management about the obstacles that need to be overcome if work teams are going to succeed in their strategic mission.

- ✔ Review all company policies and rules to ensure that they're compatible with team goals and priorities.

- ✔ Publicly recognize and reward team successes.

Developing Employee Recognition Programs

Employee recognition programs have been a staple in the HR professional's tool kit for decades, and it's easy to see why. When recognition programs are planned intelligently and implemented with care, they're a proven method of enhancing performance, increasing morale, and building employee loyalty. And the best part is that recognition programs don't necessarily have to be costly. The idea and the spirit behind the programs — the mere fact that a company is singling out and showing gratitude toward employees who are doing a great job — can be as motivational as the material rewards that may be given.

You don't need a formal program to take advantage of the power of recognition. As Kenneth Blanchard emphasized years ago in that classic — and still compelling — book *The One Minute Manager* (William Morrow and Co., Inc.), one of the hallmarks of a good manager is his willingness to bestow timely praise when employees have done a good job. And when you take a close look at the culture of those companies in which employee satisfaction levels are notably high, you invariably find a management style built on catching employees doing things "right" rather than continually taking "corrective action."

As you may expect, human resources professionals should play a key role in any recognition initiative. For example, the rationale behind any reward mechanism needs to correlate to your company's overall business goals and objectives. The traditional recognition programs, such as length of service awards, attendance, and safety, still have a place in most companies. But in today's performance-driven business environment, the trend is toward recognition that is productivity-based, which can have a more direct impact on both the company's bottom line and the employee's commitment.

Problems and pitfalls in team situations

Even under the best of circumstances, the road to successful teamwork is filled with minefields. Here's a look at the pitfalls you need to be aware of:

- Dissension and disagreement among team members.

- Abuse of authority by team leaders.

- Individual resentment, especially by highly talented and ambitious workers, of group-based advancement and rewards.

- Management interference, especially when an individual manager is not committed to team concepts.

- Conflict between team mission and company policies.

- Resentment by workers not included in teams, which can cause morale and productivity problems.

- Team practices that conflict with existing union contracts.

- Legal problems. (Team activities that involve both exempt and non-exempt employees may create payment/scheduling situations in conflict with the Fair Labor Standards Act and other similar laws.)

- Failure to monitor team practices to ensure compliance with EEO and civil rights laws, especially in the area of work assignments and training opportunities.

The decisions involving the actual mechanics of the employee recognition programs — budget, in particular—should be well-coordinated and equitable. Otherwise, you run the risk of creating discord between those teams or departments in your company that have recognition programs and those that do not.

One final note: Regardless of how much money and time you're willing to commit to it, no recognition program can overcome morale and productivity problems that are tied to a poor working environment. In other words, a recognition program is not a panacea for systemic management-related problems. On the contrary, introducing these programs into an atmosphere that is permeated with low morale — without addressing the underlying problems — may turn out to be a very costly mistake.

Assuming, however, that a poor working environment isn't an issue at your company, here are some guidelines for developing effective recognition programs:

- **Think it through carefully.** Before you actually launch any formally structured program, make sure that you, or whoever will be administering it, have thought through every aspect of it, particularly the criteria you intend to use as the basis for the rewards. Ideally, the performance targets you set up for each program ought to be challenging enough to instill an extra measure of motivation, but not so challenging that they're considered out of reach. At the other end of the spectrum, if too many people meet the criteria for special recognition, you'll dilute its impact.

Make sure, too, that all employees eligible for formal rewards are made aware of how these decisions will be measured — and who will do the measuring. Finally, consider the possibility that the same person or group of people may win the rewards repeatedly.

✔ **Make sure that the recognition means something.** Regardless of what form they take — a certificate, an acknowledgment in the company newsletter, or an all-expenses-paid trip to Tahiti — all rewards or gestures of recognition should be directly tied to actions or achievements that warrant special acknowledgment. Keep in mind that the fundamental purpose of a recognition program is to motivate exemplary performance. As a result, rewards should have real value to recipients, regardless of how much money is spent. A paperweight or elegant plaque, for example, can be meaningful and motivational because they're visible to all coworkers — not to mention the recipient — indefinitely.

✔ **Share the wealth.** Formal reward programs ought to be as all-inclusive as possible. If you've set up a program for one group of employees — sales reps, for example — give thought to instituting a reward program for nonsales/back office personnel as well. The nature and amount of the rewards don't necessarily have to be the same for every group, but if your company is truly customer-focused, everyone has the potential to contribute and should therefore be eligible for formal recognition.

If your company is moving toward team-based operations, make sure that your recognition program supports that change. Singling out one individual in a team effort may very well breed group resentment.

✔ **Communicate the criteria.** One of the downsides to recognition programs is that occasionally employees will feel that the "winners" are not deserving. The best way to protect yourself is to make sure, early on, that the criteria for rewards are not only well-defined, but communicated clearly to all employees. Another suggestion: Get as much employee input as possible when you're setting up the program.

✔ **Spread the news.** To get the most mileage out of a recognition program, you need to do a good job of publicizing it. If your company has a newsletter, designate a section that regularly announces the winners. Other ways to communicate details of the program include color brochures, company-wide memos, bulletin boards, or notices on your company's intranet.

Budget-conscious reward programs

The success of a recognition program isn't determined solely by the monetary value of its prizes. With a little imagination and employee input, you should be able to develop dozens of rewards that are easy and inexpensive to administer — and that most employees will appreciate. If you're looking for a good source of ideas, check out Bob Nelson's *1001 Ways to Reward Employees* (Workman Publishing), a best-selling book that first came out in 1994 and was updated in 2005. I'll also politely recommend my book *Motivating Employees For Dummies* (Wiley Publishing). In the meantime, here's a quick list of some of the popular rewards that are in place today:

- Time off or extra vacation days
- A note or letter of appreciation from the company president
- Dinner (for two) at a local restaurant or a group lunch for an outstanding department
- A designated employee-of-the-month parking spot
- Lunch or dinner with the company CEO (provided that the CEO enjoys these functions; otherwise, it can make for an awkward session)
- A photo and brief article in the company newsletter
- A press release to the local newspaper
- Inexpensive plaques or paperweights
- Special gear (T-shirt, tote bag, and so on) with the company logo
- Movie tickets

Chapter 17

Handling Difficult Situations

• •

• •

*R*egardless of how good a job you've done in organizing the human resources function in your company, and regardless of how diligently you handle your day-to-day challenges, you're engaging in wishful thinking if you expect your organization to be entirely free of personnel-related concerns. Even your best employees are going to make mistakes from time to time. So are your best supervisors. Even the most closely knit and harmonious group of employees is going to get into occasional squabbles. And unpleasant though the prospect may seem, inevitably, you or the managers in your company will be obliged at some point to take some sort of corrective action — including termination — against an employee whose job performance or conduct falls short of company expectations.

Of course, you are rarely the one responding directly to the problem because the ultimate responsibility for evaluating job performance normally lies with the employee's immediate supervisor or manager. Nevertheless, as the person responsible for HR in your company, you still have a crucial role to play. It's up to you to see to make sure that job performance and workplace conduct issues are handled promptly, intelligently, and fairly — and in a way that doesn't diminish productivity, accelerate turnover, or deplete employee morale. And most important perhaps, you (more than likely) have to make sure that your company's disciplinary and termination policies minimize your company's exposure to wrongful discharge lawsuits.

In this chapter, I look at the challenging side of HR management — but with an upbeat message. Most human resources problems are solvable, as long as you're alert to the early danger signs and you respond promptly with a clear sense of purpose.

This chapter, as well as Chapters 2, 8, 10, and 15, provides you with a significant amount of legally sensitive information, prepared with the assistance of the law firm, O'Melveny & Myers. But this area is not one where you can afford to be your own lawyer. Employee disciplinary action, termination, and layoffs are matters that require advice tailored to your particular company and situation. My advice: Hire an attorney.

Establishing an Ethical Culture

The best overall way to reduce the number of difficult situations you have to deal with is to prevent them from happening in the first place. You can never hope to avert all employee improprieties, poor judgments, and disputes, of course, but establishing a culture based on ethical behavior can go a long way in diminishing these situations in your organization.

From the "tone at the top" on down, become a company that emphasizes the critical importance of employees' ethical behavior in all interactions, whether externally with customers and vendors or internally among each other. People will always find ways and excuses to commit wrongdoing just as they will always be capable of making honest mistakes. But including integrity and consideration of others as one of your core values not only prevents many unpleasant situations from occurring, but also helps you develop a reputation as a business people want to work for.

It's very important that managers be every bit as accountable as employees. Your company should have a formal code of conduct that is not buried on a shelf, but actively reinforced by all of your managers. When employees hear one set of values but see another enforced — or, for that matter, neglected — by managers, the inconsistent messages confuse them or, cause them to question your commitment to your basic principles. As a result, they will likely become less committed to the overall organization.

Fleshing Out the Meaning of At-Will Employment

Ever since horse-and-buggy times, employers in the United States have operated under a doctrine generally known as employment-at-will. *Employment-at-will* (sometimes referred to as *termination-at-will*) means that in the absence of any contractual agreement that guarantees employees certain job protections, you (as an employer in the private sector) have the right to fire any of your employees at any time and for any (or no) reason. In other words, you may terminate an employee with or without cause and with or without notice. At the same time, your employees have the right to leave at any time, for any (or no) reason, even without giving notice.

You should note that the concept of at-will employment is specific to the United States. Other countries have their own sets of requirements concerning termination, but the policy of employment-at-will is practiced only in the United States. At-will employment is, however, subject to a number of significant limitations. If your company is unionized, for example, your employees' jobs are likely subject to contractual constraints.

Court decisions involving wrongful discharge cases, particularly in recent years, recognize employment-at-will so long as the employer's actions do not violate certain public policies. For example, you can't terminate an employee for refusing to forge reports to the government or to violate antitrust laws. So, yes, your company still has the right to set behavioral standards, take corrective action when those standards aren't met, and fire employees who don't perform their job duties. However, you must be sure that in the process of carrying out these practices, you're not impinging on public policies.

Staying Out of Court

According to the Bureau of National Affairs, the number of wrongful discharge suits working their way through local, state, and federal courts more than doubled during the 1980s, and the trend continues today. Even more sobering is the fact that plaintiffs win most wrongful discharge suits that reach trial largely because juries tend to favor employees over employers. How does a company protect itself? In short, protection comes from preventive action. Here are seven key principles to bear in mind:

> ✔ **Review all company recruiting and orientation literature to ensure that no statements, implicitly or explicitly, "guarantee" employment.** Be especially careful about the use of the word "permanent" in any employee literature or in conversations that occur before an employee is hired. Courts have held this term creates an implied contract of employment. If you need to differentiate between classes of employees, "regular" or full-time are better terms. The term "probationary" should be avoided for similar reasons; some courts assume that after an employee is no longer on probation, the employer then must have good cause to terminate the employee.

✓ **Establish and document specific, easy-to-understand performance standards for every position in your company and make sure that every employee is aware of those standards.** You may need to update these standards as each position evolves.

✓ **Train managers to maintain careful, detailed records of all performance problems and the disciplinary actions that have been taken in response to those problems.** Keep in mind that the verdict in many wrongful discharge suits hinges on whether the discharged employee was given "fair warning." Juries do not like it when they think an employee was surprised when terminated.

✓ **Make sure that all disciplinary and dismissal procedures are handled "by the book"—** in a manner consistent with your company's stated disciplinary and termination policy.

✓ **Make sure that all the managers and supervisors in your company are well-versed in your company's disciplinary and termination procedures.** Confer with them on a regular basis to ensure that they're following procedures. If you discover they're not, talk with them immediately, letting them know emphatically that failure to follow proper disciplinary and termination procedures is unacceptable and can prove extremely costly.

✓ **Seek legal advice whenever you are uncertain about any aspects of your company's disciplinary or legal policy.**

✓ **Be sensitive to the possibility that an employee who leaves your company voluntarily as a result of a change in assignment or work practices may be able to convince a jury that the change in assignment or work practices represented a deliberate attempt on your company's part to force the employee to quit.**

Developing Disciplinary Procedures

Some companies like a formalized disciplinary process, one that reasonably and systematically warns employees when performance falls short of expectations.

A formal disciplinary procedure works best in companies that are highly centralized, where personnel decisions for the entire company are made within one department (most likely HR), which makes sure that each step of the disciplinary process is implemented properly. The advantage is that the rules and regulations of job performance are consistently communicated to everyone. The disadvantage, however, is that if your company doesn't abide by these self-imposed rules, not even a lawyer can help you.

On the other hand, some companies don't like such a process. Using a formalized disciplinary process doesn't work as well for organizations that are decentralized, where personnel decisions are made within each office or department on a case-by-case basis in accordance with a company's general expectations. In these situations, ensuring that each office or department follows the same disciplinary procedure is difficult.

The specifics of a formal disciplinary process can take a variety of forms, but most practices are structured along similar lines. To one degree or another, they all mirror the following phases:

1. **Initial notification:** The first step in a typical progressive disciplinary process is informing the employee that his or her job performance or workplace conduct isn't measuring up to the company's expectations and standards. The employee's manager typically delivers this initial communication verbally in a one-on-one meeting. Details from this and all later conversations should also be documented. The report needn't be lengthy; a few bullet points highlighting the main topics are perfectly acceptable.

2. **Second warning:** This phase applies if the performance or conduct problems raised in the initial phase worsen or fail to improve. The recommended practice is for the manager to hold yet another one-on-one meeting with the employee and accompany this oral warning with a memo that spells out job performance areas that need improvement. At this stage in the process, the manager needs to make the employee aware of how her behavior is affecting the business and what the consequences are for failing to improve or correct the problem. The manager needs to work with the employee to come up with a written plan of action that gives the employee concrete, quantifiable goals and a timeline for achieving them.

3. **Last-chance warning:** The "last-chance" phase of discipline usually takes the form of a written notice from a senior manager or, in smaller companies, from the company president. The notice informs the employee that if the job performance or workplace conduct problems continue, the employee will be subject to termination. What you're doing here is applying the heat.

4. **Corrective action:** Corrective action is some form of discipline administered by the company prior to termination. In union contracts, for example, this action may take the form of a suspension, mandatory leave, or possibly a demotion. In small companies, disciplinary actions become a little trickier to implement — so much so, that corrective action can become termination itself.

5. **Termination:** Termination is the last step in the process — the step taken when all other corrective or disciplinary actions have failed to solve the problem.

These progressive disciplinary steps serve as general guidelines and aren't intended as a substitute for legal counsel.

However you decide to structure your disciplinary plan, the process itself — apart from being fair — should meet the following criteria:

- **Clearly defined expectations and consequences:** Every employee in your company should be aware of the expectations and standards that apply to her particular job. These standards should be measurable and attainable. Employees also need to know how not meeting these standards and expectations affects the company's operations. Your company needs to communicate standards and expectations early on in the employee's tenure. The same principle applies to workplace rules. Courts have repeatedly held that employers can't fire employees for violating rules of which they were unaware.

- **Early intervention:** This nip-the-problem-in-the-bud principle is that an employer steps in as early as possible when an employee's job performance or workplace conduct isn't satisfactory. Failing to provide pointed performance feedback early on can hurt you in two ways:

  - Employees can interpret the lack of any intervention as an implicit sign that they're doing just fine.

  - If you take action against another employee who is having similar problems, you leave yourself open to charges of favoritism or discrimination.

The discipline needs to be appropriate for the offense. If your company is ever called upon to defend its actions, one issue that has a profound bearing on the final ruling is the relationship between the severity of the offense and the type of discipline. The general principle here is that you need to draw a clear distinction between those offenses that deserve disciplinary action and those that are sufficiently serious to warrant dismissal. You also need to factor into all disciplinary decisions — termination, in particular — the overall performance and discipline record of the employee or employees involved.

- **Consistency:** You need to apply your company's policies and practices consistently — no favoritism or bending of the rules allowed! Solid, legitimate, nondiscriminatory reasons are the only justification for deviation.

- **Rigorous documentation:** The phrase "get it in writing" takes on extraordinary importance in any disciplinary process. Cumbersome though it may be, the supervisors and managers in your company must get into the habit of recording all infractions and problems, along with the steps taken to remedy those problems. Lacking detailed documentation of what the company has done throughout the disciplinary process seriously weakens its case, regardless of how justified the firing may have been. When deciding whether to terminate an employee, review evaluations, warning notices (if any), personnel policies or work rules, witness statements, witness evaluation notes, and other relevant documents, such as customer complaints, production reports, and time cards. If the documentation is not deemed sufficient, ask the manager for more information and hold off on taking action until you've determined you have sufficient documentation.

Defusing Grievances

An effective, well-balanced disciplinary process does more than provide a means for dealing with problem behavior among employees. It also gives employees an opportunity to speak up (and be heard) when they're not happy with the way things are going in the workplace. This disciplinary process is known in union parlance as a *grievance procedure.* In unionized companies, the grievance procedure is a multistep and often cumbersome process that begins with an employee airing the complaint to the union steward. The grievance may not be resolved until many months later by an independent third party.

Chances are, your company doesn't need a highly structured series of steps to resolve complaints, but you do need to provide employees with the opportunity to voice their complaints without fear of repercussion. Here are suggestions on how to implement such a process.

- ✔ **Offer complaint-reporting options.** As a general rule, instruct employees to bring their complaints to the attention of their immediate supervisors. If the complaint involves the supervisor, however, employees should have the right to break the chain of command. In certain circumstances, directing complaints through a different channel, such as a trained and designated member of the human resources department, may be appropriate.

- ✔ **Stress the importance of prompt response.** Everyone in the company who's responsible for receiving employee complaints should make it a point to address the complaint as promptly as possible. Ideally, an employee should know within 24 hours that you've received his complaint and you're handling it. Don't worry; that doesn't mean you have to provide a complete answer in a day, but a swift initial response demonstrates your concern and commitment to resolving the issue. Of course, determining how long a problem takes to resolve depends on how complicated the issue is. Promptness is particularly important whenever the

complaint involves an alleged serious workplace safety or health violation, sexual harassment, discrimination, or criminal activity. In these
cases, alert senior managers immediately. Ignoring any complaint that
deals with serious issues greatly increases your company's exposure.

✔ **Investigate with an open mind.** Until you have reason to believe otherwise, consider all information important. Never assume that simply
because your company has never experienced a particular problem
before that the problem doesn't exist.

✔ **Report back to the employee.** Whether the complaint is substantiated
or not, you need to keep the employee who registered it informed of
what you're doing to deal with the situation. If you ultimately find that
the complaint isn't substantiated — We have no evidence to suggest that
someone is poisoning our water supply — explain why you feel more
action isn't warranted.

If the complaint is justified, indicate that corrective action is being
taken. Depending on the circumstances, such as workplace safety, you
may even want to communicate the nature of the action to the complainant. On the other hand, given privacy considerations, don't communicate to the complainant the nature of the disciplinary action taken
against another employee.

✔ **Protect the employee from reprisals.** Ensure employees that if they
follow the company's recommended procedure for filing complaints,
they will not be penalized in any way — regardless of the nature of the
complaint, if it is offered in good faith. When handling a complaint,
remind all parties involved of your company's antiretaliation policy. And
if you need to resolve a dispute between an employee and a supervisor,
caution supervisors about taking any actions that may be perceived as
retaliatory, such as unfavorable work assignments, an inappropriate
transfer, or a demotion, while an investigation is underway or shortly
after its completion. If the supervisor was addressing performance
issues prior to a complaint being filed or feels she needs to address
them during the current investigation process, encourage her to work
with you in determining the appropriate performance management
approach.

Settling Disputes

Depending on your point of view, disputes among employees and between
employees and supervisors are either a big headache or a great opportunity to
strengthen the internal fabric of your organization. Left unresolved, conflicts
often escalate into major disruptions, but if you can resolve these disputes,
you can create the kind of atmosphere that fosters open communication and
innovative thinking. The key is to settle any workplace dispute fairly, dispas-
sionately, and quickly.

The dispute resolution procedures in this section are designed only for the usual personality conflicts that arise in the workplace. They do not address or resolve complaints of illegal conduct, such as discrimination or sexual harassment. For those types of complaints, see Chapter 3.

Whenever possible, settle disagreements or disputes at the local level. Encourage employees who are in conflict with one another to come to an agreement themselves with help from their manager or a fellow team member trained in dispute resolution procedures.

For many companies, alternative dispute resolution (ADR) is an appealing alternative to the costly and unpredictable court action in wrongful discharge suits. ADR involves the same options as traditional conflict resolution strategies: mediation or arbitration. Both mediators and arbitrators typically have legal backgrounds, a vital skill given the extremely sensitive and potentially expensive implications of the termination process.

Mediation and arbitration can also be implemented on their own and are processes best conducted by outside firms or professionals who specialize in these areas. Here's more on how each works.

- ✔ **Mediation:** The objective of *mediation* is to resolve a dispute by bringing in a third party who, presumably, has no ax to grind and whose job is to help the two parties come up with a solution that is acceptable to both parties. The key qualities of an effective mediator are patience, listening skills, and the ability to find common ground between differing viewpoints. To verify if indeed the mediator has these skills, it's best to ask for references. The advantage of mediation is that the process generally (though not always) leaves both parties at least reasonably satisfied. The downside of mediation: This time-consuming process doesn't always guarantee a resolution.

- ✔ **Arbitration:** As with mediation, *arbitration* requires the participation of a disinterested third party who listens to both sides of the story. But unlike a mediator, an arbitrator has the power to impose a financial settlement. The key precursor to any arbitration arrangement is the willingness of both parties to accept the judgment of the arbitrator as final.

Firing Employees Is Never Easy

Even when you have ample cause for doing so, firing employees is always a cause for heartache — not only for the employees losing their jobs and the supervisors making the decision, but the coworkers as well

You can do only so much to ease the pain and disruption that firings create. You can do a great deal, however, to help ensure that your company's approach to firing meets two criteria:

✔ It protects the dignity and the rights of the employee being terminated.

✔ It protects your company from retaliatory action by a disgruntled former employee.

The standard (and recommended) practice in most companies is for the immediate supervisor to deliver the termination notice. The message should be delivered in person and in a private location. Depending on the circumstances, include a third person, such as another supervisor or member of the human resources department, at the meeting. Do not involve coworkers. (*Note:* Some union contracts require the presence of a third person, such as a union official.)

Regardless of why an employee is leaving your company, keep the termination meeting as conclusive as possible, which means you need to prepare prior to the meeting. The following list covers some issues to consider.

✔ **Final payment:** Ideally, any employee being dismissed should walk out of the termination meeting with a check that covers everything he is entitled to, including severance. (Some states, such as California, impose penalties for failing to pay all wages due at the time of termination.) Depending on your company's policy — and on the circumstances that led to the employee's departure — the amount of the final check probably includes money from some or all of the following:

   • Salary obligation (pro-rated to the day of dismissal)

   • Severance pay, if applicable

   • Any outstanding expense reimbursements due to the employee

   • Money due from accrued vacation, sick days, or personal days

✔ **Security issues:** Think about company security, including keys, access cards, and company credit cards. If the employee has been using a password to access company files, ask your IT department or consultant (or whoever sets up your computers) to change it on the system. Do the same with credit-card privileges.

✔ **Company-owned equipment:** The employee should return any company-owned equipment immediately. If the equipment is off-site (a computer in the employee's home, for example), arrange for its pickup.

✔ **Extended benefits information:** If your company is subject to COBRA regulations (See Chapters 2 and 23), you're generally obligated to extend the employee's medical coverage — with no changes — for 18 months.

Who pays for the benefits — your company or the employee — is your call, though you're under no legal obligation to pick up the tab. Make sure, though, that you have all the information the employee needs to keep the coverage going. Also resolve all questions regarding an employee's 401(k), pension or stock plan during the meeting, providing up-to-date information on what options, if any, the employee has regarding those benefits.

✔ **Notification of outplacement or other support mechanisms:** If your company has set up outplacement arrangements (or any other services designed to help terminated employees find another job), provide all the relevant information. In some companies, the outplacement counselor is already on the premises and is the first person the terminated employee talks to following the meeting.

Delivering the news

No perfect script lets employees know that they're being discharged, but the news ought to be delivered as soon as the termination meeting starts.

Employees being discharged have the right to be told why the decision was made, even if you've had a previous discussion about problems and infractions. Tact and sensitivity are important, but so is honesty. Keep the conversation short and to the point and don't try to fill in awkward silences.

Remind managers that whatever they say during the termination interview (for example, "It wasn't my idea. Management is simply trying to cut back.") can come back to haunt your company in a wrongful discharge lawsuit.

Keep any discussion of the employee's shortcomings brief — one or two sentences at most. The termination meeting is not the time to engage in a lengthy discussion of the employee's faults. So much has occurred prior to this stage that it's best to let the decision speak for itself and not over talk.

Post-termination protocol

If your company hasn't developed one, work with your management to develop a disciplined, clearly defined procedure for what happens after you discharge an employee. Make the break as clean as possible — albeit with respect to the feelings and the dignity of the person being fired. Harsh and humiliating though the practice may seem, accompany the dismissed employee back to her office or work station, give the employee a chance to collect personal belongings, and escort the employee out the door. If the company has confidentiality agreements, remind employees — in writing — of their legal obligations. Also advise employees that they're no longer authorized to access the company's computer systems and any online accounts

Generally speaking, holding the meeting early in the week (not the weekend) and at the end of the work day works best. If you conduct the termination meeting on Monday or Tuesday, you make it easier for the dismissed employee to get started immediately on a job search and for you to begin searching for another employee. By delivering the news as late in the day as possible, you spare the employee the embarrassment of clearing out his or her office in front of coworkers.

A waiver of rights

Some companies ask a discharged employee to sign a statement that addresses confidential agreements and also releases the company from legal liabilities. Often called a *severance agreement,* firms require employees to sign this document and return it by a specified date before they receive a severance payout. Note that this payout is separate from any compensation regulated by state or federal law, such as accrued benefits or regular compensation. Due to the differences in the time requirements between final compensation for time worked or accrued benefits versus a severance agreement, there can be two separate checks involved.

The value of this practice is obvious. Although some people believe that employers who present waivers of rights while terminating employees can communicate that they're worried about the legality of their actions, it's quite common practice in many companies and a useful business tool. Keep in mind, though, that such a document should be closely reviewed by your legal counsel and the employee encouraged to consult legal counsel as well. In fact, it is a good practice to discourage employees from signing the document during the exit interview. This is because an argument may be made later that the employee signed the document while under duress. Telling the employee to take time to consider the document and to consult legal counsel helps further dispel the notion that the company is trying to hide something.

Easing the Trauma of Layoffs

Layoffs differ from firings in a variety of ways, but one critical aspect comes to mind: The people being let go haven't done anything to warrant losing their jobs. Layoffs occur for a number of reasons, which can include

✔ Seasonal shifts in the demand for a company's products or services

✔ An unexpected business downturn that requires the company to make drastic cost reductions

✔ A plant/company closure

✔ An initiative that restructures work practices, leaving fewer jobs

✔ A merger or acquisition that produces redundancy in certain positions

REMEMBER

Generally, when someone is *laid off,* there is no expectation that she will be returning to work. Some companies use the term in a different sense, however. When business is slow and they don't need the entire current workforce, some firms (particularly those operating in a unionized environment) notify workers that they will be placed on "furlough" for a period of time and will be offered the opportunity to return to work on a certain date or in stages. Some companies (especially seasonal businesses and those for which losing a major project creates a significant worker surplus) call this arrangement a "layoff" even though they plan to bring people back to work if and when conditions allow. Depending on the nature of the business — and their affiliation with unions or public versus private sector obligations — many companies today steer away from suggesting that a layoff is temporary because it can be difficult to determine with certainty whether or when employees will be recalled to work. Layoffs (sometimes called "Reduction in Force," "Position Elimination" or "downsizing") are far more common when they refer to employee terminations that are final. One thing that all these approaches have in common, however, is that they are involuntary and considered to be *no fault of the persons affected.*

Just cause

Certain employee infractions and misdeeds are so blatant that you can generally terminate the employee without going through the normal disciplinary channels. Your orientation literature should spell out the offenses that lead to immediate dismissal. Here's a list to get you started:

✔ Stealing from the company or from other employees

✔ Possession or use of drugs

✔ Distribution or selling of illegal drugs

✔ Blatant negligence that results in the damage to or loss of company machinery or equipment

✔ Falsifying company records

✔ Violation of confidentiality agreements

✔ Misappropriation of company assets

✔ Making threatening remarks to other employees or managers

✔ Engaging in activities that represent a clear case of conflict of interest

✔ Lying about credentials

Whatever the reason for a layoff, the pressure on the HR function is the same. You need to help your company navigate this difficult turn of events with as few long-term repercussions as possible. The following sections guide you through the process.

View layoffs as a last resort

You should always view layoffs as the last resort in responding to any change in the business environment. When you or your management are weighing the possibility of layoffs, make sure that the management team is considering more than the bottom-line implications and thinking about the impact on customers and remaining staff members. Layoffs may turn out to be inevitable, but management should be aware that the short-term cost-cutting benefits of layoffs may well be offset by the following factors:

- ✔ Severance and outplacement costs for the laid-off employees (including accrued vacation and sick pay)
- ✔ The impact on your company's future unemployment compensation obligation
- ✔ The effect on morale and productivity
- ✔ The impact on future recruiting efforts

Know the law

If the number of full-time employees in your company exceeds 100 (fewer in certain states), your layoff strategy needs to consider the Worker Adjustment and Retraining Notification Act (WARN). As I explain in Chapter 2, WARN obligates companies with 100 or more full-time employees to give 60 days' notice of a mass layoff or reduction in hours. A *mass layoff* or *reduction in hours* at a single site is generally defined as one that affects 500 or more workers or 50 or more workers if they comprise at least 33 percent of the active, full-time workforce. A reduction in hours is a 50 percent cut in hours worked each month for six months or more.

Employers covered by WARN don't have to comply in the case of smaller layoffs. Beware, though, that multiple layoffs in a short period of time — for example, 50 days — may trigger WARN obligations. And also note that a number of states have their own WARN-like laws. These matters can be tricky, so consult your legal counsel.

Think through the criteria

The simplest (and, to some degree, safest) way to determine which employees should be let go and which employees should remain whenever layoffs are necessary is to establish some criteria, such as seniority or a percentage of head count in each department. The problem with this strategy, however, is that the combination of people you're left with may substantially weaken your company's ability to compete.

The better way is to precede any wide-scale layoff decision with a careful analysis of your company's strategic needs and to base the layoff criteria on which employees are best equipped to meet those needs.

One word of caution: You should be prepared to defend the rationale behind the criteria. You need to be careful, too, that in the process of carrying out this more strategically driven approach, you're not laying off a disproportionately high number of employees who are in any group protected by Equal Employment Opportunity Commission (EEOC) legislation. (For more details on EEOC, see Chapter 2.)

Ease the burden

Moral considerations notwithstanding, it is in your best long-term interests to do whatever is reasonably possible and fiscally responsible to ease both the financial and psychological pain that layoffs invariably create. Be as generous as you can with severance packages — that's a given. But you can take additional steps — for example, help in resume writing, financial planning, networking, and so on — that won't cost you much money but will nonetheless help employees get back on their feet again.

Hire outplacement specialists

Outplacement is the term used to describe companies that specialize in helping dismissed employees (usually middle managers and above) regroup and find new jobs. In a typical outplacement program, managers who've been let go get an opportunity to attend seminars or one-on-one sessions in such areas as career counseling and in job-hunting basics (how to write a resume, network, and interview, and so on). Typically, too, the job seekers are given office space, access to a phone, and administrative help for a predetermined period of time.

Outplacement can get expensive, particularly if you're dealing with large numbers of dismissed managers, but it's one of the best ways to help those managers who've been with your company a long time and need the support. In major companies that conduct large-scale layoffs, outplacement services tend to be the rule, not the exception.

Take advantage of staffing services

Staffing companies can help workers get back into the workforce with opportunities for project-based and full-time positions. These firms maintain existing networks with many employers and may even specialize in particular industries, such as high-tech, legal, or finance. The big advantage is that they don't charge your company or the worker. When the employee is placed by the staffing firm, his or her new employer pays the staffing firm's placement fees. Some firms even provide tips on resume writing and interviewing, similar to outplacement specialists.

Address the concerns of those who remain

Layoffs are traumatic not only for the people who are laid off but also for those who remain. Quite apart from the sympathy they might feel for colleagues, remaining workers must generally take on increased workloads. Regrouping after layoffs as quickly and effectively as possible and giving your new, smaller staff a renewed sense of purpose and opportunity is key to your future. If, at some point your company finds it necessary to conduct layoffs, keep the following pointers in mind (or encourage line managers in affected departments to do so):

- ✔ **Honest, open communication is critical.** Bear in mind that what you don't say to employees can be as disconcerting and worrisome as what you do say. It's important for managers to have team meetings very soon after layoffs have occurred, not merely to justify what's taken place but also to set goals, clarify roles, and, most of all, genuinely listen to concerns. The more a manager can create an open, honest environment for communication during this difficult time, the better off your entire organization will be as time goes on.

- ✔ **Treat employees as adults.** Explain why the layoffs were necessary, why current staff members were chosen to stay on, and what you are expecting from them in the future. Make everyone aware that their contributions are now more essential to the company's continued success than ever before.

✔ **Focus on the future.** You'll need to clearly explain why downsizing was an unavoidable move for your company if you're to remain competitive. But instead of focusing too much on what employees have *lost* in terms of colleagues, focus on what they're *gaining* in terms of a stronger, more stable company. Explain that the contributions of everyone on the now-smaller team are critical to the business's future success. Some employees will be able to work in new areas and acquire additional skills. Some may have greater chances of promotion.

✔ **Consult a staffing firm.** Just as staffing services can help your displaced employees find new work, they can also help you bring in skilled supplemental workers to maintain continuity and prevent burnout on the part of remaining full-time staff.

Reduce the need for layoffs

Obviously, the best approach to layoffs is to know how to avoid them in the first place — without repercussions to your business. The better you become at understanding and focusing on true business needs and creating workforce strategy around these key needs, the more likely you'll be able to avoid layoffs.

One of your primary roles is continually considering your company's strategic priorities and determining their staffing implications (see Chapter 3). You also must ensure that all staffing decisions you make clearly support your company's strategic priorities. If you keep an eye on how the business is going, as well as workforce needs and costs, you can proactively slow down full-time hiring yet maintain productivity through alternative staffing approaches (such as the use of contingent workers, as I discuss in greater depth in Chapter 13). This step allows you to reduce the workforce via attrition rather than layoffs.

Dealing with Workplace Violence

Workplace violence isn't a pleasant subject, but these days, you can't avoid the topic. Violence in the workplace is an issue that no company today — regardless of how large or small the company or where it is located — can afford to ignore. Workplace homicide is the fourth leading cause of work-related deaths.

Alternatives to layoffs

If the purpose of the layoff is to cut down on costs (as opposed to reduce redundancy), you may want to explore options that, at the very least, can reduce the number of people who need to be terminated:

✔ **Temporary pay cuts:** Reducing salary costs is probably the simplest and most direct way to cut staffing costs without cutting staff. The key to this strategy is to ensure that everyone — including senior managers — shares the pain. Many companies, in their efforts to ensure equality, vary the percentage of reduction according to the amount of salary an employee is earning, with higher salaried workers surrendering a higher percentage of their regular pay checks than their lower salaried counterparts.

Downside: No matter how justified the cuts and how many jobs you save, some workers will resent losing pay — and the decision to cut back on pay may induce your best and most mobile workers to quit. Keep in mind, too, that employees who agree to pay cuts will expect the salary to be restored — and then some, when the business turns around. If your company doesn't meet that expectation, you'll likely soon encounter decreased employee commitment and, down the road, a higher turnover rate than desired. Though there is no legal limit on the duration of a temporary pay cut, the sooner you can communicate when wages will be restored, the more positive the impact on morale.

✔ **Work week reductions:** This option is worth exploring for companies that have large numbers of hourly workers. You maintain the same hourly rates, but employees work fewer hours. As an inducement to accept the lower take-home pay, most companies pledge to maintain benefits at full-time levels.

Downside: Reduction of hours has no effect on salaried employees and managers who are not paid by the hour.

✔ **Early retirement:** An often-used method of reducing payroll costs is to encourage early retirement, generally through financial incentives. Because senior employees are usually the most highly paid, trimming their ranks can result in significant savings.

Downsides: Senior employees are often your most valued, and losing too many of them at one time can significantly weaken the leadership of your firm. Remember, too, that under the Age Discrimination in Employment Act, it is illegal, with rare exceptions, to force anyone to retire.

In addition, in order to avoid charges of age discrimination, early retirement offers usually have to be extended to wide classes of employees rather than selected individuals. This option can sometimes backfire when large numbers of employees you may want to keep accept the offer.

The vast majority of workplace homicides — 85 percent, according to the U.S. Bureau of Labor Statistics — are the result of a robbery or other ordinary crime, not terrorist attacks on office buildings, ports, or other places where people are employed. What's more, an additional 5 percent of homicides that occur in the workplace arise out of a family or personal dispute and aren't directly related to workplace issues. Even so, the remaining 10 percent result from a violent coworker or client.

What steps can your company take to provide reasonable protection for your employees? Your best source of information on this matter is your local police department. Most police departments have specialists in crime prevention who can survey your business and make recommendations. Other good sources for crime prevention strategies are violence-prevention experts, insurance companies, or private security consultants. In any case, you need to take a twofold approach of both protecting your employees from the violent acts of outsiders and protecting your employees from the violent acts of fellow employees.

Here are some tips on protecting against outside threats:

- ✔ Pay your employees by check, not cash. Better still, encourage direct deposit of pay into employee bank accounts.

- ✔ Keep building perimeters and parking lots well lit.

- ✔ Limit access to strangers. Consider implementing an access-card system for employees. If appropriate for your business, ask visitors to wait in the reception area until an employee is available to escort them. If appropriate, identify visitors with a special badge and escort them at all times. Instruct employees to notify the security office about strangers with no identification.

- ✔ Safeguard valuables. Provide lockers, desk drawers, or other safe areas where employees can secure valuables.

- ✔ Plan for emergencies. Work out emergency procedures in advance. Post security and police numbers by every telephone.

Here are ways to protect your employees from internal threats:

- ✔ Establish and communicate to employees a strong, unequivocal policy of zero tolerance for violence. Include as causes for immediate dismissal threatening gestures, fighting words, and physical actions. This policy should be included in your company's employee Code of Conduct.

- ✔ Do everything reasonably possible to eliminate potentially violent or unstable employees from the running during the recruiting process. If you have any reason to suspect that a candidate has a history of violent behavior, don't hire him or her.

- ✔ Provide counseling and other assistance — possibly through an Employee Assistance Program (EAP) — for troubled employees or those with personal, financial, or substance-abuse problems.

- ✔ Be constantly aware that certain workplace situations, such as disciplinary meetings and termination interviews, always have a potential for violence. Take precautions accordingly.

✔ Be alert to the following signs that suggest an employee may someday turn violent:

- Evidence of alcohol or substance abuse problems

- Frequent displays of anger, abusive language, or threats of violence against coworkers or managers

- Any attempt to bring a weapon to work

- Other extreme behavior, such as avoidance, isolation, or deteriorating hygiene

Forms on the CD

Employee Emergency Notification

OSHA Information Posting

Protecting the safety and health of your employees

American employers are legally obligated to provide a workplace in which neither the environment nor the work practices subject employees to any unreasonable risk in safety or health. The safety- and health-related regulations vary considerably, of course, within an industry and according to state or federal regulations. (A good resource is the Occupational Safety and Health Administration, also known as OSHA. I discuss OSHA a bit more in Chapter 12.) Consequently, no one single standard and or list of safety- and health-related regulations apply across the board to every company. At the very least, though, it's your responsibility as your company's HR specialist to make sure of two things:

✔ Your company is in compliance with the federal and/or state safety and health regulations that apply to your company.

✔ Your company is doing everything that is reasonably possible (independent of your legal obligations) to protect the safety and health of your employees. (For a sample Employee Emergency Notification form, see the CD-ROM.)

The safety and health area is a complicated one. The regulations that apply depend on your particular company and industry. In addition, although the federal Occupational Safety and Health Act is applicable throughout the United States, it permits states to implement their own plans with requirements above and beyond the federal regulations. More than 20 states have adopted their own plan, so it's important that you familiarize yourself with both federal and state laws regarding safety and health. (See the CD-ROM for an OSHA Information Posting, which you can find on the OSHA Web site at www.osha.gov.) When in doubt, consult an attorney.

Part V
The Part of Tens

"I've never been good at this part of the job, which is why I've asked 'Buddy' to join us. As you know, business has been bad lately, and, well, Buddy has some bad news for you..."

In this part . . .

Every *For Dummies* book ends with top-ten lists, and this one is no exception. In this part, I offer ten keys to becoming an HR strategist. I also list ten HR-related Web sites and associations you should know about.

Chapter 18

Ten Keys to HR Success in the Future

In This Chapter

▶ Maximizing staffing

▶ Staying ahead of the pack

*T*he old saying that "the inventory goes out the door every night" is echoing through the halls of the business world louder than ever. The reason is quite simple: The most successful companies are seeing more and more that their biggest competitive advantage lies in their ability to get the most out of their workforce. As the person responsible for taking care of the HR function in your company, you play a major role in accomplishing that objective. Your skill at building human resource strategies and policies that reinforce strategic objectives helps ensure your company's long-term success. In this chapter, I give you ten ways you can help ensure your company's future success.

Adopt a Strategic Approach to Staffing

Hiring smart today means hiring *strategically* — taking the time and effort to make sure that each staffing decision matches the goals and operational needs of your company. The traditional approach to hiring — finding the one person who best fits the specs of a particular job — is losing ground in contemporary companies to a much more fluid and flexible model in which the goal is to determine what the job really requires and what combination of resources best meets that requirement.

If you follow this model, you begin the process by developing a clear picture of your company's strategic goals. You then focus on the skills and competencies that you need to accomplish them. Armed with this knowledge, you can target your search for the "right" people far more efficiently, and your search is more likely to produce the business results that you're seeking.

Be Aggressive and Resourceful in Recruiting

With skills shortages in many fields, no company can afford to take a laid-back, business-as-usual approach to recruiting. In recent years, of course, nothing has changed the recruiting process more than the Internet (see Chapter 5). Everything from e-mail referrals to job centers to easily accessible databases of candidates has made it possible to identify a wider range of prospective employees than ever.

Keep in mind that traditional recruiting methods — job postings, classified advertising, and personal referral networks — still have their place.

Most of all, you need to constantly explore and experiment with new ways to find superb candidates. Internship programs, job fairs, staffing firms, and campus recruiting are all valuable means. The key is to be as broad-based as possible in your overall approach. No single recruiting strategy works for all situations. And in a tight labor market, you may need to devote more resources to your recruiting efforts — and become increasingly innovative in your practices.

Seek to Create a Healthy Culture

Every company has a *culture* — a working style and general environment that influences how it carries out its business and how employees relate to one another. The big question is whether the culture that prevails in your company is healthy — and whether senior management has a clear idea of the kind of culture it wants to create.

Healthy, dynamic company cultures —seen at firms that rate high with employees, such as Starbucks, Nordstrom, and Eli Lilly — don't evolve overnight. Nor can you create them with a single speech or the introduction of one or two policies. Clearly, however, such cultures, whether you're a Fortune 500 company or a small business, take their cue from senior management.

An essential first step to creating a positive cultural change in your company is to get senior management's vision of the ideal environment. Only then can you formulate values necessary to create such a workplace. After management identifies those values, you and others within the company can examine individual practices to evaluate whether they reflect the company's desired "personality." This task isn't easy, but the long-term dividends are well worth the time and effort.

Get the Most Out of Contingent Staffing

The astonishing growth in the last two decades of the *contingent workforce* — people working as consultants, independent contractors, and temporary employees — has given companies of every size and in every industry staffing options that weren't previously available. (The opportunity, for example, to hire a former CFO on a project basis to help you take your company public is one such option.)

But if you want to derive the benefits these project-based or contingent workers provide, you need to incorporate them into your overall human resource strategy. You need to be careful, too, that you're making a clear enough distinction between your employees and independent contractors. The safest option is to hire an outside staffing firm to address your contingent hiring needs, because such firms handle all compensation, payroll taxes, and, in many cases, benefits for their own employees.

Take a Proactive Approach to Regulatory Compliance

The legal ins and outs of the human resources function are becoming more confusing — and more restrictive — by the day. And all signs point to a trend that's only going to intensify in the future. Your challenge is twofold: Not only must you keep pace with changes in employment law, but you also must make sure that you're constantly bringing other key people in your organization up to speed as well.

Court rulings in recent years make clear that companies who aren't taking an aggressive and proactive approach to communicating regulatory information to employees may still be held accountable for violations that individual employees commit. The moral is that, in keeping people in your organization informed about employment law, there is no such thing as overkill.

Make Work/Family Balance a Priority

Creating family-friendly policies is more than a simple act of company altruism. A smart policy toward work and family has become a bottom-line-driven "best practice" among some of today's most successful and respected companies. Recent survey data from a variety of sources suggest that policies such as flex time, child-care support, and telecommuting can produce measurable improvements in employee morale, employee satisfaction, and productivity and, at the same time, can reduce turnover and absenteeism.

Even if some industries lend themselves more than others to these practices, your company needs to explore any workable options available to you. Top candidates in any economy can largely dictate which companies they want to work for, and lifestyle factors often play a key role in their decisions.

Keep Pace with Changing Demographics

As you take on the HR function, you become, in some sense, the psychologist of your workplace. It's a key part of your job to understand what makes people tick and see how individuals can productively work together.

But I urge you to borrow from another social science discipline, too. To be effective, you must also, at least to some degree, be attuned not just to individuals but to the broader, shifting demographics of our society. For the first time in history, the current workforce includes four distinct generations, each with its own set of desires, strengths, and work styles. They range from the oldest — the Silent Generation born before World War II — to the baby boomers, Generation X, and, the most recent addition to the workforce, Generation Y. As I discuss in Chapters 1 and 11, you need to understand how these groups differ from each other in terms of workplace approaches and preferences and how you can help them most effectively interact. To take advantage of your staff's variety of viewpoints, creativity, and talents, make knowledge-sharing a priority.

While awareness of these trends can be helpful in designing management policies and approaches (your benefits package, for example), be careful not to fall into the stereotype trap when considering generational differences. You and company line managers should develop individual relationships with staff to get an accurate picture of the attributes of each.

Demographic shifts are producing another challenge for the HR function. Although many baby boomers say they plan to work beyond the traditional retirement age of 65, large numbers of this group will inevitably leave the workforce. Companies, therefore, face the loss of some of their most experienced workers, as I discuss in Chapter 1. Many companies are recognizing this potential "knowledge drain" and are taking steps to compensate for the departure of baby-boom-age workers. In your HR role, you'll have to boost recruitment efforts to attract new talent, but you also need to capture as much of the institutional knowledge of the boomers before they leave. The time to begin identifying your company's next generation of leaders and beginning the transfer of critical wisdom is now. Organizations that do the best job of preparing for the anticipated exodus put in place well-thought-out programs and policies for knowledge exchange.

I'm not saying you need to create new programs for every societal change you read about. But you as a business owner or the managers you work for will want to keep up with shifts in the composition of the workforce in your area that may affect employee concerns and priorities. That kind of "big picture" understanding is precisely the kind of thinking that's making the HR profession so dynamic these days.

Play It Safe When It Comes to HR Technology

One of the great success stories of the last ten years has been the way HR professionals have been able to maximize the benefits of information technology. Although the Internet has drastically changed the face of recruiting, it's only one piece of the HR puzzle. You can manage everything from payroll to benefits administration to staffing matrices quite efficiently on your desktop. So here's the key question: With all these bells and whistles at your disposal, what should be your priorities in maximizing their value?

Probably the most important factor to keep in mind these days is security. With so many people in the organization now having access to more information, any system you use must be properly safeguarded against intrusion. This security is especially important in human resources, which houses such sensitive information as employee compensation, performance reviews, health records, and other important data.

Your second priority: the ability to consistently, smoothly and affordably upgrade and integrate technology into the rest of the organization. Because HR professionals work with every department within the company, you want to make sure that any software products you implement are easily understood and used by others. Consider the pitfalls, for example, if a finance executive finds reviewing the latest corporate guidelines difficult. You want your resources to be easily accessible.

View Training as an Ongoing Investment

Training in progressive companies has a new face. It's no longer an event — a group of employees filing into a classroom to attend a one- or two-day workshop that they signed up four months earlier. Training is now an ongoing process, fueled by the notion that the one skill employees need to develop today, above all, is the ability to learn. Employees' ability to learn enables the companies they work for to keep pace with the relentless demands of today's competitive, rapidly-shifting economy.

The good news is that the Internet has made this ongoing learning process far easier. You can download engaging, interactive training courses and materials to help more employees take advantage of new programs you and your colleagues create.

Handle Discipline and Dismissal Carefully

Bad things can happen to even the best of the companies. So regardless of how innovative and leading edge you want to be in your HR policies, don't lose sight of the basics, especially involving disciplinary action and dismissals. Wrongful termination suits are increasing at an exponential rate — with juries frequently showing a penchant for favoring the dismissed employee. (For details, see Chapter 17.) When handling these difficult situations, apply fair and consistent practices and show respect for the dignity of individuals involved. The manner in which disciplined or dismissed staff are treated provides a message to the remaining workforce that can directly affect employee motivation, morale and commitment.

Chapter 19

Ten Ways to Become an HR Strategist

- -

- -

*U*nquestionably, the last and current decades have been an incredibly dynamic time for HR professionals. Just consider what has changed in your job in recent years. Every business discipline has become increasingly sophisticated. Corporations have created new management models and workplace cultures. New approaches to hiring, evaluating, supervising, retaining, and motivating employees are developing constantly. Nations around the world are grasping the consequences of an increasingly global economy.

Not surprisingly, the role of the HR professional has changed to keep up — and largely for the better. The strategic implications of your job create many challenges. You need to stay on top of trends and new developments — both within your company and in the HR profession. Senior managers are looking for you to provide input on a wider variety of issues than ever. They're also counting on you to come forward with new ideas.

Amid the change and challenges, which are likely only to accelerate in the coming years, you need to keep certain principles in mind. This chapter covers ten signposts for success as an HR strategist.

Develop a Business Orientation to HR Initiatives

The leading HR professionals keenly grasp how their work fits into their organization's overall business. How? By understanding the complexities and operating challenges that set their company apart from its competitors. (See Chapters 1 and 3)

A basic understanding of business finance is essential. (Quick test: Can you read a P&L statement?) More important, you need an in-depth understanding of your company's products and services, the competitive challenges it faces, and the strategic initiatives that are underway to meet those challenges. The best way to gain this knowledge is to ensure that you're in on any meetings and discussions involving these initiatives. Make sure to keep close track of monthly sales reports and to set up meetings with line managers or other colleagues to find out about their strategic goals.

Position Initiatives as Bottom-Line Benefits

Human resources departments are traditionally viewed as cost centers. In more recent years, though, a growing appreciation for the bottom-line benefits of sound, innovative HR practices has emerged. You can reinforce this appreciation by providing more insight into the bottom-line implications of any HR initiative that you plan to recommend — everything from training programs to hiring practices and, difficult as it is, employee termination procedures. Work with the financial analysts in your company to establish some concrete ways to attach a dollar value to the contributions your department is making to the company's bottom line.

Develop a Marketing Mind-Set

You typically need to aggressively "market" and "sell" leading-edge HR initiatives to all segments of your internal customer base: senior management, supervisors, and all staff employees. The key is to focus your communication efforts on the benefits that these initiatives deliver as opposed to the mechanics of the initiatives. As you're "selling" these initiatives to senior management, stress competitive advantage. If your audience is supervisors, stress the operational advantages of the initiative — how it can ease their day-to-day burdens.

As with any marketing initiative, you need to know your audience and base your approach on their needs and concerns. Worth remembering: Whenever you're introducing a new initiative to a group of employees who are already under tremendous time pressures, anticipate resistance — even though the new program may be designed to ease those pressures in the long-run.

Share Your Expertise

Your background and training has helped you develop skills that you may take for granted, but that many managers in your company may lack. Chief among these skills are the abilities to conduct an effective selection interview, resolve disputes, and facilitate team meetings. Your company may not have the time or budget to provide formal training in these skills, but you can still accomplish a great deal through informal training sessions and one-on-one coaching. The bottom line: Don't sell yourself short as a resource. (See Chapters 7, 16, and 17.)

Serve as the Model

One of the best and most easily controlled ways to increase your leverage and credibility in your company is for your own actions — and the actions of your staff members — to represent the model for other departments. If you're trying to get line managers to adopt a less authoritarian, more collaborative management style, for example, demonstrate the benefits of that approach through how you manage your own people.

Be particularly careful about the quality of the people you hire. Make sure that your own staff recognizes that all employees in the company are internal customers.

Stay on the Leading Edge

As with everything else in today's marketplace, the challenges that confront HR professionals are changing at warp speed. You need to dedicate a portion of your work week to remain current on new developments. Following are some ideas on how to stay ahead of the curve:

- Subscribe to the major HR publications (both national and regional) and maintain a file of articles that are relevant to your company.

- Join your local HR group and actively involve yourself in programs and committees relevant to your work.

- Attend seminars and conferences geared specifically for HR practitioners.

- Stay informed about legal issues that can affect your policies — through the Internet, through occasional conversations with lawyers, and by monitoring news stories and legal cases that will likely have HR implications.

- Regularly patrol the Internet for articles, books, Web sites, discussion groups, blogs and other venues for information that's relevant to your company and the overall business environment. (*Blogs,* short for weblogs, are frequently updated Web sites containing personal thoughts, news, opinions, and almost any information that individuals — and increasingly companies — want to make available to the Web-savvy public. It's a way for these individuals and businesses to connect with a variety of stakeholders on a more direct and personal level.)

- Pay close attention to your competitors' HR practices — compensation and benefits, in particular. Remember that these differences may be giving them an edge in attracting high-performing employees.

Develop Your Communication Skills

Any measures you can take — courses, seminars, personal coaching — to enhance your communication skills pay enormous dividends for you in almost every aspect of your job. Remember that as a human resources professional, you want to make a contribution to the growth of the company — and that in turn requires constantly winning acceptance for the initiatives you create. Your own skills as an effective speaker and writer greatly influence your ability to generate support for your initiatives.

Avoid the Flavor of the Month Pitfall

Regardless of the pressure you may be under to "solve" pressing problems, resist the tendency to rely on stopgap measures, such as a hurriedly assembled presentation to explain a fundamental change in benefits policy. Do your best to make sure that any initiative you undertake — whether a training program or a fundamental change in work practices — is well-thought out and enjoys the enthusiastic backing of senior management.

If you establish a pattern of introducing HR programs that lack follow-through, you lose credibility with the workforce and make winning acceptance for future programs all the more difficult for yourself. It's much better to tackle a few that succeed than spread yourself too thin.

Choose Consultants with Care

If your company is typical of most organizations today, you don't have enough internal resources to carry out certain key HR initiatives, such as training, and so to fill the gap, you must rely on the outside consultants that staffing firms often provide. You need, therefore, to make sure that whomever you hire is not only technically qualified to do the work, but also is willing to take the time to learn about your company.

Job skills aside, never engage a consultant unless you first take the following steps:

- You or your staffing firm, depending on your source for outside help, meet personally with any consultants you plan to use to gain a sense of how they may interact with others.

- You receive a written document that outlines the services the consultant is to provide, what results you can reasonably expect, and how much the service is going to cost.

- You obtain reliable references.

Be Sensitive to the Needs and Agendas of Line Managers

Even if HR initiatives have the blessing of senior management, never assume that your line managers are going to support these initiatives simply because doing so is "their job."

One reason many initiatives bog down isn't for lack of a blessing from senior management, but because line managers haven't been shown the value of these ideas. Anticipate resistance and be patient. Any HR initiative that you need to "force" on people is doomed to fail.

Chapter 20

Ten HR-Related Web Sites Worth Exploring

• •

In This Chapter

▶ Identifying workplace disability issues and laws

▶ Finding resources to continue your HR education

• •

*A*s is the case with virtually every subject these days, you can find information relating to human resources in staggering abundance on the Internet and other online resources — with the volume growing daily. A recent search our firm conducted on the term "human resources" revealed more than 450 million results. Fortunately, the number of sites that are of general interest (that is, sites that don't focus on one specific region and that don't represent a consultant or a university program) is manageable. This chapter identifies and summarizes information on ten sites that every HR professional should know about — and use.

U.S. Equal Employment Opportunity Commission (EEOC)

```
www.eeoc.gov
```

Categories on this site include background on the commission; facts about employment discrimination and enforcement; litigation information; and areas that summarize EEOC policies for small businesses. If you like, you can access both the full text of EEOC legislation and summaries of the key provisions.

Occupational Safety & Health Administration (OSHA)

`www.osha.gov`

Given the scope of OSHA's mission, the fact that this U.S. government-operated Web site is unusually large and varied is no surprise. Departments include an OSHA newsroom; sections on laws, regulations, and compliance; a reading room; outreach material; and easy links to the Department of Labor Web site. The categories the site covers are voluminous, with nearly 60 entries in the index — everything from asbestos to hazardous waste to workplace violence. A typical entry consists of a summary of the topic, along with an extensive list of links to other information sources. In some cases, you can download entire slide presentations, complete with overheads. Some information that you find throughout this Web site comes from sources other than the government, but you can download and copy nearly all of it without restriction. The library gives you online access to most OSHA documents.

The ELAWS Advisor

`www.dol.gov/elaws`

ELAWS (Employment Laws Assistance for Workers and Small Businesses) was developed by the Department of Labor (DOL) and enables employers and employees alike to interact with on-line "advisors" about employment issues. The advisor is a mechanism that simulates the interaction you might have with a DOL employment law expert. It asks questions, provides information, and directs you to the appropriate resolution based on your responses.

Americans with Disabilities Act (ADA) Document Center

`www.usdoj.gov/crt/ada`

As the name implies, this Web site devotes itself exclusively to information relating to the Americans with Disabilities Act of 1990 (ADA). In addition to a full text of the ADA, you get access to the technical assistance documents and manuals prepared by the EEOC, the Department of Justice (DOJ), the National Institute on Disability and Rehabilitation Research (NIDRR), and the

Department of Labor. One of the best features of this Web site is that it provides you with links to other Internet sources of information concerning workplace disability issues.

Bureau of Labor Statistics (BLS)

```
www.bls.gov
```

If you like to engage in long-range, global thinking and are a numbers junkie to boot, this Web site is a potential goldmine. It contains a ton of information on specific industries, regions of the country, economic figures throughout the U.S., business costs, demographics, and more. Other elements include a steady flow of news releases, research papers, and online access to the DOL's publication, the *Monthly Labor Review.* The data is well-organized — the site groups news releases, for example, according to major BLS statistical categories, such as Employment and Unemployment, Prices and Living Conditions, and so on — and most of the statistical data comes with concise explanations provided by the Bureau of Labor Statistics economic staff.

State Department Travel

```
http://travel.state.gov
```

As exciting it is for many businesses to be expanding all over the world, you need to be mindful of matters related to procedures, safety, and health. This State Department Web site provides tips for traveling abroad — from information on passports and other required documents, to healthcare advisories from around the globe, to updates on potential security threats in various nations.

Society for Human Resource Management (SHRM)

```
www.shrm.org
```

This Web site is run by the Society of Human Resource Management (SHRM). SHRM provides much of its information to nonmembers, although you need to join to gain access to all articles and sections. The various departments include an "HR Talk Discussion Center," a "Knowledge Center" with dozens of papers and studies, and online access to articles that originally appeared in the organization's publication, *HR Magazine.*

Among the most appealing features of this Web site is its own search engine of other HR-related Web sites as selected by SHRM's editors and updated on a weekly basis. After you navigate to this section of SHRM's site, you're given a choice of categories, with a multitude of options within each category.

WorldatWork

    www.worldatwork.org

Formerly the American Compensation Association, WorldatWork has emerged as a superb resource for news, research, educational resources, networking opportunities, and many more human resources topics. The cost of joining is well worth it, as the site covers a wide range of valuable publications and materials.

As an HR professional, you may find yourself particularly interested in WorldatWork's professional certification program, which covers such fields as Certified Compensation Professional (CCP), Certified Benefits Professional (CBP), Global Remuneration Professional (GRP) and the new Work-Life Certified Professional (WLCP).

American Society for Training & Development (ASTD)

    www.astd.org

ASTD numbers some 70,000 members from more than 100 companies. Access to most of the Web site's categories is limited to members, but nonmembers can browse through the library and get useful information on a variety of training-related topics. Members have access to current and past articles from Training and Development, ASTD's monthly magazine, as well as the normal features of a professional organization Web site, including discussion groups, buyer's guides, and job-related information.

Workforce Online

www.workforceonline.com

Workforce Online was created and is run by the editors of *Workforce Management* magazine and takes a broad-based approach to its subject matter. Although you must register (it's free) to access the information on this site, after you log in, you can find a great deal to explore. The information database, for example, includes more than 500 articles covering every aspect of the HR function, and you can access the database by keyword or subject. Other departments include a software directory, a buyer's guide, and job postings. Daily updates include a tip-of-the-day and a legal digest.

Chapter 21

Ten HR-Related Associations You Should Know About

● ●

In This Chapter

▶ Identifying compensation and benefits facts

▶ Promoting flexible employment opportunities

● ●

*I*n this chapter, I offer contact information for ten nonprofit organizations, each of whose mission, services, and activities relate to the human resources function. Some of these organizations offer a great deal of information through their Web sites. You may want to consider membership in those groups that are most relevant to your position and needs.

Benefits

Employee Benefit Research Institute (EBRI)
2121 K Street, NW, Suite 600
Washington, DC 20037-1896
Phone: 202-659-0670
Fax: 202-775-6312
Web: www.ebri.org

The Employee Benefit Research Institute is the source of a wide array of benefits facts and figures, Web links to its own and other online resources, and a range of programs that make benefits information easily available.

Compensation

Employers Council on Flexible Compensation (ECFC)
927 15th Street NW, Suite 1000
Washington, DC 20005
Phone: 202-659-4300
Fax: 202-371-1467
Web: www.ecfc.org

The Employers Council on Flexible Compensation provides information on flexible compensation programs to members, national opinion leaders, and the general public to help create a positive climate for the growth of flexible compensation.

Contingent Workers

American Staffing Association
277 S. Washington Street, Suite 200
Alexandria, VA 22314
Phone: 703-253-2020
Fax: 703-253-2053
Web: www.americanstaffing.net

The American Staffing Association has been promoting flexible employment opportunities since its founding in 1966. Its members provide a wide range of employment-related services and solutions, including temporary and contract staffing, recruiting and permanent placement, outsourcing, training, and human resource consulting.

Employee Assistance Programs

Employee Assistance Professionals Association
4350 North Fairfax Drive, Suite 410
Arlington, VA 22203
Phone: 703-387-1000
Fax: 703-522-4585
Web: www.eapassn.org

Established in 1971, the Employee Assistance Professionals Association publishes the *Journal of Employee Assistance* and offers training and other resources to enhance the skills and success of its members and the stature of the employee assistance profession.

Equal Employment Opportunity

Equal Employment Advisory Council (EEAC)
1015 15th St. NW, Suite 1200
Washington, DC 20005
Phone: 202-789-8650
Fax: 202-789-2291
Web: www.eeac.org

The Equal Employment Advisory Council, founded in 1976, is the nation's largest nonprofit association of employers dedicated exclusively to the advancement of practical and effective programs to eliminate workplace discrimination. Members rely on the EEAC's staff of attorneys and compliance professionals to help them meet their EEO and affirmative action compliance obligations. Membership is corporate, meaning that anyone employed by a member company is eligible to benefit from EEAC's array of member services.

General HR Management

American Management Association
1601 Broadway
New York, NY 10019-7420
Phone: 212-586-8100
Fax: 212-903-8168
Web: www.amanet.org

The American Management Association provides a full range of management development and educational services to individuals, companies, and government agencies worldwide. The organization features seminars, conferences, current issues forums and briefings, as well as books and publications, research, and print and online self-study courses.

Society for Human Resource Management (SHRM)
1800 Duke St.
Alexandria, VA 22314
Phone: 800-283-SHRM (7476); 703-548-3440
Fax: 703-535-6490
Web: www.shrm.org

The Society for Human Resource Management (SHRM) is the world's largest association devoted to human resource management. Representing more than 200,000 individual members, the Society's mission is to serve the needs of HR professionals by providing the most essential and comprehensive resources available. SHRM has more than 560 affiliate chapters, both in the United States and abroad, and provides additional programming and networking opportunities in local areas.

WorldatWork
14040 N. Northsight Blvd.
Scottsdale, AZ 85260
Phone: 877-951-9191 (toll free); 480-922-2020
Fax: 866-816-2962 (toll free); 480-483-8352
Web: www.worldatwork.org

Founded in 1955, WorldatWork focuses on human resources disciplines associated with attracting, motivating, and retaining employees. The WorldatWork
family of organizations provides education, certifications, publications,
knowledge resources, surveys, conferences, research, and networking opportunities.

Information Technology

International Association for Human Resource Information Management
(IHRIM)
P.O. Box 1086
Burlington, MA 01803-1086
Phone: 800-804-3983; 781-791-9488
Fax: 781-998-8011
Web: www.ihrim.org

The International Association for Human Resource Information Management
provides HR technology professionals with news, knowledge, and networking
opportunities. IHRIM is a community of practitioners, vendors, consultants,
students, and faculty.

Training and Workforce Development

American Society for Training and Development (ASTD)
1640 King St., Box 1443
Alexandria, VA 22313-2043
Phone: 703-683-8100
Fax: 703-683-8103
Web: www.astd.org

The American Society for Training & Development is the world's largest association dedicated to workplace learning and performance professionals. Its
members and associates come from more than 100 countries and thousands
of organizations of all types and sizes.

Chapter 22

The Ten Most Important HR-Related Laws

In This Chapter
▶ Identifying discriminatory practices
▶ Assisting employees with family responsibilities

*T*he list of HR-related laws and regulations employers must follow these days is longer than it has ever been — and getting longer by the year. With each new law (and each new wrinkle to an existing law), your job handling HR for your company becomes a little more challenging.

In this chapter, I cover the ten most important federal employment laws. Keep in mind that, depending on the number of employees in your company, your firm may or may not be subject to the regulations. And don't forget you're subject to state laws as well. For more information, consult Chapter 2, the CD-ROM that comes with this book, or, best yet, a lawyer.

For more on these laws and how they may affect you, see Chapter 2 and the Cheat Sheet.

Age Discrimination in Employment Act (ADEA)

This act protects individuals who are 40 years of age or older from employment discrimination based on age.

Americans with Disabilities Act (ADA)

Your company's hiring or promotion policies can't discriminate against individuals who suffer from disabilities. Moreover, you must be willing to take reasonable steps in the workplace (at your expense) to accommodate the special needs of disabled applicants and employees who are otherwise qualified.

Consolidated Omnibus Budget Reconciliation Act of 1985 (COBRA)

Most employees covered by your company's group health-insurance plan who then leave the company can retain medical coverage under the plan — at their own expense — for up to 18 months after they leave.

Employee Retirement Income Security Act (ERISA)

Any pension and retirement programs that your company offers must include safeguards to ensure that employees receive what they're entitled to. And you're not permitted to show favoritism to employees based on the size of their salaries.

Equal Pay Act

Covered companies must prevent any discrepancies in pay between men and women who are assigned to or perform the same job.

Fair Labor Standards Act (FLSA)

Any company that engages in interstate commerce is bound by these minimum wage standards, overtime rates, and other salary-related regulations.

Family and Medical Leave Act (FMLA)

Employees faced with a critical family responsibility — the birth or adoption of a child, their own serious illness, or the illness of a member of the immediate family — are entitled to up to 12 weeks of unpaid leave during any 12-month period. The employee's job and benefits are protected during this period.

Federal Unemployment Tax Act (FUTA)

Employers must contribute to the government program (usually state-run) that offers temporary benefits to employees who are discharged.

IRCA: Immigration Reform and Control Act (1986, 1990, and 1996)

Employers who knowingly hire illegal aliens can be penalized. IRCA has become more important since the 2001 creation of the Department of Homeland Security.

Title VII of the Civil Rights Act

An individual's race, color, sex, religion, or national origin can have no bearing on any company decision regarding hiring, compensation, promotion, or dismissal.

Note: The Civil Rights Act of 1991 gives employees who believe they've been intentionally victimized by discrimination the right to seek compensation and damages before a jury.

Appendix

About the CD

*H*ere's what you can find on the *Human Resources Kit For Dummies* CD-ROM:

✔ More than 30 documents — policies, forms, contracts, and laws

✔ Adobe Reader, for viewing the documents in PDF format

System Requirements

Make sure that your computer meets the minimum system requirements shown in the following list. If your computer doesn't match up to most of these requirements, you may have problems using the software and files on the CD. For the latest and greatest information, please refer to the ReadMe file located at the root of the CD-ROM.

✔ A PC capable of running Microsoft Windows 98 or later; or a Mac running Mac OS X or later

✔ A CD-ROM drive

If you need more information on the basics, check out these books published by Wiley Publishing: *PCs For Dummies,* by Dan Gookin; *Macs For Dummies,* by David Pogue; *iMacs For Dummies* by David Pogue; *Windows 98 For Dummies, Windows 2000 Professional For Dummies, Microsoft Windows ME Millennium Edition For Dummies, Windows XP For Dummies*, and *Windows Vista For Dummies,* all by Andy Rathbone.

Using the CD with Windows and Mac

To install the items from the CD to your hard drive, follow these steps.

1. **Insert the CD into your computer's CD-ROM drive.**

   The license agreement appears.

   Note to Windows users: The interface doesn't launch if you have autorun disabled. In that case, click Start⇨Run. In the dialog box that appears, type **D:\start.exe**. (Replace D with the proper letter if your CD-ROM drive uses a different letter. If you don't know the letter, see how your CD-ROM drive is listed under My Computer.) Click OK.

   Note for Mac users: The license agreement does not appear. Instead, the CD icon appears on your desktop. Double-click the icon to open the CD, and double-click "Start". Skip Step 2 and proceed to Step 3.

2. **Read through the license agreement and then click the Accept button if you want to use the CD.**

   After you click Accept, the License Agreement window doesn't appear again.

   The CD interface appears. The interface allows you to install Acrobat Reader and read and print the HR forms with just a click of a button (or two).

3. **Open the PDFs folder on the CD and double-click the icon of the document you want to open, or drag the icon into the Adobe Reader window.**

   The files are named according to the chapter they appear in. For example, 02-01.pdf is from Chapter 2, and it's the first document mentioned in that chapter.

What's on the CD

The following sections are arranged by category and provide a summary of the software and other goodies on the CD. If you need help with installing the items provided on the CD, refer to the installation instructions in the preceding section.

Shareware programs are fully functional, free, trial versions of copyrighted programs. If you like particular programs, register with their authors for a nominal fee and receive licenses, enhanced versions, and technical support.

Freeware programs are free, copyrighted games, applications, and utilities. You can copy them to as many PCs as you like — for free — but they offer no technical support.

GNU software is governed by its own license, which is included inside the folder of the GNU software. GNU software has no restrictions on distribution of. See the GNU license at the root of the CD for more details.

Trial, demo, or *evaluation* versions of software are usually limited either by time or functionality (such as not letting you save a project after you create it).

Adobe Reader, from Adobe

Freeware

For Windows and Mac. You can access all the forms and documents on the CD using Adobe Reader.

For information about all the features and controls in Adobe Reader, be sure to check out the Adobe Reader Help file.

The documents on the CD

I've organized the forms and documents on the CD by the chapter in which they're mentioned or explained. Here's a chapter-by-chapter reference list for you:

Chapter 2

Equal Opportunity Posting Requirements: This document specifies what EEOC information must be posted by all employers who engage in interstate commerce.

Sample EEO Posting: This form is an example of an acceptable EEOC posting.

Discrimination Guidelines: This document lists the major provisions of the Age Discrimination in Employment Act and other discrimination guidelines.

Americans with Disabilities Act of 1990: This act gives people with physical or mental disabilities increased access to public services and requires employers to provide reasonable accommodation for applicants and employees with disabilities.

Key Provisions of the Family and Medical Leave Act: This document summarizes one's rights under FMLA.

Title VII of the Civil Rights Act of 1964: The entire text of this important law is included on the CD.

Sample Policy Statement on Harassment: This document is a sample policy on harassment that your company may want to issue in its communication with employees.

Chapter 4

Blank Job Description Form and Sample Job Descriptions: The sample job descriptions should serve you well because you can use the blank form to develop your own job descriptions.

Chapter 5

Sample Skills Inventory Form and a Blank Form: The form can serve as a model for a database template for an employee skills inventory.

Acknowledgement of Receipt of Resume/Job Application Form: This letter is an example of an acknowledgement of receipt of a resume and/or job application.

Chapter 6

Rejection Letter: This document is an example of a "thanks, but no thanks" letter to an unsuccessful applicant.

Chapter 7

Interview Q&A Form: Use this form to write down questions you want to ask a candidate, record answers, and jot down any comments.

Employment Inquiries Fact Sheet: This fact sheet contains suggested guidelines for managers involved in the hiring process.

Blank Candidate Interview Evaluation Form: Use this form to record your general impressions of a job candidate.

Chapter 8

Candidate Rating Form: This form allows you to rate candidates on criteria that are important but may not be part of the specific job description.

Reference Check Letter: You can place this letter on company letterhead and send it to your prospective employees' former employers to request reference information.

Employment Inquiry Release: With this form, a prospective employee grants the employer permission to make investigative inquiries on the background of the prospective employee.

Consent to Criminal Background Check: With this form, a prospective employee grants the employer permission to do a criminal background check on the prospective employee.

Background Check Permission (Comprehensive) for Prospective Employee: This document is a sample form in which a prospective employee grants the employer permission to do a comprehensive background check on the prospective employee.

Disclosure and Authorization Regarding Procurement of Investigative Consumer Report for Employment Purposes: Under the federal Fair Credit Reporting Act, an employer must offer this form (and obtain authorization) regarding the procurement of an investigative consumer report from a consumer reporting agency.

Disclosure and Authorization Regarding Procurement of Consumer Report for Employment Purposes: Under the federal Fair Credit Reporting Act, an employer must offer this form (and obtain authorization) regarding the procurement of a consumer report from a consumer reporting agency.

A Summary of Your Rights Under the Fair Credit Reporting Act: If an employer performs a credit check on a prospective employee, the employer must supply this form.

Confirmation of Receipt of the Summary of Your Rights Under the Fair Credit Reporting Act and the Copy of Consumer or Investigative Report: Under the federal Fair Credit Reporting Act, an employer must provide a prospective employee with a copy of the official summary of rights under the act issued by the Federal Trade Commission, and with a copy of the consumer report or investigative consumer report, prior to taking any adverse employment action based in whole or in part on information in a report.

Disclosure of the Adverse Action Based on Information in a Consumer or Investigative Report: Under the federal Fair Credit Reporting Act, an employer must present this document if it has taken any adverse action based in whole or in part on information in a consumer report or an investigative consumer report.

Offer Letter to Prospective Employee: This sample letter offers a job to a prospective employee.

Employment Agreement: This form is a sample employment agreement for a senior-level employee.

Chapter 9

Onboarding Checklist: This list of onboarding criteria can serve as a measuring device for determining the effectiveness of your orientation process.

E-Mail Policy: This sample e-mail policy gives employees guidance as to the use of the company's e-mail system.

Drug-Free Workplace Policy: This sample policy statement informs an employee of the company's position on illegal drugs.

Employee Handbook Table of Contents: This document can serve as a model for an employee handbook you may want to create for your own company.

Employee Handbook and At-Will Employee Status Acknowledgment: This document is a sample form in which a new employee acknowledges receiving and agreeing to the matters contained in the company's employee handbook.

Chapter 11

Employee Statement of Benefits: This form lists all the benefits that a company provides to an employee.

A Look at 401(k) Plan Fees for Employees: This document answers common questions that employees have about 401(k) plans.

Sample FMLA Posting: This document summarizes one's rights under the Family and Medical Leave Act.

Employer Response to Employee Request for Family or Medical Leave: When an employee requests family or medical leave, use this form to respond.

Certification of Health Care Provider: A healthcare provider completes this form upon an employee's request to implement FMLA rights.

Chapter 12

Employee Satisfaction Survey: Use this survey, to be distributed to employees, to gauge worker satisfaction and determine areas of needed improvement.

Exit Interview Questionnaire: A company representative can use this questionnaire when an employee voluntarily leaves the company.

Chapter 15

Essay Appraisal Form: This employee appraisal form requires evaluators to write out statements that describe an employee's work performance.

Job Rating Checklist Appraisal Form: This employee appraisal form asks evaluators to rate an employee's performance based on a prepared list of criteria.

Chapter 17

Employee Emergency Notification Form: Employees fill out this form to indicate to the employer whom to notify in the event of an emergency.

OSHA Information Posting: This document lists the major provisions under the Occupational Safety and Health Act.

Troubleshooting

While these programs work on most computers with minimum system requirements, your computer may differ, and some programs may not work properly for some reason.

The two likeliest problems are that you don't have enough memory (RAM) for the programs you want to use, or you have other programs running that are affecting installation or running of a program. If you get an error message such as Not enough memory or Setup cannot continue, try one or more of the following suggestions and then try using the software again:

- ✔ **Turn off any antivirus software running on your computer.** Installation programs sometimes mimic virus activity and may make your computer incorrectly believe that it's being infected by a virus.

- ✔ **Close all running programs.** The more programs you have running, the less memory is available to other programs. Installation programs typically update files and programs, so if you keep other programs running, installation may not work properly.

- ✔ **Have your local computer store add more RAM to your computer.** This step is, admittedly, drastic and somewhat expensive. However, adding more memory can really help the speed of your computer and allow more programs to run at the same time.

If you have trouble with the CD-ROM, please call the Wiley Product Technical Support phone number at (800) 762-2974. Outside the United States, call 1(317) 572-3994. You can also contact Wiley Product Technical Support at `http://support.wiley.com`. John Wiley & Sons provides technical support only for installation and other general quality control items. For technical support on the applications themselves, consult the program's vendor or author.

To place additional orders or to request information about other Wiley products, please call (877) 762-2974.

Index

Wiley Publishing, Inc.
End-User License Agreement